To Catch the Moon from the Bottom
of the Sea

Dorothy and I at home.

To Catch the Moon from the Bottom of the Sea

A Memoir

Peter McEwan

Glengarden Press

Published by Glengarden Press

ISBN 978 0 9547552 3 2

British Library Catologuing-in-Publication Data
A catalogue record for this book is available from
The British Library

By the same author: F5 McE

Modern Africa (with R B Sutcliffe)
Africa from Early Times
Nineteenth Century Africa
Twentieth Century Africa
Industrial Organisations and Health (with F Baker and A Sheldon)
Retirement (with A Sheldon and C Ryser)

The Dictionary of Scottish Art and Architecture
Art Words: McEwan Handbook of Art Related Terms

Published and distributed by Glengarden Press
Ballater, Aberdeenshire AB35 5UB
www.glengardenpress.com
Tel: 013397 55429

Printed by SCA Print & Supply Chain Solutions, Glasgow
Bound by Hunter & Foulis, Haddington

CORRIGENDA

Illustration page 3, Gafic Club caption - should read 'L to R, Doug Smith, John Fuller, Ken Lindford, Christopher Morahan, the author, John Wurr, Rodney Tucker, Bingham Hobson and Ken Shaw

Page 140, line 9 – should read 'the will to transgress and the fear of terrorist reprisal'

Page 158, line 8 – the asterisk relates to footnote [1]

Page 172, five lines from foot – should read 'icy slopes'

Page 206, line 3 – 'chance' not 'change'

For Dorothy, Feona, Malcolm & Rhod

Acknowledgements

A long the way, stagnant memory has been resuscitated and verbal infelicities rectified by some warmly appreciated advice and help.

Hazel Knorr and our son Malcolm spent hours delving into the genealogical circumstances of a very convoluted lineage; my dear old friend the late John Fuller and another fellow Old Cholmeleian, Bingham Hobson, relived some of our old school capers; Philip Laundy refreshed some caducous Rhodesian memories; Bob Sutcliffe recalled interesting moments when our careers several times converged; Vivien Macmillan provided encouragement from, as it were, the outside world; David Hamilton, from his experience as an author, printer, publisher and surgeon, provided many invaluable corrections and suggestions; Peter Hodgkiss patiently, promptly and professionally transformed the printed text into appropriate book format – transmogrification with a touch of magic; Elizabeth Lowson typed the first draft with great good cheer and electric speed while Moira McDougall helped me through the seemingly endless proof reading stage and shaped the final drafts with unerring accuracy and patience.

A very big thank you to my daughter Feona and younger son Rhod for their endeavours to introduce a greater degree of sanity, for their help in organising the illustrations, and – most of all – I owe an enormous debt to my ever tolerant wife Dorothy, who has extended all the boundaries of love and forbearance in her lifelong understanding of a difficult case.

For all the cacologies and errors that remain, of which I hope there are but a few, I am alone responsible.

Introduction

Writing an autobiography requires if not an apologia certainly an explanation. In my case a medley of motives mingle. There is the belief that over eighty very varied years there have been enough experiences to make at least some of them of general interest and, perhaps more important, there may be hidden lessons to emerge that might occasionally provoke and often resonate.

This also provides an excuse, if one is needed, to offer some thoughts that seem to me important and worthy of further reflection.

Looking back I realise the over-riding importance given to friendship and an almost excessive sensitivity to place. Whilst it is impossible to convey the warmth and camaraderie of true friends, and to portray characters with the accuracy they deserve, an attempt has been made to do them justice in all their rich variety.

As to place, the environment has always been more significant for me than the work to be done therein. I find it hard to understand how so much accomplishment in the world is achieved in so many unrewarding environments.

An added reason for recording people, places and events is that it is just possible that these details may be of interest to those who follow, even though genealogical information about the family remains thinner than its diversity merits.

Along the way many folk have suggested that a more lasting record should be made of some achievements that would otherwise only be noted in some forgotten ephemera, if at all.

Opening one's cupboard is a salutary undertaking. The contents, the circumstances bringing them about and their consequences, have been portrayed as honestly as one person's inevitable subjectivity has allowed.

Apart from a brief spell after school and again during the first six months of becoming a countryman, I have never kept a diary, a severe disadvantage when ransacking memory. Again, as Dorothy will readily testify, I have always found it easier to recall the good things than to remember the bad, to recollect the happy events and the good people rather than remember the disappointments and the disagreeable. That is the only recognisable bias to which I confess.

Join me, then, in a roller coaster journey along life's pathways, through many different terrains, along surfaces sometimes smooth, sometimes extremely rough, but always strangely unpredictable.

CHAPTER 1

Early Days

Its terrifying to think how much research is needed to determine the truth of even the most unimportant fact.

[Stendhal]

The past is the only dead thing that smells sweet.

[Edward Thomas]

Life, liberty and love. Three beacons which in their varying guises have illuminated and sustained all the more important episodes and deeper thoughts of my life.

The gift and mysteries of life led to my philosophical home.

A constant hankering after liberty, the freedom to do one's own thing without any formal constraints coloured everything one sought and has been the necessary condition for everything worthwhile I may have achieved.

Love comes in many forms, enriching all it embraces and is always infinitely rewarding.

* * * * * * * *

A large part of the joy and sorrow of family research lies in discovering the unexpected. If family legend is to be believed, the hidden genealogical lines on both sides owe as much to curiosity as they do to mystery. Unravelling the many skeins of such a cosmopolitan bunch is a daunting task, one that still haunts my thinking whilst all the while building a stock of frustration.

My paternal grandfather was in some way a kinsman of the cricketing playwright James Barrie. Albert McEwan was a successful timber merchant carrying on business at 282 Old Street in the city of London from 1902 until 1930. Old Street has changed beyond recognition but one of my earliest memories is of my maiden aunt Lal seated on a high stool tending the firm's books in a small ante room, the resinous smell of the sawdusted floor, beyond a yard stacked with tall ranks of timber. But by this time grandfather McEwan had died, having departed this life before I was born. For reasons unknown to me, although probably not uncommon at the time, he was an ardent Germanophile, so much so that he dispatched his only son to school in Germany where, unable to speak a word of the language, my father sent letters home, obviously intended for his mother, stained with tears. But this failed to move grandfather and when school days were over, my father, having narrowly avoided expulsion for hoisting a Union Jack on the school flagpole, then went on to Heidelberg University, becoming bilingual and rowing in their eight, the former a facility that would stand him in good stead in later life. When grandfather became ill his German predilections led to his demise for, electing to enter the German hospital in London, he died from post-surgical complications.

Father carried on the business with his sister and a small band of devoted staff but when, in 1930, the dark days of recession had taken its toll, my soft-hearted father, although at first battling on, resisting all advice to reduce the staff, was eventually forced to sell the business.

All we know of his parents is that his grandfather, a Scotsman, probably a Glaswegian, married a Hampshire girl, Sara Bignell, whose mother's maiden name was Newlyn, thus explaining how this name first entered the line, being among the Christian names of both my father and our younger son Rhod.

I remember my paternal grandmother as a lovely lady with a wonderful sense of humour and infinite patience. Contrary to Nancy Astor's dictum that all women marry beneath them, it was thought that her husband had married, in the language of the time, beneath him. Gaga, as I called her, lived to be 104, tended to the end by her devoted daughter Lal with whom she had spent all her life.

Mother's family was extraordinarily mixed, with a chapter of unanswered questions still waiting to be unravelled. Her father, a prosperous Jewish jeweller and erstwhile milliner, was born Michael Cohen, but during the recession changed his name to Rose. A direct relation was Alice Cohen, the first Lady Reading and Vicereine of India. For some years after the first war Michael ran a millinery business in Shaftesbury Avenue, Aunt Gladys ('Gar') being the designer, her older sister Renée the book-keeper, while my mother, the youngest daughter, looked after the customers among whom were a number of celebrities including Elizabeth Bowes-Lyon, the future Queen Mother.

The major skeleton in our cupboard, so we were often told, was the infamous Goodman Levy, Michael's maternal grandfather. In the Derby of 1844[1] the first horse past the post was called *Running Rein*. Although owned by Levy, the horse ran in the colours of a Mr Wood, an Epsom corn merchant, to whom Levy was in debt. The horse's real name, however, was *Maccabeus*, a four year old purchased by Levy as a yearling. He changed the name of these two horses in 1842 and in 1843 transferred ownership to Wood, but not before *Maccabeus* had won a race for two year olds at Newmarket. The Duke of Rutland, who owned the runner-up, lodged an objection, supported by Lord George Bentinck, whose agent, a dubious character called Harry Hill, knew most of what was going on in the racing underworld. At the subsequent enquiry the objection was over-ruled when the stable lad who had been present when the real *Running Rein* had been foaled, incorrectly confirmed that the winner was indeed the real *Running Rein*.

Thereafter Levy held his fire until imprudently entering *Maccabeus* (now re-christened *Running Rein*) for the Derby which he proceeded to win by three quarters of a length at 10-1. The

---

[1] For a full account see R. Mortimer; *The History of the Derby Stakes*, Cassell, London 1962

owner of the second horse, *Orlando*, was Colonel Peel, brother of the Prime Minister. Peel, encouraged by the relentless Bentinck, claimed the stakes. In the ensuing legal action, Wood withdrew from the case and *Orlando* was declared the legitimate winner causing my great-great grandfather, the nefarious Goodman Levy, who had stood to gain £50,000, to flee the country. The horse, the subject of a painting by Herring, never raced again, ending his life on a Northamptonshire farm. Bentinck was awarded a substantial testimonial for his efforts from which was founded the Bentinck Benevolent Fund for the dependants of impecunious jockeys and trainers.

Disgraceful as it was, scandals in the racing world at this time were rife. In the same race *Running Rein* had struck a horse called *Leander*, breaking *Leander's* leg. A veterinary examination disclosed that *Leander* was also a four year old whereupon his owners, two German brothers called Lichwald, were barred for life from racing their horses ever again in England. The brothers were extremely angry, denouncing the English as liars, exclaiming that their horse was not four but six! This was not all. The favourite was declared a victim of foul riding while the second favourite was not only nobbled on the eve of the race but was pulled up by his jockey to make doubly sure of its failure.

A curiosity of which I knew nothing and the family never spoke, concerned my maternal grandmother's grandfather. Septimus Hoskins was an architectural surveyor. On October 8th, 1866, when he was 64 years old, he went for a drink at the still standing Railway Tavern in Kentish Town. The landlady, waiting to come out from behind the bar, attempted to lift the hinged counter, which it was alleged Septimus for some reason resisted. It seems the landlord decided the old man had insulted his wife and ordered him to leave the premises. When Septimus attempted to object, the landlord ordered him out still more vehemently. Two days later Septimus returned for a drink in the hope of clearing up the matter, but strong words ensued. The landlord then thumped poor Septimus from behind the counter before leaping over the barrier and, according to the victim's son, hammering Septimus's head while the poor old fellow lay on the ground. The next day Septimus died. The nature of the original insult was never explained but at the ensuing inquest[2] the landlord was charged with manslaughter. At the subequent trial, held in the Central Criminal Court (Old Bailey), the publican was acquitted. This seems to have been due to the fact that two independent witnesses alleged that the principal prosecution witness, a sixteen year old girl, had perjured herself.[3]

It has always been a source of regret that my interest in our antecedents only came to light after all remaining close relatives were no longer with us. All that I knew were family legends, seldom spoken about, of which Goodman Levy was the darkest and the only one that subsequent probing firmly established as a kinsman. Septimus was unknown and most of the legends have still no clearly defined connection, among them Lady Reading; Nelly O'Brien, *dame horizontal*, Mistress of George III and the Earl of Bolingbroke, whose portrait by Joshua Reynolds adorns the Wallace Collection in London; and the notable seventeenth century miniaturist, John Hoskins. Hoskins died in 1665 while the earliest traced Hoskins in our family was Ephraim, born in 1726. John had a son, also a miniaturist, but the generation gap between him and Ephraim is one we have so far been unable to close from either end.

One legend, however, we have managed to clarify, although slightly flawed, the flaw lying in the Bohemian nature of the relationships which makes accurate family research almost impossible. Alfred Concannen's family came from Galway. *The Irish Independent* spoke of this graphic artist as a 'sociable and hot tempered character, described abroad as an archetypal Irishman'[4]

After marrying one of two sisters, known as the Devonshire beauties, their relationship festered and broke. He next consorted with, and probably married, Sarah Cohen, my great-great-aunt. They had two children, one of whom, Violet Eileen, married

---

2   Camden & Kentish Towns Gazette Nov 10 1866
3   CCC Proceedings First Session 1866-7, pp 84-92
4   *Irish Independent*, Feb 15, 2003

Edward de Marney in 1915, after they had begat the actors and film producers Derrick (1906-1978) and Terence (1908-1971). Although best known for his role in *Dangerous Moonlight* (1941), with Anton Walbrook and Sally Gray, Terence appeared in 39 other films as well as directing, producing and writing scripts and composing part of the soundtrack for *Dangerous Moonlight*. An abiding regret is that I never knew these last remaining contacts who died less than thirty years ago.

* * * * * * * *

Into this maelstrom of contrasting cultures and lifestyle, I first appeared at the family home 2 Briardale Gardens, Hampstead, in November, 1924, having been delivered by a New Zealand gynaecologist called Kennedy. By this time both grandfathers had died. My parents took me to their new home in Brookside Road, Golders Green. It was here that, aged three, I contracted typhoid fever, an illness which in those days was prolonged, incapacitating and frequently fatal. I was nursed at home by my devoted mother, surviving, the medics told her, only by dint of her unremitting care and the infant's strong will to live. Standing in a cot having a blood test lingers as my very first albeit faded memory. Significant consequences were the onset of bronchial asthma, which has never properly left me, and the excessive protectiveness of my mother, exaggerated by the fact that she had been warned against having any more children.

Looking back on those early childhood days I realise what an odd contrasting assortment of humanity was our family circle, a fact to which I would have to grow accustomed. Father and his family, partly Scottish but mostly English, were dependable, phlegmatic and stable. Father's centenarian mother was one of the most modest, patient, undemanding people you could wish to meet. She loved nothing more than a good laugh and teaching me many variations of Patience, or the mysteries of crocquet and how to knit with four needles, skills that were a source of comfort during my frequent bouts of asthma.

* * * * * * * *

Father's unmarried sister Lal devoted her life to her mother, surviving only a short time thereafter. My dear father, a natural gentleman, was intensely patriotic, serving in both Great Wars, proud of his Scottish blood, but always proclaiming himself first and foremost British. His rock-like stability must have attracted my mother whose single sisters always sought his advice and help whenever a real or imagined problem arose, a circumstance of unfailing regularity. Mother and her several sisters were artistic, excitable and socially perceptive, creating a kind of Jewish or Mediterranean type environment within a shrill cacophony of exclamations and blandishments. Thinking of mother's attitude to her only son reminds me of Lord Goodman's experience with his own mother, 'She found it difficult to believe that a more remarkable creature could ever have been conceived. This was, of course, at times embarrassing, because whenever she encountered anyone who was not acquainted with and therefore had not had the opportunity of detecting my remarkable intelligence and virtue, she proceeded to describe it in great detail' (Lord Goodman's *Memoirs*, p. 7).

A crisis arrived in 1929 when the breathless five year old was banished to a mixed private boarding school in Cliftonville, near Margate, where the bracing East Coast climate was expected to alleviate if not cure the condition. Lying in bed trying to pen a letter on kindergarten paper in the depth of despair at what seemed abandonment comes vividly to mind, a memory which seventy years have failed to expunge. After a week or two several redeeming features emerged, among them travelling in an old Wolseley car to learn how to ride a horse, and becoming proficient at roller skating in winter which was greatly enjoyed, racing along the deserted winter boulevards above Cliftonville beach. But the asthma did not respond so it was back to our new home at 39 Briardale Gardens, at the opposite end of the street in which I was born. A short time later mother succumbed to emphysema and pneumonia, her life saved by a resilient disposition and some wonderful care at the Brompton Hospital.

These miseries behind, I was old enough for enrolment at the Hall prep school near Swiss Cottage. But a sickly young lad who had often to be wheeled to school by his mother was a natural butt for bullying and within a year I was taken away to join York House at the foot of Maresfield Gardens, in Hampstead. The headmaster, a merry clergyman, was known to all the boys as the Owl. Each morning as we arrived we called out 'Good morning Owl !'. For the head, sitting in his study at an open door, this ritual replaced the need for a formal roll call. Then there was Mr Davson, the maths master who often stayed behind after school to discuss the latest motorcars and sometimes joined us boys in a game of spillikins. And George Rust, he of the fish monogram, the scoutmaster. Our scouting sessions were held in Finchley Road, at a site I located decades later as the place where a century earlier, when it was still rural, Sir Edwin Landseer had completed his first known drawings.

Apart from the dominie, I remember a red-headed Irish boy called Morrison who had a tantrum, whether feigned or real we never tried to fathom, whenever he hear the word 'orange'; a fifteen minute banishment outside the classroom for talking, the longest quarter of an hour of my life which it seemed was never going to end; and a pleasant young man called Ali Reza Zarrenkash who, we were told, was the son of the Persian Ambassador. For his birthday he proudly announced to his mates the parental gift of a brand new bicycle, a present so great that to the rest of us seemed beyond our wildest dreams.

Every year on Ash Wednesday all the school snaked their way to the Owl's church, near Swiss Cottage, although why the expedition was always on Ash Wednesday[5] we were not told. This was my first experience of going to church and the curiosity of it all has stuck. But none of these things diminished our fondness and respect for the Owl.

Occasionally I would stay with maternal aunt Mabel and her family in their Chiltern Court corner flat overlooking Marylebone and Baker Street. One day in 1931 a span of Marylebone Road from the top of Wimpole Street to its junction with Baker Street

---

[5] It is, of course, the first day of Lent, named after a custom in the Western Church of sprinkling ashes on the heads of penitents admitted to penance on that day, a practice thought to have originated with Gregory the Great.

was banned to traffic, the roadway lined with straw. This, I was told, was to dampen the noise of the funeral cortège of the novelist Arnold Bennett. I wondered if this was the last time London had straw strewn on any of its streets, although I now believe that this was for the funeral of Winston Churchill. In spite of being only seven at the time, the incident left me wondering who this remarkable man was to deserve such public and solemn treatment. The only fragment of information I gleaned was that Bennett's favourite sounding phrase in the English language was 'cellar door'.

An advantage of being an only child was that, thrown upon one's own resources, all manner of imaginative amusements had to be invented. Among the main props were the cigarette cards offered at this time by all the leading tobacco manufacturers. These became race horses as they were shuffled across the floor or, when I was in bed with one of my bronchial attacks, across the blankets, with race-cards and bookmakers' odds prepared and recorded in advance. Variants included having each card transmogrified in to a contemporary golfer who then did battle in open matchplay or into current tennis stars who fought over the Davis Cup, the cards being manoeuvred in a variety of different ways. The fact that cigarette cards were part of primary school leisure culture meant that there was ample opportunity to swap and even to accrue during the various games played during the break and after hours.

* * * * * * * * *

The first summer holiday I recall was in Norfolk at Sheringham and Walcot. My father, who had served as a cavalryman with the Honourable Artillery Company in the first war, used to visit Sheringham where lived one of his surviving wartime friends, an estate agent who owned a small stable of horses and a garden pond with a punt, over which sometimes hovered the most beautiful but to a small urban boy terrifying, dragon flies.

Father's favourite mount in Palestine had been called Peter, after whom I was named, and many happy hours were spent galloping along the Norfolk beach. One day mother's riding proclivities were sorely tested when her horse bolted and she went careering across the sands scattering placid sun bathers in her wake, making hysterical calls for help as my father galloped after her, eventually calming the situation. At the time it seemed hilarious but for my mother it had been deeply traumatic and she never rode again.

It was during these prep school years that two events occurred of lasting influence. In 1937 we went on a family holiday to Scotland, with the Gairloch Hotel as our main base. In those days the hotel, which had hosted Lloyd George's cabinet during the first Great War, was a place of considerable luxury with a sweeping drive around a grass forecourt looking across the sea to Skye, a kilted concierge at the door welcoming arrivals.

The first time I experienced panic was when excitable mother and placid father took me fishing for whiting in the bay. As we lay peacefully at anchor there came upon us the sound of a stream cascading into the great ocean. But we were some distance from land or any stream. The next thing we knew were plumes of vapour rising from the sea beneath unmistakable fins which belonged, we were afterwards told, to a grind of bottle-nosed whales. We had no life jackets, none of us could swim, there were no other boats visible and mother was becoming increasingly hysterical. When we eventually reached land, father having rowed as if Satan was at his elbow, I felt more a coward than a hero but the feeling of powerlessness and the hidden dangers of the impersonal, relentless ocean remains.

We travelled north again the next year, this time with two cousins and two large tents, a joyful expedition that was repeated in 1939 with grandmother ('Gaga') and Aunty Lal. These journeys opened eyes and heart and soul to the beauties of rural life, most especially the Scottish Highlands.

The sport that attracted my father and I most was athletics. Many happy hours were spent at the old White City stadium and it was while we were in Gairloch that the late Stanley Wooderson broke the world record for the mile, a gleeful moment to savour. The walk down the brae from the old post office as we read the wonderful news made the holiday.

In 1936, as well as Hilda, a sonsie young maid from Sunderland, we had taken into the family a young Finnish au pair girl, Aune Saarinen. Aune and I developed a happy friendship. When her year was up I was heart broken, the only child had lost the nearest he ever knew to a sister. Four decades went by until in the 1990s I thought how nice it would be if I could find out what had become of Aune. All I remembered was her maiden name and her home town. To my great surprise, with the help of the Finnish Church and its excellent parish records, she was located living in Tampere, by this time an elderly widow and grandmother. Although we have never seen each other since 1937, more than seventy long years ago, we remain in frequent touch, my oldest and much treasured, earliest surviving friend.

By 1938 the world had become a more serious place and with advancing adolescence, life was entering a more intense phase. Carefree exuberance was being replaced by the arousal of passions, passion about family and home, passion about one's sporting heroes, a greater awareness of the pitfalls and pleasures of life, a sensitivity for achievement, failure and loss, an awakening response to the beauties of art, friendship and the natural world, and with these, a profound appreciation of occasional solitude which perhaps only an only child can fully appreciate and understand.

Animals held a strong fascination. My first intimate encounter was with two guinea pigs, housed in a converted orange box, pending the arrival of a more substantial home. Hours were spent just watching them, perched in the dining-room table in their temporary home, a great joy, especially when they produced babies and became tame enough for an occasional cuddle, and watching them skedaddling around the drawing room floor. But one day tragedy struck, I had succumbed to one of my regular bouts of infection and this time the virus passed to my babies and all of them died.

I have always loved dogs, feeling a close affinity with Cesar Millan the celebrated Mexican 'Dog Whisperer', whose knowledge of canine psychology is unsurpassed as anyone who has seen his programmes will testify. Not only does he understand and love dogs, of which he owns more than twenty, but he is equally good with their often neurotic and naive owners. Though without his skills, I was always fearless in my approaches; this and the guinea pig saga nurtured ambitions to become a vet. Mother was quite modern in matters of health and well-being and persuaded Dadna, as I always called my father, to have me psychologically assessed by a vocational psychologist. It did not take the consultant long to report that a lack of manual dexterity had to exclude further thought of such ambition, but the seeds of animal husbandry had been sown, with unexpected consequences.

An incident from this time happened one summer afternoon when searching for four leaf clovers outside Vernon Court off the Finchley Road. Mother had stopped for a chat with a pleasant youngish lady. Mother was always stopping for a chat with someone or other but for a young boy this diversion was rather special. The lady was Amy Johnson, the aviatrix. In 1930 a few years before this chance encounter, she had become the first woman to fly solo to Australia. The following year she set a record for a solo flight to Tokyo, followed a year later with another record, this time to Cape Town. She joined the Auxiliary Air Force in 1939 and was tragically lost when her plane disappeared on a routine flight over the Thames Estuary.

In 1938 I became a weekly boarder at Highgate School, able to continue the pleasure of prolonged sporting activities denied to day boys, but with the love and security of going home for weekends. The guinea pigs had gone, Shredded Wheat replaced by porridge. My class teacher was a genial, rotund, bald man whom we thought of as eighty but was probably fifty. He was known to everyone as 'Eggy' on account of the appearance and shape of his head. In our youthful ignorance of the ageing process, it seemed astonishing that this ageing, plump gentleman had once gained a soccer blue at Oxford and later played in the English first division.

Then came the Munich crisis when war seemed imminent. A tearful farewell as, trying to be men, the school assembled on a Paddington Station platform, satchels and gas masks at the ready, en route to the relative safety of Ilfracombe. I remember some makeshift lessons in a hotel lounge presided over by the head of school, a very earnest, well groomed young man called Lawrence, who later became a Senior Clerk in the House of Commons.

The crisis over, albeit temporarily, a happy year was spent after our return to Highgate, enjoying cricket and soccer above all else, under the tutelage of Aubrey Howard Fabian, cricket blue and Derby County footballer. It was fun being the only new bug to get into the house soccer team, which won the inter-house cup, thanks largely to an athletic diving save by our goalie. The summer term ended as the shadow of war grew darker. The day war was declared we were on our way home from a third summer holiday in distant tranquil Gairloch. Whilst there we had made the acquaintance of Peter Thomson, a farmer in whose field we had camped, a meeting which was to have a major impact on my life. On the last day of our broken journey, we were lunching in Stamford when Prime Minister Chamberlain made the fateful announcement that Britain was now at war. Within a week I was back at school, one of the large majority whose parents had elected to have their sons evacuated to Westward Ho! in North Devon.

Our home of so much nostalgia at 39 Briardale Gardens was placed on the market and my parents moved to a mezzanine flat in Chiltern Court, two doors away from aunt Mabel and her family, and – although we never knew it at the time – opposite Dorset House wherein lived two of my very different heroes: Bertrand Russell and Apsley Cherry Garrard. Chiltern Court was considered especially well built, owned by London Transport and designed to withstand the continuous rumblings of the Underground which ran beneath. The flats had their own so-called bomb-proof shelter, certainly a safer place then an ordinary house in suburban Hampstead.

At about this time mother's two unmarried sisters, sensitive, intelligent, neurotic, wide-eyed Renée and glamorous but duller goldilocks Gladys ('Gar'), and my deaf but stately grandmother, also decided to leave London and could think of no better place to go than to follow the example of the school. So for the next four years they moved from one rented furnished house in Westward Ho! to another. By this time, although fully adjusted to boarding school life, with its rationing of jam, sugar and other goodies – each boy had a small jar for his jam and another for his sugar which had to last a month – it was refreshing to visit my relations for an occasional teatime break – how tasty was the hot buttered toast and marmalade, and more important, I was able to remain in the village during all the holidays, my patriotic father, who had served throughout the first war, having volunteered to join the RAF and moved with mother to his first posting with Training Command in Torquay.

Westward Ho! was, of course, the scene of Kipling's boyhood classic 'Stalky and Co' (1899) which, if we agree with *The Concise Cambridge of English Literature* 'is an unpleasant book about unpleasant boys in an unpleasant school'[6]. For us, a century and half later, life in an evacuated boarding school was very different from the popular image of life in such a place. In deference to the day boys who had now perforce become boarders, fagging was abolished, school prefects were no longer allowed to beat other boys, and with no more than the rudiments of organised sport, free time became available for a multitude of escapades. We revelled in our emancipation. In the 1940s Westward Ho! was a small village at the end of the beaten track[7]. An extensive beach was furnished along its straight mile long stretch by an unbroken backbone of medium sized stones, called the pebble ridge, maintained by locals known as pot wallopers. The purpose of this ridge is to guard the low lying ground on the landward side whereon lies the Royal North Devon Golf Club, an establishment with a distinguished history no master or resident ever mentioned. In later years this brought to mind how many places and peoples we casually encounter in life, experiences which would have been enriched if only we had known more about them at the time. A steep hill above the main village rose up to the tors, a ribbed keel of land, which ran parallel to the pebble ridge and the shoreline far below.

When very young I had an alter ego called Pang Hey although where this name came from no-one knew. Whenever I attracted

---

[6] p. 959
[7] Today it lies despoiled by development, recently voted the worst English holiday resort.

parental opprobrium I replied that it wasn't me but Pang Hey who had done it. Some years later, exploring our new base in the village, I was intrigued to note the vicar's name – the Reverend Mr Pinhey.

School House was encamped in Bellevue, an ivy-clad old mansion, and the only school unit on top of the hill, so that every excursion to classes, to cafés and to my aunts, involved a steep descent and an asthmatic climb back up to base.

My best school buddy was John Fuller, a bond having been formed on the first day when as new boys we waited together on the front door steps wondering what to do and where to go whenever the first bell should sound. John was a warm, angular, slightly nervy, sincere young man. We found ourselves in the same class, in the same dormitory, and when they eventually met, our two excitable mothers got along very well. We shared a disregard for work and an inclination to embark on any idiosyncratic adventure which presented itself. I was a hopelessly untidy young fellow and whenever a fly button was undone or an odd pair of socks appeared beneath the trousers, our maths master, Mr. Gibbon, would shout 'Fuller, take him outside and dress him'. Items of dress with which I could never cope were puttees, worn as part of our uniform in the compulsory OTC (Officers' Training Corps). Parades were called to a halt, Private McEwan was summarily dismissed in disgrace and barred from any hint of promotion, the recalcitrant long strips of khaki cloth cascading down both legs. But in my final year, by dint of becoming a first-class shot and managing to remember the seven duties of a sentinel, my military career ended as a lance-corporal, 'serving' beneath Murray Walker, our exalted sergeant major.

One Saturday afternoon, the tide being out, John and I, with the unexpected company of his small dog Garbo who had mysteriously appeared, strolled along the beach until we reached the sand banks at the mouth of the Torridge River. Suddenly the sea was eddying and surfing around us and our route to the shore was cut off. Carrying Garbo under his arm, John and I, both non-swimmers, managed to wade through deepening pools as the tide came racing in. It was a close run and frightening experience and from that day onwards the headmaster declared the coastline and the river out of bounds.

Our preferred method of transport for half-term adventures was hitch-hiking. One summer half term we organised a private race among a few friends to reach a country inn I had noticed on a previous expedition, returning in time for evening roll-call. Unfortunately, my map reading was sadly deficient so that nowhere along the extent of the appointed Devonshire lanes was there any sign of an inn. John and I persevered the longest but there was little traffic to help us and we were back at Bellevue at about ten. All the doors were locked, the only entrance being through an upstairs window reached by standing on top of a rubbish bin before shinning up a drainpipe. Unhappily, but inevitably, the lid fell off with an almighty clatter, leading to inevitable discovery and the choice of either a headmaster's beating (he was known to us all as the Pate on account of the shape of the head of his predecessor), or the docking of the next half-term. We both elected the former punishment, duly delivered and recorded above our dormitory beds, where a VC was the reward for a beating, a DSO for a master's punishment, and an MC for a prefect's punishment. I have to confess that although never indulging in anything as sinful even as smoking, I boasted a VC and bar, DSO and MC triple bar, all for untidiness, unpunctuality, or lack of classroom diligence.

Aside from all these pranks and peccadilloes, two developments shone through, illuminating all memories of school. We were a friendly bunch in School House and very early in our evacuation, while still billeted in Torridge House, our original base, on September 20th 1939 several of us decided to form a club. This we called the Gafic Club, 'G' for golf, 'A' for athletics (we held our own games), 'F' for football, 'I' for indoor games (snooker, Totopoly, bridge and chess), and 'C' for cricket. In addition to John and I the foundation members were Gordon Bell, Ian Baines (son of the comedian Stainless Stephen), Martin Pegg, and Richard Parsons. With the removal of School House to Bellevue in 1940, the character of the club changed, becoming more organised. Outsiders were challenged at eleven different events varying from football to bridge, while most summer evenings during term we took on the prefects at touch handball on the back lawn as well as organising a competitive inter-dormitory league.

Once settled in Bellevue we made a large cycle track around the slopes of the vegetable garden with the object of racing one at a time around the perimeter against the clock. One day someone sped out of control disappearing near the top, landing slap in the middle of a tea party being given by the Pate for a number of VIPs including the Bishop of Exeter and a posse of refugee European Professors. We were, of course, severely reprimanded, but the saga had not ended, for one of our punishments was to move a large shed from Bellevue to the garden next door. Luckily, Laurie Buck, one of our number, came to the rescue by producing a horse and cart borrowed from one of his farming friends. But, alas, our efforts only succeeded in arousing another bout of magisterial wrath for instead of moving the shed we succeeded only in knocking it down.

When in 1942 members began to leave school the character of the club changed again, its purpose and value becoming quite different. A constitution had been framed at Edgehill, on the summit of Buckleigh, with regular reunions. By 1946, by which time most of the members had left school, membership had risen to 28, the star among them being my old French teacher, Theodore Mallinson, known to everyone as 'TGM'. He was the only member of staff ever to be honoured with membership, the best teacher I ever had, happily still with us, and, although now in his nineties, he remains the school archivist and very much the soul of the school[8].The club produced a booklet in 1947 as well as having its own stationery printed with the club's motto 'Sincerity'.

During the early part of our evacuation, I was fortunate enough to win the confidence of an unusual character who was the owner of private indoor and outdoor double squash courts near the village centre. He kindly entrusted me with the key to the indoor court, so that in addition to learning the sport – he had

---

[8]   Since these words were written, 'TGM' sadly died, in his 99th year, on Oct 11, 2008.

a wooden leg and had mastered a technique whereby whenever retrieving the ball against a side wall his right leg fell away, thus avoiding serious damage to the leg or injury to its owner – members of the Gafic Club revelled in this refuge, enjoying many private teas and escape from the discipline of the classroom as we disported ourselves in measured tones on the dusty balcony of the indoor court.

We developed a code for forbidden activities closest to our heart. '1' was cigarette smoking, a vice I personally never shared, preferring a pipe and St Bruno during the holidays, '2' referred to a glamorous young blonde called Anne Tompkins, whom we adored but none of us knew, being too shy to ever find an excuse to make her acquaintance, and '3' was for any activity such as clandestine visits to the cinema in Bideford that entailed absence without leave.

The second source of great enjoyment was our piggery. As part of the war effort, John, Laurie Buck and I hit upon the idea of forming a consortium for the purpose of acquiring two sows. The money was raised by selling 2/6d shares on the understanding that the investment would be repaid plus 100% profit, if possible. We were allowed to keep the pigs on a nearby farm. This was all very well but feeding them every day involved collecting swill from the various school and other houses, cooking it on a primitive fire, before sloshing the resultant brew into the troughs. Since the farm was a mile away up a hill with hedgerows full of yarrow and wild horseradish, the time involved was considerable. During term the chore was shared by the three of us in rotation but in the holidays it all devolved upon me as, thanks to my two aunts, I was the only Highgate boy left in the village. One of the fondest Yuletide memories of my life was Christmas day 1941, spent walking up the hill to the farm, preparing the food and enjoying the swine's company, all in quiet rural isolation, the deep grey sea beyond the green cliffs, with the outline of mysterious Lundy island far away across the bay.

The following year the shadow of school certificate exams was upon us, so that, with great reluctance, when our two pigs were ready for market, no replacements were allowed. However, all was not lost, for we managed to persuade the headmaster, who was also our house-master, to allow us to keep rabbits. During the holidays I carried them down to my aunts where they lived amid the luxury of an overgrown garden with dandelions in profusion. But one holiday John volunteered to take them home to London. When the train arrived at Paddington John called to his mother 'can you help me with something I have in the guards van ?'. Faced with five large hutches and their occupants, his mother was not amused, 'I dread to think what father will say', but the rabbits survived to face another term.

These essays in animal husbandry had a lasting effect for two of us. When he left school Laurie Buck remained for the rest of his life in Devon, marrying two local farmer's daughters in quick succession, acquiring the accent and dialect of a true Devonian and remaining in the Bideford/Barnstaple axis. For me the effect, as we shall see, was not altogether dissimilar.

Adolescent years are formative times and beyond the classroom, several life-long interests and passions were taking shape. In Bideford there was a treasure house of literature, Harper's Bookshop, now – alas – no more. It was here that many hours were spent browsing and my first books were bought: Adam Smith's *The Wealth of Nations* and Fridjof Nansen's *The First Crossing of Greenland*, the latter beside my elbow as I write, the price of 1/6d (18p) still visible on the blank front end paper, beside my childish signature and first book-plate.

Other awakening interests were classical music (I had long been a sentimental devotee of Vera Lynn and Charlie Kunz), dashing to my aunts to listen to *Music While You Work*[9], devouring tales of the heroic age of polar exploration, and learning a little more about the game of chess. During the holidays I listened to every possible concert and with it the dawn of understanding about how a grown man could weep on hearing Sibelius Symphony No 2 for the first time, as once reported on the radio, while during term Scott, Shackleton and Co were read avidly by

---

[9]   Readers old enough to remember this programme will be interested in a recent book, *Music While You Work, An Era in Broadcasting*, Brian Reynolds, Book Guild Publishing, 2006.

torch-light beneath the bedclothes after lights out. Chess yielded to a more gradual approach, it was not until later that I began to play through the games of the masters and learn the openings, gleaning an understanding of tactics and strategy.

Looking back on these days one recognises how those of us living in Britain during the 1920s and early 30s were extraordinarily privileged to have had the opportunity to appreciate and enjoy, at the summit of their powers, in music the genius of Frederick Delius (1862-1934), Edward Elgar (1857-1934), and Ralph Vaughan Williams (1872-1958); among conductors and musical giants the incomparable Sir Thomas Beecham (1879-1961); among dramatists George Bernard Shaw (1856-1950); and in philosophical thought Bertrand Russell (1872-1970). What a towering group, all born within twenty-three years of each other. Surely a galaxy of musical and literary genius unsurpassed before or since in our nation's history.

* * * * * * * * *

Visits to the wonderful BBC Promenade Concerts were always a source of delight. Once, when standing in the auditorium before the concert had begun, I heard a termagant behind me exclaiming to her neighbour 'someone has been smoking Belgian cigarettes'. Alerted by the comment my attention was drawn to steam drifting from my right-hand trouser pocket, a packet of Swan Vestas having combusted.

It was during late adolescence, when emotions begin to enflame, that I attempted to write poetry, a catharsis that was intensely enjoyable. Unhappily, of the few that were published and others in precious notebooks, many have been lost. *'No waters flow that musing can alone distil'* is the only single line I can recall.[10]

Chess was a growing enthusiasm, reaching its zenith a few years later playing for Scotland and ardently supporting the now defunct Chess Educational Society (CES). After that it very soon reached a level of self-torment following a defeat so that it ceased

---

[10] Since this was written an old notebook has come to light with a selection of verses, some of which appear as an appendix.

to be fun and became an ordeal. With the arrival of computers every master game is recorded and can be referenced. This is extremely time consuming and encourages obsession. To be a serious contender it is first necessary to understand and be able to apply rudiments of opening theory. The size of the task can be gauged by the fact that at the latest count there are 701 different named openings. Several decades later our younger son Rhod passed through a similar phase, becoming joint winner of one of the annual Open Civil Service tournaments, but he too then abandoned serious play, enjoying just the occasional 'friendly' game.

On one of our weekend camping ploys we pitched tent in heavy rain beside a river. After two of our party had gone for a swim, Laurie Buck and I lit a bonfire to dry both the bathers and our own soggy bedding. Unfortunately, matters got out of control for as well as drying some of the clothing, most of the shirts and underwear were burnt. After spending a cold night beneath layers of newspaper, without pyjamas or shirts, although I did have my yellow kapok eiderdown, we were early awoken by a herd of cows. They were curiously aggressive, pulling down the tent, splitting the canvas and breaking the central pole. On the way home the eiderdown came to grief on the main Barnstaple road, becoming caught in the front spokes of my bicycle, showering kapok like confetti across the highway. Somewhat crestfallen and very hungry, we found a baker's shop which we entered to buy cakes for tea. We had to leave very quickly when John noticed that I was standing in the middle of a large wooden tray full of cream buns, which some unthinking soul had carelessly left on the floor. Luckily, the baker couldn't run fast enough to catch our cycles. I was never fond of Barnstaple.

Little has been said about the masters because our extra-mural activities and adventures seemed so much more exciting and lessons, English and history excepted, seemed ineffably boring. There was dear diminutive Miss Heather, the science teacher, based in what in peace time had been Twose's Garage, physics in the attic and chemistry in the workshop. She found keeping discipline a task too many; we did not rag her but ribald inattention was rife and absenteeism common. 'Jumbo' White, rotund, merry and bright, retained our attention prancing around the schoolroom bringing history to life as he described the good guys and lambasted the villains. He was a master of the lampoon, a wagger-pagger-bagger need never be a waste paper basket again. We never doubted the truth of his claim that, as a putative kinsman of the clan Campbell, upon revealing his name he had once been denied accommodation at a B & B establishment in Glencoe.

For a term we were privileged to have teaching us biology, E L Grant Watson (1885-1970). Though no-one ever thought to tell us, Grant Watson was a distinguished anthropologist, pseudo-Lamarckian biologist, and author, combining the scrutiny of a scientist with the insight of a poet.

The headmaster, Geoffrey Bell, the 'Pate', was fearsome, though whether his stern demeanour was genuine or assumed we boys could never decide. We had no idea and would have been surprised to know that, as an Oxford blue, he had once played first-class cricket for Derbyshire. His slight wife Marjory, who lived to be 104, was a charming, auburn-haired mother figure, attractive, sympathetic and warm. There was a temporary dashing young master called White, reputedly Marjory's cousin, and in a school play, with the insightful wickedness of youth, we composed a ditty, one verse of which ran:

> When the headmaster goes to town,
> Our sorrows are but slight;
> It brings great joy to Mrs Bell,
> And Mr Gordon White.

But our favourite man, and the only one in the whole wide world who could have tutored me successfully in French, was the aforementioned T.G.M., his quirky enthusiasm striding across the desktops mouthing French epithets endeared him to generations of school boys long after all those years ago in Westward Ho!

One aspect of school life that always repelled me was church-going. The school ethos was firmly Christian, fervently upheld by the Pate, with prayers every morning and grace before meals. Elementary metaphysics had interested me from a very early age, Christian beliefs struck me as deeply flawed and, probably tinged with adolescent arrogance, I perceived the large unthinking majority to be either piously hypocritical or perversely conventional.

This came to a head at confirmation time when upon reaching the age of sixteen, regarded as the age of discretion, there took place the religious rite of confirmation, confirming a person to be a member of the Christian faith. I asked to be excused and, although no words were ever spoken, the effect was to bar me from prefecthood. This was of little concern as I have always felt uneasy in the face of authority, whether as recipient or wielder. However, in my last term I was exalted to the level of dormitory prefect, almost certainly a *faute de mieux* appointment.

Once the rabbits had been dispersed, it was possible to spend the holidays with my parents. On one occasion, at the height of the London blitz, while Dadna, who had not yet joined the RAF, was out fire fighting with the Home Guard, Mother and I were sheltering in the underground Chiltern Court air-raid shelter, when there was an enormous explosion, a direct hit on Madam Tussaud's next door. I have never heard a louder or more sinister noise.

Occasionally I went to play chess in the evening with Dadna's best friend, Mr Pullen, manager of Hamleys toy shop in Regent Street. As he too was a fire-fighter we had to play on the top floor so that whenever the mournful air raid sirens sounded he had to repair to the roof in case of incendiary bombs. Fortunately none fell during any of our games. Among his idiosyncrasies Pullen was a numerologist, telling me that my special number was nine, a superstition that remains with me, having a curious sequel that will appear later[11].

The following year Dadna, although over age, volunteered to join the RAF and found himself posted to an Air Training wing in Torquay. One of the holiday pursuits developed by three school

---

[11]   Years later I learned that nine is the mystical number found everywhere in the fanciful works of the old heraldic writers – there were nine degrees of rank, nine ordinaries, nine furs and nine colours.

friends and I was a war game that involved the map of Europe, whereby we each fielded different countries. No references were made to the actual war. We circulated to each other moves in rotation. My responsibility was the British Air Force for which I prepared imaginary postings with imaginary names and a detailed record of the state of play, including details of aircraft and crew. Taking these papers one summer holiday to the hotel where my parents were posted, with the arpeggios of the pianist Moura Lympany practising in the room above, my war papers were found on a table by a junior officer who must have immediately alerted the Air Ministry because shortly afterwards my father was called in by a member of the Intelligence to account for detailed logistics that had been uncovered in a book with the name McEwan on the cover. My usually phlegmatic father was more furious than I had ever seen him when, to my intense embarrassment, immediately after dinner in the dining room he stood up and demanded to know who in the present company had had the stupidity to report the obvious nonsense of a school boy's imaginary games to the Intelligence Service when any fool should have recognised their amateur, unreal and unsophisticated nature. A horrible hush descended on the dining-room. I never discovered whether the culprit had owned up.

Proceeding along the road from Bellevue, just before descending to the village from the tor, there was a long, six foot high stone wall. Behind this barrier lived the McConnochies, elderly mother, son and daughter. The son was a recluse, very shy, completely bald, and sensitively conscious of his enormous bulk. A glandular problem commonly ran in the family for mother and daughter were as thin as my friend was huge. Somehow, in a way now forgotten, I came to know this enormous, puckish poultry farmer, enjoying the privilege of his company. Many were the afternoons spent collecting eggs, feeding hens and learning something of the fascination of P G Wodehouse, of whose books McConnochie was a fervent admirer. I have often wondered what became of this man, his family and his hens.

Another piece of local village history about which we were never told was the position in the pantheon of English golf held by the Royal North Devon Golf Club of Westward Ho! This was the golf course where, in my ignorance, I learnt to hack, where the Gafic Club held its first tournaments, justifying the 'G' in its title. A barren but invigorating wide open space during the war with scarcely a player or green-keeper in sight, seriously deep bunkers, sheep gently grazing, the distant roar of the ocean in the background. But within its bosom there lay hidden three claims to fame. First, it regards itself, perhaps rightly, as the cradle of English golf, having been founded in 1864 making it arguably the oldest course in England. Second, it nourished the skills of John Henry Taylor, born in Northam overlooking the course, the man who, alongside Harry Vardon and James Braid, dominated the professional game for thirty years. But for me its very special place is not because of either of these things but because of what happened one October morning in 1934, the whimsicality of which has never been equalled, certainly not surpassed, on any national sporting field.

Alistair Cooke once described the scene in one of his famous broadcasts. 'It was the first day of the English Ladies Championship – a larger crowd than usual had gathered round the first tee because a rumour had gone round that one unknown woman was about to outrage some convention of the game ... nobody knew who she was or what she was up to. There whisked into sight a large yellow Rolls Royce, and out of it stepped a Miss Gloria Minoprio. She had two shocks to administer. The lesser one – she was carrying just one club, an iron. That was it – she was going to play the championship with one club. She did, but the big shock that made the journalists stagger, Miss Minoprio [her face whitened with powder] was wearing a neat little black beret, a polo-necked white sweater, and, wait for it, tight fitting midnight-blue trousers, fitting the shapely – the very shapely – Miss Minoprio who, as Damon Runyon remarked 'had bumps where dolls were supposed to have bumps'. She was a stunning sight, an outrage to presiding authority – the Ladies Golf Union – which put out an instant notice deploring anyone who 'departs from the proper decorous costume of the traditional lady golfer'." Well, Gloria lost that day but she returned next year, still with just the one club, and won, but was defeated on the Tuesday, giving rise to Henry Longhurst's jibe 'sic transit Gloria Tuesday'. But, as Cooke said, 'lets hear it for Gloria Minoprio, who struck the first blow for woman's liberty on the links'[12]. And to think that a mere five years later we young lads were never told a thing about it!

* * * * * * * * *

The time came to leave school and acquire some money. The war was still raging, my parents were away following Dadna's career training RAF air-crew, my two aunts and grandmother remained in Westward Ho! so I stayed with them. School friends had gone except for lanky Laurie Buck who wasted no time in courting and eventually marrying the cross-eyed daughter of a wealthy farmer, but other friends in the village remained, especially McConnochie with whom I shared and certainly understood a small proportion of his reclusive mentality.

The first job I found was as a farm hand earning the princely sum of 45/- a week. My elderly fellow labourer with whom I shared lunch breaks in an empty pigsty, had such a strong Devonian accent that conversation was impossible. The only task I can now recall was scything and burning clumps of nettles and other weeds in a large field when, at the end of a long hot day, the fire I had started spread to a haystack. I was saved from whatever further ignominy lay in store by contracting an attack of pharyngitis which led to my resignation on medical advice, a case of jumping before being pushed, for a combination of asthma and allergic pharyngitis was not a healthy one. Thus ended my first attempt at gainful employment, which had lasted just two hay-fevered weeks.

There followed a short spell teaching at a run down-prep school in Bideford before finding my last and most mentally rewarding job in Devon. This was back in Westward Ho! helping to run a small intensive one acre market garden owned by a kindly, quiet, unassuming man who had had part of his face shot away in the first war. Respecting his disfigurement, I enjoyed learning about the finer points of digging, the amount of liquid manure

---

[12] Alistair Cooke, *Letter from America*, 5 July 1999

to bestow upon artichokes and onions, the cultivation of lettuce, carrots and beans, and the more difficult task of how to deal with the public when they came to buy their brassicas.

In the village a friend of my aunts had introduced me to herbal tobacco. With ordinary St Bruno becoming increasingly difficult to obtain, this was supposedly less harmful. Apart from the fact that the mixture sparked, smelled like burning hay, and was occasionally garnished with maggots, to a young pipe smoker it was a comforting substitute for the real thing.

So it was that on one of my excursions to the Highlands, camping in a field above Tomidhu farm, near Balmoral, with two fellow Gafficers, a soldier from one of the nearby anti-aircraft batteries, pretending to defend Balmoral Castle, came to our tent one evening to ask if he might have a fill of the tobacco, the aroma having reached their gun site. This I gladly provided only to be told the following morning by a pale looking young recruit that, although grateful for the bounty, he had been sick most of the night.

The next day we cycled the seven miles into Ballater to watch a gymkhana being given around and beyond what is now the second hole of the local golf course. The performers were a company of mounted Indian artillerymen training for service, we were told, in Norway. They were billeted in Nissen huts on what is now Monaltrie Park.

With School Certificate having been passed sufficiently well to merit university entrance, life was not all work, there was music to exercise the soul, an occasional flutter on the horses, letters to Gafic members, chess by correspondence, books to search for at Harpers. And in due course there arrived Joan. Mrs Fisher, another evacuee, was a friend of our family, Joan was her only daughter and for weeks on end the two headless families planned and plotted to have us meet. Eventually my shyness succumbed. Joan became a good platonic friend and when the war was over we continued to meet, mainly on the tennis court, until in due course, after she had joined the BBC and married into the RAF, our paths no longer crossed.

Chapter 2

Life Begins in Earnest

They never taste who always drink
They always talk who never think.

[Matthew Prior]

A warm attraction to the countryside, allied to an obvious love of animals and what my parents recognised as a comprehensive inability to engage in any sort of business activity, persuaded us all that in spite of health concerns, farming was the preferred vocation, and that a university qualification would help compensate for shyness, a genetic legacy from the McEwan side of the family. The alternative was law but in those days Latin was the pre-requisite, a subject I had abandoned years before. Although very much a home bird, five years of boarding school lessened the trauma of bidding farewell to my parents in London as I set off for Edinburgh. I arrived at Waverley Station one raw October evening, sat sipping coffee in the station restaurant beside a copy of *The Scottish Farmer,* charting how many days and hours would elapse before it was time to return home. Early attempts at finding digs were not encouraging. The first landlady, a genteel elderly widow, had rooms full of equally elderly lace and antimacassars. These only added to my feeling of bewildered home sickness so, after an uneventful night, I rendered my apologies, abandoned the good lady and, armed with *The Scotsman,* went in search. I settled on an establishment in exclusive Heriot Row, with a bed-sitting room on the first floor, large enough to hold a concert. In a degree of luxury totally inappropriate for an impecunious first year student I examined my finances. It at once became clear that if I remained in Heriot Row my capital would be exhausted in two weeks and classes had not yet even begun. Thus, after a memorable week, common sense prevailed and it was off to a very much smaller abode with the family of a manual worker in Inverleith Row, conveniently adjacent to the Royal Botanic Gardens, where the botany lectures were held. Here I remained for the year, comfortable and well looked after, the only downside being my landlord's habit of spitting into the fire rather than soil a handkerchief, a quotidian performance which he propelled with unerring accuracy.

My first undergraduate year was disastrous. First year agriculture comprised four subjects: physics, chemistry, botany and zoology. Physics and chemistry left me unequivocally cold without creating any interest whatsoever and, having no interest, they were rejected. Botany was taught in a very boring way, with endless lists of classifications to be found in, I recall, the botanical students' bible, *Bentham & Hooker*. Furthermore, the ability to draw even an apple, still less the ovary and placenta of a wall-flower, extended my artistic ability beyond its natural limit. The only redeeming feature was the attractive blond laboratory assistant who did her best to tutor my ailing, failing pencil. Zoology was the least repellent subject probably because Professor James Ritchie was such an inspiring teacher, but here too there were 'practicals'. Dissecting the inner recesses of a lately deceased frog or locating the breeding apparatus of an earthworm were irreconcilable with my dormant scientific sensitivities. Inevitably, the exams were either failed or ignored altogether. The basic laws and truths of science would for me have to remain forever unopened. Memory dominated thought and lacking any inclination to employ memory for topics lacking interest, my fledgling agricultural career was doomed.

But the year was not entirely disastrous. Three of us in the class forged a firm friendship. Walter Davies was a fiery, aquiline Welshman who worked hard but shared our humour and rebellious *Weltanschauung*. In due course he developed a successful business in Wales as an agricultural contractor. R.P.B. (Bob) Paine, the son of a Colonel of Marines and himself an inveterate adventurer, shared my disaffection with the course and whenever possible the two of us ventured to the squash courts or the mountains or anywhere to get away from the city.

A memorable two days were spent over the February break tramping twenty miles across the glorious Perthshire hills culminating in an ascent of Ben Vorlich, our trousers frozen solid as we devoured sandwiches on the freezing but exhilarating summit. We slept the first night in Monachyle Youth Hostel (does it still exist?) and, with blisters on every toe, the second night was spent on a hard wooden bench in a deserted railwayman's signal box near Falkirk. The hills were truly alive with the sound of music and even today, more than fifty years later, whenever I hear Beethoven's Pastoral Symphony, my mind returns to that inspiring, exhausting but wonderful, blisterful journey.

When eventually the year came to an end Walter and I never saw each other again but Bob's path would later cross with mine in an unexpected way.

The battle for Europe was still being fought and, having volunteered for the Navy, an appointment for a medical examination was demanded on the 9th day of the 9th month at 9 a.m. The details reminded me of Pullen's belief that my 'lucky' number was 9! Having failed to pass because of bronchial asthma and myopia, the state allowed me the option of either going down the mines as a Bevin boy or becoming a school teacher, a choice not difficult to make. Enquiries were immediately launched with Gabbitas and Thring, a leading educational consultancy. The most interesting vacancy seemed to be at a prep school in the West Riding of Yorkshire. Surprisingly, my application was accepted, helped perhaps by a few friendly words from the Pate who must have forgiven or forgotten my assorted peccadilloes.

I travelled north to take up the appointment without a prior interview. Wood Hall traced its history back to the Norman Conquest. The first Norman owner was a Mr Malgar Le Vavasour and for several hundred years it remained with that family. The original mansion had been situated on the banks of the River Wharfe which flows through the grounds. This was destroyed by Cromwell during the Civil War, the stones jettisoned into the river.

The building which greeted me in 1944 had been built in 1750 by the Scott family of Leeds. In 1911 it changed hands and in 1935 a school was launched. The prospectus boasted an encomium from an Archbishop of York whilst among the parents had been the cricketer Sir Len Hutton, and the Bishop of Norwich. It clearly regarded itself as an elite establishment with pupils ranging from five to fourteen and with fees high, for those days, at £70 per term. Looking back, this was a turning point in my life, a kind of *rite de passage* from the carefree irresponsibility of youth to the more demanding seriousness of life. What a relief this must have been to my parents, especially my father.

In addition to the Headmaster and the Matron, there were three assistant masters, D.K.M.Yorke, a tall, ungainly young classicist with thick spectacles who hailed from Kent, and whose acute myopia rendered him incapable of military service, Mr Weissler, an equally earnest young German Jewish refugee who played Schubert impromptus most beautifully, and myself. Since neither of my colleagues nor the headmaster were particularly interested in games I managed to assume responsibility for boxing, cricket and soccer. The best all-round sportsman among the boys was James Guthrie, son of a Ceylon tea planter and the only cricketer I ever had the privilege of coaching who went on to play first-class cricket. Although Hutton's son Richard had attended the school this was before my time.

As far as teaching was concerned I was met on arrival with the question 'What are your subjects ?' 'English, history and geography, sir', I replied. 'Right', said the headmaster, 'that fits in well, you will be responsible for Latin, mathematics and a little geography'.

Luckily, the three of us, lodged in an adjacent stable block, got along very well in spite of Yorke's passive homosexuality. But it did not take long to find out that there was a worm at the heart of the apple. The first indication was the discovery that the headmaster was a narcoleptic. Without any warning, in the classroom or at table, he would suddenly and disconcertingly fall asleep. Maintaining discipline at such times was difficult. Then we realised that our end of term reports were edited so thoroughly as to be quite misleading. But what brought matters to a head was the realisation that Common Entrance papers were being tampered with. Apart from the cheating, a consequence was that upon entering a public school, often Eton, pupils were placed in an inappropriate class or, still worse, had failed to reach the required standard for entry at all. The three of us decided that something had to be done. It was agreed that I should seek the advice of a Leeds solicitor. Having selected a name at random, an appointment was duly made and, within the environs of an austere brown city office, I explained what had brought me. 'I have to tell you, Mr McEwan', replied the lawyer, 'that Mr Leeson happens to be one of our clients. You would therefore be advised to seek advice elsewhere'. It was a deflated young man who reported to his colleagues later that afternoon. After due reflection, and with the end of the school year in sight when we would all be leaving, we decided to forget lawyers, instead submitting a report to the Professional Schools Association of which Wood Hall was a member. An enquiry was eventually launched but up to the time of our departure no decision had been reached and I never knew the outcome although rumours circulated that the school had been struck off from the Association's membership list. However this may be, I believe the school survived until 1966 when the property was purchased by the diocese of Leeds to become the first pastoral and ecumenical centre of its kind in Britain, Mother Theresa being among its first visitors. In 1988 it was transformed into a luxury hotel and spa, with a Carmelite Monastery retained in the back premises.

I was asked by the Bishop of Norwich to spend part of the summer holidays tutoring his son but the attractions of reading some philosophy and psychology at home, with bouts of chess, snooker and the occasional cricket match, proved to be a stronger pull and the intriguing offer was gratefully declined.

* * * * * * * * *

It was at about this time that I made the acquaintance of the philosopher and broadcaster Cyril Joad. He was at the height of his fame with the BBC Brains Trust, before his subsequent fall from grace. This bearded, highly articulate man was a keen chess player, not averse to encouraging serious but immature philosophical neophytes like myself. He kept a salon in the L-shaped library of his home high up on Hampstead Heath, a haven of intellectual conversation and frequent chess soirées.

To an aspiring under-graduate, these were moments of intoxicating Elysium. This experience emphasised the vigilant need for clarity in thought, echoed in Joad's favourite, well-worn phrase 'it all depends what you mean by. .', or in the words of T S Eliot

> *That was a way of putting it – not very satisfactory,*
> *A periphrastic study in a worn-out poetical fashion,*
> *Leaving one still with the intolerable wrestle,*
> *With words and meanings. The poetry does not matter.*[1]

* * * * * * * * *

The eventful summer of 1945 was drawing to a close, Dadna was among a chosen group of officers selected by Montgomery to form the nucleus of a British Military Government in Berlin, and it was time for me to leave the haven of home. The uncongenial experience of my encounter with elementary science had neither dented my fondness for Scotland nor diminished my attraction to the charms of Edinburgh. I had been accepted to read the honours course in philosophy with psychology as the main subsidiary. Within a week of arrival the professor of Logic and Metaphysics, A. D. Ritchie (no relation to the zoology professor) asked to see the five of us who were hoping to embark on the honours course. 'I would warn you', he told us, 'that, however well you do, there are very few openings these days for philosophy graduates, unless you plan to enter the church. Even a first-class honours degree would not guarantee an academic position, so great is the competition and limited the opportunities'. Three of the group were indeed aspiring clerics, but two of us were not, so the fourth chap and I accepted the implication of this advice, transferring from philosophy to psychology while retaining philosophy as our main subsidiary.

---

[1]   Four quartets, *'East Cocker'* pt. 2

Accommodations during the four year course were a source of joy. After a short spell in a guest house adjacent to Murrayfield wherein lodged two elderly ladies, addicts of *The Scotsman* crossword puzzle, who initiated me into the arcane mysteries of these puzzles, explaining the idiosyncrasies of the various compilers, so for the first and only time in my life I devoted some energy to their solution. After a short time I moved to the home of Mrs Law in Corstorphine. Mrs Law was the epitome of Scottish couthiness, intelligent, kindly, loving and totally without pretence. With her I remained for two happy years leaving only when gaining a place in Cowan House, then the main men's hall of residence, with its own tennis court and the added attraction of being adjacent to Masson Hall, the corresponding residence for ladies. With the destruction of these establishments in later years to make way for a new library, an intrinsic microcosm of what undergraduate life should encompass disappeared. George Square lost much of its beauty and charm, all in the name of progress.

At the outset of my first year, dormant pseudo-political tendencies came to the fore when, with the confidence of having tasted Edinburgh University already, I was elected as the first year Arts representative on the Students' Representative Council. Thus began four years as a Council member with a number of unexpected but important consequences.

In the late 1940s and early 1950s undergraduate culture was very different from today's, not only because of general cultural change but because of the leavening provided by ex-service men and women, people of a mature age who had passed through the darkest tunnels of life. They worked harder because they were so keenly aware of both the privilege of having survived the war with now the opportunity of learning rather than fighting, and mature enough to recognise the importance of achieving professional success. Whereas today a dedicated, serious minded student may be regarded by his peers as a 'geek', in 1946 any student who neglected the opportunity to get involved in serious exchanges with his/her colleagues was regarded as a 'noodle'. A stark example of the change is shown by the characters chosen for selection as chairman and students' representative on the University Court, a once cherished

Scottish tradition. Past Edinburgh Rectors include Kitchener (1914), Lloyd George (1920), Baldwin (1923), Churchill (1929), Allenby (1935), and Sir Alexander Fleming (1951). The most recent Rectors since 1985 have been Archie MacPherson, Muriel Gray, Donny Munro, Dr Malcolm MacLeod, John Colquhoun, Robin Harper, Tam Dalyell and Mark Ballard.

My second year was momentous, a period with everlasting consequences. One of the committees of the Students' Council was 'Ways and Means', responsible for every aspect of raising money during the University's Charity Week. Elected to this committee I found myself alongside an attractive, vivacious but serious final year language student. Apart from her good looks she had the *je ne sais quoi* that set her apart from all the other lovely degagé denizens of the Old Quod. Dorothy Turnbull, a daughter of the manse, and I fell in love and after fifty-nine years it is wonderful to report we remain happily together. She recalls our first meeting when a dishevelled young man arrived late (as usual) for a committee meeting, wearing an old brown mackintosh, dripping with rain from every pore.

On frequent visits to Dorothy's lovely home in her father's rural Dumfries-shire manse, her father one day suggested a round of golf. The weather having cleared after a very wet day before, the ground still very sodden, especially in places where golfers naturally stand, we motored over to Dumfries. Teeing off at the first hole the Reverend Turnbull lost his footing on the drive, such was the intensity of the shot, and fell flat on his back. Being the unassuming, humorous gentleman that he was we enjoyed a quiet laugh before moving on. When we arrived back at the manse, however, my mother-in-law was less than pleased at finding her husband's mud-spattered back torso and leggings considerably less funny than the cause of their besmirchment.

My first visits to the Manse had needed delicate treatment on both sides, especially as the Sabbath approached. I explained my attitudes as best I could and these were received with slightly pained understanding by Dorothy's father and by unspoken disapproval from her mother. But once we were all reunited before the roast beef and tatties the differences of the morning dissolved. The fact that Dorothy's existing brother-in-law was also a clergyman added piquancy but as he too was a model of good humour and tolerance there was never any question of a rift in the family. And for Dorothy herself, although going to church when at home, this was more in respect for her father than through any abiding religious commitment.

This was also the time when a number of enduring male friendships were forged. John Watson, a young Yorkshireman of great good sense, humour and dependability who shared my enjoyment of wild places, was a fellow budding psychologist. Apart from the lecture theatre and the Students' Council, there was an exceptionally talented Philosophical Society founded by John Hick and I. Two of its undergraduate members, James Torrance and Ian Pitt-Watson, became Moderators of the Church of Scotland, while John Hick, now an internationally recognised and highly regarded Professor of Divinity and the philosophy of religion, Gifford lecturer, and author of many important seminal books, was my hill walking companion. George Rankin and I were two sceptical non-churchmen. John, one of the leading theologians of his generation, is the most cerebral person it has been my privilege to know.

One cold February weekend John Hick and I, with a charming dilettante Irish serial student called Alec Stewart, planned an expedition up Glen Slugain, which old Finlay Grant, the Tomidhu farmer and part-time Balmoral stalker with whom we stayed in pre-war days, had recommended as the finest walking glen in the Cairngorms. But first we had to reach Braemar. I set off on the Friday as the lone advance party, travelling by train to Blairgowrie. There I found the shop I was looking for with bicycles for hire. Having rented one for myself I asked for two more to be reserved for student friends who would be arriving the following day. 'What are they studying ?' asked the shopkeeper, 'theology,' I told him, thinking this would be the end of the matter. 'Sorry', he replied, 'I never lend to medical or theology students'. But after some persuasion he relented and off I went. It is thirty-five miles to Braemar from Blairgowrie, over one of the highest main roads in Britain and in those days, long before skiing and global warming, the road between Glenshee and Braemar was normally considered impassable between Christmas and Easter. With my father's old leather briefcase hooked on to the headlamp holder, by the time I reached the foot of the main ascent at Glenshee my legs would no longer gyrate. The cold beef sandwich and a cup of tea in the old inn there, since burnt down, restored a semblance of energy but the long climb became increasingly snow bound. A few hundred yards from the summit in the failing winter light I caught up with a sinister looking elderly tramp who gave me the unlikely story that he was walking to Braemar in search of a job. We shared my last bar of chocolate before I had to carry the bike for the last hundred yards across the snowfields drifting on both sides of the now hidden road. What a relief it was to reach the summit as darkness was falling, free-wheeling down the last five miles to Braemar, waving to the old chap as I pedalled past him. The next day Alec and John appeared, looking remarkably fresh as they cycled into view a mile above Braemar. It appeared they had cadged a lift on an old red Rolls Royce postie van from Blairgowrie, their cycles on the roof as far as Glenshee, whilst an overnight thaw had enabled them to pedal almost all the rest of the way!

We were the very first guests in a small guest house recently opened on Chapel Brae; chatting in the evening in front of a roaring log fire with the snow falling outside was heart warming. This was in 1946 and on the way back we resolved that those of us who survived would hold a reunion on the summit of Cairnwell at the Millennium. Unfortunately, by the year 2000 Alec had vanished into the unknown and John was too handicapped by stenosis to travel. The old road, known as the Devil's Elbow, by the year 2000 had long since been by-passed, but on January 1st 2001 Dorothy and I, living only thirty minutes drive away, did keep faith and honoured the pledge. The scar on the old leather briefcase remains a treasured souvenir of a wonderful winter week-end.

On another winter's day, John and I were given a perishing hitch on the running board of a tractor between Crianlarich and Bridge of Orchy in a failed attempt to reach Fort William via Glencoe. John had been a conscientious objector in the war, serving as an ambulance driver in Greece, but nothing had prepared him for the hardships of our winter Highland journeys.

Two other members of the Philosophical Society became good friends. Harry Nagler, a fuzzy-haired Jewish mathematician who looked like a young Beethoven, was always enjoyed for his wry humour and a willingness to play bridge all night, and the slightly severe, intellectually intense Ron King-Murray, destined to become a Scottish Law Lord.

One afternoon in Cowan House there was a message awaiting me from one of my anthropology classmates, Sheila Gamlin, daughter of the broadcaster Lionel Gamlin, asking if I would care to take her to a dance. As dancing was never among my favourite activities I told her I felt sure that a fellow called Ron would appreciate such an invitation. The outcome was that (Lord) Ron Murray and Sheila were happily married for over fifty years until the dreaded Alzheimer's eventually carried Sheila away.

Other interests away from the classroom and council included a popular Gramophone Club with concerts organised by Peter Legard, an ex-army officer forestry student and myself, held every Saturday evening in Masson Hall, next door. And then there were the Pleiades, seven of us in a group named after the seven daughters of the Titan Atlas and the Oceanic Pleione who were pursued by Orion until Zeus changed them into a cluster of stars. In addition to John Watson and I the other five were Ted Whitley, Ian Noble, Mansell Prothero, Peter Weigall, and Tom Batho. The central feature was that we should all keep in touch after graduation. But first we were asked to record predictions about our respective passages though life, with particular reference to domestic issues. The secretary would then report annually on the accuracy or otherwise of these predictions. Mansell was a bubbly Welsh geographer, already a junior academic, later a distinguished professor specialising in the medical aspects of his subject. Ian Noble, another serious student with a lively sense of fun, rose to the heights of the Edinburgh legal profession, becoming senior partner in the largest Scottish law firm and Professor of Conveyancing at the University. Tom Batho did well in commerce, attaining a senior position with Shell as well as helping to organise and finance the Keep Britain Tidy campaign. The big surprise was Ted. The consensus was that he would be the last one of us to marry, if at all, and that he would remain a playboy, probably carrying a pony tail and living in France until late middle age. In fact he was the second of us to tie the knot and not only this but he married a daughter of the Bishop of Melanesia, a union that has remained steadfast. Barbara, his wife, was a colleague of Dorothy's in London, meeting Ted at one of our parties, our second unpremeditated matchmake. But unlike the Gafic Club which fizzled out only slowly, the Pleiades failed to survive as a viable group beyond graduation although John, Ian and Ted remained good friends.

1948 was, of course, the year of the London Olympics. Living in London I was fortunate to claim one of the Varsity Athletic Club's season tickets for the athletics. Esconced in a superb position beside the Royal box I sat mesmerised throughout the Games, from the opening demonstration sport of lacrosse to the final high jump and the nerve-jangling, dramatic marathon.

In sharp contrast to all the subsequent Games, culminating in the fantasies of Beijing, the opening & closing ceremonies, although in a minor key – the ravages of war were only months away – were none the less appropriately ceremonial and moving. The principal opening attraction, before the arrival of the athletes, was the splendid spectacle of the massed bands and pipes playing their hearts out. A quintessentially British sight, performed in a manner beyond compare, far more resonant than all the razzmatazz of pop singers, glitzy dancers and caparisoned acrobats.

In the marathon Etienne Gailly, a Belgian soldier, who had never run a race longer than twenty miles, was at 10 kilometres 41 seconds ahead of a chasing group comprising two Argentinians (Guinez & Cabrera) and a Swede (Ostling). Gradually tension mounted in the stadium as we heard that the field was closing on the leader so that by 20 miles Gailly was passed by a Korean (Yoon-Chil Choi). It seemed that Choi was comfortably in command for after 22 miles he led by 28 seconds, with one of the Argentinians (Cabrera), who like Gailly had never run a marathon before, alone in second place, Gailly and Guinez a little way behind. But Choi was soon to retire, having run himself into the ground, and with three miles to go Cabrera had overtaken Gailly to lead by five seconds, but Gailly was not finished and with 800 yards left he led Cabrera by 50 yards with a 38 year-old Welsh nurse (Tom Richards) a further 50 yards behind. The exhausted Belgian arrived in the stadium to a rousing reception, staggering but, just managing to stay on his feet, he covered less than a hundred yards of the track before being passed first by Cabrera and then by Richards. The crowd, I recall, was awash with emotion, partly in support of the Welshman who had seemingly come from nowhere and partly in sympathy for poor Gailly who, in a state of near-collapse, crawled across the finishing line to win the bronze medal in very gallant third place.

One early mid-week evening, with the stadium less than a quarter full, I was transfixed by the high jumpers battling it out at the far end of the field. When clearing 6'4¾" a 23 year-old Australian bank clerk from Perth (John Winter) strained his back but bravely decided to take one last jump when he promptly cleared the bar at 6'6". There were four jumpers still left in, among them two Americans (Stanich & Eddleman) who had both cleared 6'7¼" in qualification. We all watched in silence as each of the four still had three attempts left. All twelve attempts failed, leaving the injured Winter the undisputed, unexpected winner. Our own Alan Paterson finished 7th equal having cleared 6'2¾".

And there was the great privilege of seeing Fanny Blankers-Koen, probably the greatest female athlete of all time. When she came to London, already thirty and with two children, she held no fewer than six world records, then proceeded to win four gold medals, in the 100 metres sprint, the 200 metres, the hurdles, and the 4 x100 relay, and would have won the long jump as well if she had competed having jumped twenty inches further than the winner. On her return to Amsterdam she was driven through the crowded streets in an open carriage drawn by four grey horses. Her neighbours presented her with a bicycle 'so she won't have to run so much'. In 1999 she was voted the greatest woman athlete of the twentieth century. She died in 2004 aged 86.

In the 200 metres our own Audrey Williamson finished second. She recently recalled many of the athletes being billeted in barracks with her own training runs having to be completed around Cadogan Square. How pampered the athletes of the world have become and what lessons might be learned for the organisers of the 2012 Olympics !

Looking back to 1948 and comparing them to the multi-billion dollar extravaganza of the Beijing Olympics arouses serious reflection. The only two places where people from across the world forgather are the United Nations and the Olympics. But whereas the former, far from being typical representatives of their citizenry tend to be among the less desirable and unrepresentative, the Olympics provide a representative cross-section of the youth of the world. Unfortunately, the Games have always suffered from the intrusion of politics. Would it not be in the true spirit of sport and international amity if references to nationality could at least be reduced if not abandoned altogether ? Why should athletes be housed by nationality rather than their sport, why wear national costume and have national anthems blaring out their jingoistic incitements ? If London in 2012 could reduce the politicization and nurture true international fellowship, that would indeed be something we could all be proud of, a cause for thanksgiving across the world. The extent to which this may appear naive or no more than a pious pipe-dream reflects how far we have yet to travel along the road to sanity. I note that for the rights to record Beijing one American television company paid 450 million dollars, and that before the end of the first week they had recouped 500 million dollars in advertising revenue. Does money kill hope ? Forgo the flags, let us rejoice, the world together, in the harmony of nations.

* * * * * * * *

In the autumn of 1948 I was elected Senior President of the Students' Council, for what turned out to be an unusually eventful year. Debates in the Union were of a high quality, largely due to some exceptional talent in the Labour Club, two of whose members would have undoubtedly reached cabinet rank had they not been overtaken by early misfortune. The ebullient, brilliant, copper-haired John P. Mackintosh became a leading party thinker, fervent political activist and writer before his tragic early death when on the threshold of greatness; then there was Alan Thompson, an ex-service inhabitant of Cowan House, a lean, bespectacled and earnest economist whose first attempt at Parliament was fighting the safe Tory seat of Galloway. At the farewell party to his honours students, the Professor of Economics advised Alan, whom we called 'twinkle toes' on account of his unexpected dancing ability, 'go upstairs, dear boy, you will find a safe seat up there'. Eventually he was elected for Dunfermline. Unhappily, when canvassing at a later election he contracted pneumonia which left him with a legacy of asthma. Unable to pursue a promising political career, he entered academia becoming a distinguished professor, lately retired.

Late June 1949 was blessed with glorious weather. This was the time Gussie Moran was shocking and replenishing tennis enthusiasm with her revolutionary yet enticing display of frilly pants, a latter-day Minoprio of the tennis world. Peter Weigall, a mature, rather dapper ex-army officer with a devilish streak of humour joined me on a trip north. In memory I have Peter the ballywagger confused with the urbane Henry Blofeld. We pitched our tent at Shieldaig, near Gairloch, on Peter Thomson's land, hired a rowing dinghy from a nearby hotel and every day, beneath cloudless skies, we rowed across the bay to the main village to buy food and newspapers and bask a little on the golden sands of Gairloch beach. Landing one afternoon there was a mixed line of sun-bathing maidens and elderly aunts before whom it was necessary to parade in order to reach the shops. Spying an especially pretty form, who it later transpired was a receptionist at the main hotel, Peter embarrassed my pedestrian soul by engaging the nymph in jocund conversation. He went further, he invited the young lady to join us on a fishing trip the next day, an invitation she apparently accepted – I say apparently because their having reached this level of early intimacy I had withdrawn a little apart. Never, my mother taught me, be a gooseberry. The next day, our passenger duly collected, the three of us rowed away, Peter and the nymph in the bows, leaving me as the slave with the oars. It wasn't long before he had convinced the lass that I was the octoroon son of a quadroon sheikh. Naturally, for this was the purpose of his circumlocution, an explanation was required. He explained in conspiratorial tones which I was too breathless with rowing to deny, that I was, in the popular parlance of the time, a half-caste, my father being one-quarter white leaving me just one-eighth Aryan, although Peter added, I was wealthy. On hearing this the young lady was clearly delighted and towards the end of the trip – we never began to fish – Peter gallantly took hold of the oars leaving me perplexed, whether to sanitise her mind and shame him or persevere with the charade. When she asked for my address it became too hideously awkward, my last vision was of the strangely bedraggled young blonde *gobermouche* forlornly traipsing back up the beach toward her hotel, Peter smiling as contentedly and proudly as if he had laid an egg, leaving me to moan alone at his gross albeit initially amusing insensitivity. But, I suppose, if you have odd friends you must expect odd things to happen, although on this occasion it seemed to me the limit of legitimacy had been exceeded.

Peter left at the weekend and for the second week I was joined by two girl student acquaintances. The only divertissements worthy of mention were first, a photograph taken outside the tent at midnight without a flash, in order to illustrate to our English friends that in the magical north-west Highlands in mid-summer, daylight scarcely disappears. Second, one of the young ladies, I will call her A, apparently took a fancy to me which was not reciprocated, as sadly I found young lady B much more attractive. In a rather transparent attempt to inveigle me into their tent, A called out to me shortly after midnight asking if I could please rid them of a snake, a request I declined on the somewhat specious grounds that the exercise could wait until morning since snakes did not normally attack unless disturbed, but in any case only adders are poisonous and their's was probably a grass snake.

But these two weeks had been magical, a dead calm ocean, continuous warm sunshine, the mountains bathed in a soft balmy light, all within an ambience of midsummer tranquillity. Glorious.

This was not the only ploy the wicked Peter played. At about this time, we went on a walking holiday in the Grampians, staying with my old friends the Grants at Tomidhu farm, near Balmoral. There were three of us: Peter, a rather intense Jewish psychology student called Bernard Katz, and me. One evening

Bernard awoke early, complaining of an itchy rash somewhere around his extensive torso. He asked Peter to take a look. After careful scrutiny Peter pronounced his solemn verdict. On the basis of his army experience (and knowing a little about Bernard's way with girls), he informed the luckless Bernard that he knew the early sign of syphilis when he saw it. Thus distressed, an alarmed Bernard dashed off first thing in the morning to the Braemar doctor. Having told the doctor of his fear, a blood test was administered. It was not until we all got back to London that we heard the rash had gone and the report of the blood test had of course come through negative.

* * * * * * * * *

In 1949, shortly after my election, there came word that Princess Elizabeth and Philip, Duke of Edinburgh, would be visiting the University. After various daytime events there was to be a Ball in the evening at the McEwan Hall. At this time there was among the undergraduates a promiscuous, financially well endowed young lady, with high social pretentions. When she heard of the impending royal visit she organised a lavish party, almost, it was said, an orgy. I knew the girl only by sight so my invitation to attend had, I was convinced, the ulterior motive of getting her name added to my list of those to be invited to the Ball. This kind of interpersonal engineering, so rife in life, of which this was my first obvious encounter, I found, and continue to find, distasteful, and so, some might think somewhat priggishly, I excused myself.

After a splendid luncheon in the Senate Room we assembled in the Old Quod in preparation for a motor cavalcade to the Royal party's next port of call, the ladies' halls of residence in East Suffolk Road. I found myself in the back of the same limousine as Professor Tindall, dean of the Faculty of Divinity, and my liquorish junior president, John Miller. The streets were lined along the way with an enthusiastic throng of Edinburgh burghers. Encouraged by this display of public support, John insisted in opening the window of our luxurious limousine, returning their waves with copious, vigorous flourishes of his own, much to the silent but pained disapproval of the Divine Dean.

The only awkward moment came when the Duke asked if I knew what had become of a student who had been a school friend of his at Gordonstoun. It so happened that I knew the answer, leaving me with no option but to report that the gentleman in question was currently a guest in one of His Majesty's prisons.

The second major event was the election in November and subsequent Address of a new Lord Rector. Until 1859 this office had been held *ex officio* by the Lord Provost of Edinburgh. Because historically Scottish universities evolved from their Italian counterparts, where students formed the major role and hired the teachers, this form of civic control came to be resented. In 1858 the Universities (Scotland) Act placed the election of a Rector in the hands of the students. Until 1929 candidates were sponsored by the university's political parties, the last incumbent in this system being Churchill, elected at his second attempt having been defeated twenty-one years earlier. From 1932 nominations could be made by any sufficient number of students. Thus it was that in 1948 the election developed into a fight between Harold Macmillan and Alastair Sim. Sim was known as a character actor of charm and some academic experience, having been Fulton lecturer at New College, teaching budding parsons how to speak in public, in addition to running his own School of Drama and Speech Training. In the event, Sim was elected with a majority of 1,276, Macmillan came second leaving the philanthropist Sir Donald Pollock, who had run three times before and been successful twice, in third place.

The installation took place on April 27th, 1949. By tradition the 2,500-odd students in the McEwan Hall produce such a sustained din that often the address can be scarcely heard. It was my task, as chairman of the proceedings, but not blessed with a booming voice, to establish the tone. As the hooters, rattles and exploding squibs resounded around the circular hall, our procession arrived, led by the avuncular university beadle, followed by the Vice-Chancellor and members of the Court, resplendent in all their finery, with the new Rector and me bringing up the rear. The brouhaha was enormous as we walked down the aisle to take our seats with as much dignity as we could muster. I managed to lull the storm in a very brief introduction and plea for peace before the hall once again erupted. Alastair afterwards told his wife that as he stood, waiting to speak, he felt one of his knees slightly give and he thought he might fall. His first few words were heard amid only a respectful buzz and then he made his audience laugh, and, as his wife Naomi later wrote in her biography, then they were hooked. His topic was the qualified fool, the man who recognises his foolishness as compared to those who do not, and the 'enormous power words seem to have for creating harm, without anything like a corresponding power for doing good'.

"Words", he said, "have always fascinated me, either by their sound or by their power, or (at a much later date) by their sense. I became a qualified fool. . . could I play the fool and know that I was one ? Could I wring laughter even from throats unused to laugh? That is the fool's peak of achievement . . . it is possible that unqualified fools live in a paradise of their own making, but the true fool knows only a benign purgatory. . . we vaguely sense the true meaning of a few simple words like 'kindness', 'pity', 'affection', 'friendship', 'trust', words which we believe mean approximately the same to all people, and it is strange that as we ponder on these words our sense of humour returns. So we laugh. We laugh at our own folly, at the folly of each other, and the folly of absent friends. We laugh at our seriousness, our rights and our wrongs, our airs and graces, our piety, our wickedness. We come near to laughing at our fears. But not quite. Soon, to our dismay, these naively tyrannical words are calmly asking for a degree of courage, sacrifice, altruism, and faith that would leave us no time at all for pleasure, offering instead a purely hypothetical and rarefied happiness. . . we cut short the single 'initiatory' spasm and rush to take refuge again with the crowd, neglect friends for acquaintances, think again with a group mind, and quickly seek the company of inferiors in order to feel superior. Soon we are revelling in an avalanche of fine-sounding but misused and misdirected words! Slave words, but slaves decked out to look important. Words like 'freedom', 'duty', 'patriotism', 'success', 'failure' and all the rest, to name but a few inflammatory specimens. Words which elude all efforts at exact analysis, which may mean anything, everything, or nothing, according to whether they serve with discretion or rule in chaos. But they rule – and with an emotional tyranny almost beyond belief . We fools are not concerned with the rights and wrongs of the case, but we are appalled at the enormous power words seem to have. Allow me to help clarify the picture of an average, qualified and fairly competent fool. I say qualified advisedly, to distinguish him from the unqualified variety, those that are not yet aware that they are fools. They are ubiquitous and though their case may not be serious while they are young they become increasingly dangerous, as they grow older. They become drugged with the wrong words, the false analogy, the quotation out of context, they serve as the dupes and stepping-stones of personal ambition and misguided mission . . . the authentic qualified fool recognises the inadequacy of verbal communication on any but the simplest terms and the fact that words, for the most part, are used as an anodyne for the pain of thinking. For do not suppose that a genuine fool never thinks. He suffers agonies of thinking. Thinking is his vice. His intellect has been impaired through thinking. It is concentration which he lacks. Is it words that are the danger? Or is it men ? Or is it the simple truth ? Or is it fear ? Fear of the simple truth ? The fear that stirs up the illusory frenzy of self-defence. In simple things like everything that amounts to anything, not withstanding the fact that all around the simple things there is a complicated something, amounting to little or nothing, but very, very dangerous. From which he concludes that it is fine to be clever, better to be good, and to be both is asking for trouble. I would like to feel you shared with me a degree of doubt over much that is accepted, a tendency to question, even when you are told the answer. However that may be, my happiness is the greater for being sure of this: that there is one gift which we do share and shall always share, the gift of laughter."

As I wrote in my introduction to the published version, many of us did not at the time recognise the wisdom for the wit.

James Bridie, a close friend of Sim, said that of the eight Rectorials he had attended this was the first one he had heard. Thereafter the new Rector was carried on the shoulders of his supporters to the adjacent Union for tea. The Rectorial Ball that evening ended a most memorable day. Naomi said that of all the honours Alastair received, including his CBE, the one he was most proud of was being elected Rector, of having been chosen by the young.

Looking back, it is interesting to note that this election marked a transition from the election of entrenched establishment figures to the popular choice of entertainers. Alistair was a far more substantial figure than most of his acting roles might suggest, but he was also an entertainer par excellence. His Address, which was later published, compares favourably to a similar Address given by J M Barrie in another place on 'Courage'[2].

My last duty was to represent the university at the Rectorial festivities and Address in Aberdeen given by the late Lord Tweedsmuir. My only memory, apart from the melodies of Pee-Wee Hunt popular at the time, was in the dis-robing room when the Aberdeen President, a mature ex-serviceman who should have known better, drunk as a brewer's fart, turned to Lady Tweedsmuir "your husband", he mumbled, "may be very platform worthy but you are very bed-worthy". An embarrassed silence made withdrawal a welcome relief.

I have said little about my teachers. No disrespect, but I did find the companionship and quodlibetarian dialogue with friends, allied to our required ancillary reading, more rewarding than hearkening to lecturers. James Drever was, I believe, Edinburgh's first professor of psychology. A taciturn, upright Orcadian he had been trained as a philosopher, his mechanistic approach to psychology failed to ignite in me any spark of enthusiasm. He

---

[2] Since these words were written a new biography of Alastair Sim has appeared, suggesting that his love of youth might have had a sinister aspect. As one who became his friend and met many other young people in his company both at the University and in his home in London, nothing whatever at any time gave rise to the slightest suspicion. His passionate desire for privacy in an age of celebs extended to all aspects of his life. An example, not generally known, is the extent of his co-operation with his great friend James Bridie in the writing of the latter's plays. Alastair gave every appearance of being a very happily married man of immense integrity, a fact confirmed by his wife's intimate posthumous biography.

ended his academic life as Dundee University's first Principal, a position best suited to his undoubted administrative skills.

The stars in my firmament were Denys Hay, a young European Historian, later Dean of the Faculty of Arts, and the overwhelmingly brilliant moral philosopher, James MacMurray. The trouble with MacMurray was his delivery, a wealth of original ideas flowing without pause within the framework of obfuscating phraseology. So complex was his syntax that a junior lecturer had to borrow my friend John Hick's notes on MacMurray's lectures before introducing his class to the ideas of the master.

Following graduation, which I persuaded the authorities to allow me to do in absentia, 1949 was to see one more momentous event. Dorothy and I got married, a bonding that we were both determined should last a lifetime, a resolve that we have happily honoured. Dorothy had been working in Hanover and Berlin with the British Control Commission, often visiting my parents, my father having become Head of Economics and latterly Deputy Military Governor in Berlin's British Military Government wherein he was proud to be the only member of the R.A.F., while mother, who did not speak a word of German, did her best to act as hostess to assorted Russians, Germans, Americans and Brits.

When, in March 1946, it was reported that my father would be coming home from Berlin, a group of leading industrialists including the Directors of Siemens & Halske, Siemens-Schukertwerke, Allgemeine Eklektricitats-Aktiengesellschaft, Textil-Fabrikation, and Rudolf Karstadt, penned a joint letter addressed to British headquarters in Bad Oeynhausen, appealing for his retention. Some time later the London *Evening News* ran an article under the rubric 'He Remade Berlin'. 'He arrived in Berlin', wrote the article, 'just after the Russian guns had stopped firing in July 1945, and found conditions in the Western sector unbelievably chaotic. Yet in a matter of days he had driven Communist saboteurs out of the factory yards and started production lines moving again. From old gas mask holders and tin helmets he had [caused to make] cooking utensils so that Berliners could cook what little food they then had . . . He is the man credited for thinking of the Airlift which broke the Russian blockade two years ago. Berliners have the deepest respect for him and the City Council has bestowed on him the highest praise . . .'. Unfortunately father, who always resented the fact that the American propaganda machine had been so much more effective than our own, usurping all the praise for breaking the blockade, died before a book recounting his experiences was completed. For all he did during both wars, but especially during the immediate aftermath of the Second, I am immensely proud. If his relationship with the goverment in power at the time of his departure had been warmer, I believe the honour he received would have been significantly greater.

Dorothy's father was Minister of the lovely country parish of Parkgate in Dumfries-shire and it was in his church that we became husband and wife. Dorothy's sister Kathleen, a music teacher, played the organ – unfortunately the little piece of music I composed with her help was lost and never heard again – perhaps its just reward. My best university friend John Watson couldn't be best man as he had himself just married and was on his honeymoon, but John Miller, who succeeded me as senior president, proved a splendid alternative. It was good to have my dear old friend Mrs Law among the guests. The day before the wedding my parents had travelled from Berlin and I had met them by car at Dover. Thus my last night as a bachelor was spent sharing the driving with Dadna in Standard Vanguard MLT 55 up the old A1 and on to the Moffat-Dumfries road, the church and manse being a mile up a long tree-lined avenue.

The magnificent wedding cake was a gift from a member of the Gafic Club, Christopher Floris, whose firm had made the wedding cake for the Queen and Prince Philip. As Dorothy and I drove away from the reception, with John and Joyce Watson in the back, the excitement caused me to overlook the necessity of releasing the hand brake. In the consequent pantomime, my dear mother, now more certain than ever that we were driving to catastrophe, cried out "stop them Mac before they kill themselves!" But we eventually got away without further mishap, deposited the Watsons at their honeymoon hotel in Innerleithen, and, through a raging August thunderstorm, reached our destination in a hotel above the shores of St Mary's Loch. The next morning after the storm had passed the car failed to start, requiring assistance from Dumfries. The dampened plugs having been brought back to life, we eventually set forth on our honeymoon, first to Shieldaig Lodge near our beloved Gairloch, and then to Braemar at the now rather dilapidated Fife Arms Hotel wherein Gladstone once preferred to stay when visiting Balmoral and while there had resolved to undertake a new translation of the *Odes of Horace* (1894).

CHAPTER 3

Ardachie

An adventure is only an inconvenience rightly considered. An inconvenience is only an adventure wrongly considered.

[G.K.Chesterton]

After we were married we moved to London where Dorothy found a job with the International Tea Marketing Board while I filled an uninspiring niche with a trade promotion organisation. Our first home was in Hollycroft Avenue, near Hampstead Heath, conveniently close to a little tennis club hidden away in the recesses behind Finchley Road. One of the members was A.J.F.Macdonald, then Liberal MP for Roxburgh and Selkirk. He persuaded me, as a young aspiring Liberal, to seek a nomination in the forthcoming 1951 General Election. Although Feona had been born in 1950, we were not short of baby sitters, and I agreed to allow my name to go forward but only for a constituency in the Scottish Highlands, for that was where the heart was and where Dorothy and I wanted to live. A call was not long in coming, from Caithness and Sutherland, geographically the largest constituency in Britain but demographically one of the smallest. I was twenty-seven, looked fifteen, and had never been to either county, although the family's island croft bought a year or two earlier to assuage my mother's desire for a potential haven from the next war, was in neighbouring Wester Ross.

Depositing Feona with my parents and hiring an old Wolseley from my father-in-law's garage in Dumfries, Dorothy and I sallied forth. The first step was to meet the president of the North of Scotland Liberals at his attractive modern home high above Culloden Moor.

Guy Senior was a plump, genial, cherubic, enthusiastic, retired company director who proceeded to explain, in a very positive but honest manner, the nature of the challenge that lay ahead.

Before the war Caithness and Sutherland had been represented by Sir Archibald Sinclair, later Viscount Thurso, Secretary of State for Air during the war. Internationally respected and perhaps a little vain in his aristocratic gravitas, he had unexpectedly lost the seat in 1945 when he had been beaten into third place by Gander Gower, an engaging right-wing Independent. It was said locally that the defeat had been largely due to Sinclair's inability to maintain the detailed tabs on his constituents that he had kept so assiduously before the war. This was a deficiency viewed locally as evidence that their Member of Parliament had become too big for his boots, too important to concern himself any more with the minor problems of local people. Then, at the election in 1950, to his immense chagrin, Sinclair lost again, this time even more heavily. He now lost stomach for any further fight. His handsome son and heir, probably realising that he would be no more successful than his father, declined to stand. Furthermore, Guy Senior told me that the constituency party was now defunct and was without an agent. After trawling Inverness among his many contacts, Guy eventually located a recently qualified young lawyer willing to rise to the challenge. So off went the three of us to establish a campaign headquarters and residential base for Dorothy in a Wick hotel.

Speaking at 72 meetings in 29 days, it had been an interesting and enjoyable experience, meeting many fine people I would never see again and exploring the countryside and West Highland coastline with its myriad of crofting hamlets and small fishing villages. We had been well supported by many local doctors, ministers, and teachers with energetic campaigning from a strong band of warriors including, among them, Lady Glencoats and the Editor of the Sunday Express. The one incident worthy of note was an adventurous visit across the stormy Pentland Firth to the Island of Stroma – the only candidate to reach there. Stroma is a small rather desolate treeless island, at the time supporting a small, cohesive population, but now sadly uninhabited. Returning to the mainland I had an unpleasant tea in an elderly supporter's home at John O' Groats when the Swiss roll was covered in a bitter green mould which there was no way of avoiding.

The following day a foray to Wick agricultural market coincided with the visit of the Labour candidate. As he found himself without anyone to introduce him, I did so myself.

In these days with no television, meetings had far more significance than they have today. Apart from the nightly party political broadcasts on the radio, local candidates occupied an unique forum to cover all contemporary local and national topics and were judged accordingly, question time being particularly important. Which is why there were more idiosyncratic independent MPs than is nowadays possible.

1951 was a disastrous election for the Liberals, retaining only six seats and saving their deposit in only a further nine, mine included.

I am not sure what lessons the experience taught me. I always found it easier addressing an impersonal audience of a hundred rather than a more personal one of ten. It gradually became clear that political life was not for me, partly because one would have to be away from home so often and partly because I could never trim the sails of belief necessary to navigate a party line. As for the constituency, in 1964 it was won back for the Liberals by George Mackie, later Lord Mackie. He held it for only two years, and several elections later, in 1981, the victor, Robert McLennan, transferred his allegiance from Labour to the Social Democrats thus, under its changed name, restoring Liberal hegemony.

* * * * * * * * *

1952 was an eventful year. In January Malcolm was born, Dorothy having had her pregnancy unobserved throughout the campaign, and later that month our lease in Hollycroft having expired, we moved back to the house where I was born and which still belonged to my two unmarried aunts René and Gar (Gladys). It was in London that I saw my maternal grandmother for the last time. She survived a cancer operation when in her nineties but a heart attack killed her when she was ninety-six. We had enjoyed many chats together, her curling tongs often on the flame, in Westward Ho! and fed many tufted duck from her wheelchair in Regents Park. It was also the last time we would see our friends Alastair and Naomi Sim.

It was clear that I was a misfit in London. My dear father, back in town after his hectic but extremely rewarding time in Berlin came to my rescue. On a limited but realistic budget, Dorothy and I embarked on a voyage of discovery that would take us back to the Highlands to search for a suitable farm. A farm without much arable but with potential for livestock, especially pigs, their husbandry being the one branch of farming about which I knew anything. Dorothy had vowed she would never marry a clergyman or a farmer but she was gracious and long suffering enough to concede just once, at least on an experimental basis. After two disappointing inspections, one near Huntly and the other above Pitlochry, we motored over to Loch Ness-side passing through Grantown-on-Spey on September the 29th where billboards announced that John Cobb had just lost his life, killed on Loch Ness when attempting a new world water speed record. Cobb had hoped to be the first man to exceed 200 mph on water. Travelling in his jet-powered all-aluminium *Crusader*, at an estimated speed of 240 mph, the speedboat's front plane collapsed causing the boats' instant disintegration. Although Cobb was rescued from the water alive, he died almost immediately, supposedly from shock. A white post on the east shore, marking the start of the measured mile, can still be seen, almost directly opposite the stone memorial cairn.

When camping with my parents in Shieldaig before the war, it will be recalled we had made friends with farmer Thomson in whose field we had camped. Twelve years later having heard of our agricultural intent he mentioned a small estate that had recently come on the market near Fort Augustus. Ardachie.

It was love at first sight. Half a mile from the village, wedged between two large sporting estates, Glendoe to the north-east and Culachy to the south, up a twisting rough track through woodland, rounding the third corner there came a dramatic vision: arable fields lying beyond a rustic boundary gate, an entrance that could not have been more unpretentious if it tried, a pair of cypress trees standing sentinel beside a substantial if rather sombre ivy-clad lodge. In addition to the main house there was a game-keeper's cottage nestling beside the River Tarff, a shepherd's house and fank perched high on the hill, a walled garden, a steading, two arable fields and 1,700 acres of hill, with a hirsel of Cheviot sheep. Approaching the lodge, rhododendrons flanked the oval lawn beside which nestled a small pond while in the distance, beyond the dark waters of Loch Ness, rose the majestic height of Mealfourvonie.

Lily Bruen, the owner since 1924, had died and her son, an officer in the Fleet Air Arm, had no interest in running an estate. Although our offer was accepted, disagreement arose over the value of the sheep. This required an independent assessor, and with agreement eventually hammered out, transfer was arranged for December.

Such is the unquestioning behaviour of young men, especially those momentarily flushed with enthusiasm, that it was another fifty years before I learnt something of the history of Ardachie, which translated means 'high field'. For almost three centuries, Ardachie had been the seat of a senior branch of the Lovat family. Alexander, the 6th Lord Lovat, had three sons – Hugh his heir, Thomas of Knockie and Strichen, who later possessed the Lovat estates, and James, the progenitor of Ardachie. James received a Charter of Ardachie in 1552. There followed seven generations before Thomas Fraser, a Collector of Customs at Campbeltown, had a son who succeeded his father to Ardachie in 1754 by which time he had become a general. It then passed to his son General Hastings Fraser (1795) and thence to his younger brother General James Stuart Fraser (1852). The military tradition of the place was now established, ending only with the latter's son, another General Hastings Fraser, 12th of Ardachie, who had inherited the property in 1869 and died in 1892. In 1866 General Fraser published *Our Faithful Ally the Nizam* and in 1885 *Memoir and Correspondence of General James Stuart Fraser*, two volumes I have never been able to find. The latter at least must surely have been written on the premises. After General Fraser's death the estate was assigned by

Ethelreda Fraser of Beaufort Castle, presumably a Trustee, to the Hon. Francis Oswald Lindley, a diplomat, in 1902. After various Fort Augustus clerics appeared to inherit or be appointed to the trusteeship, in 1909 the estate passed to Lt. Col. James Ramsay Campbell of the 85th Light Infantry (Shropshire Regiment), and thence to Mrs Lily Bruen in 1924.

And so it was that on the first day of the Great London smog I left Dorothy, Feona and Malcolm at our Hampstead home, the taxi driver only just managing to negotiate the dense fog on our way to Kings Cross Station. That week it was estimated that 4,000 people died in London due to the dreadful pollution.

For us the great escape had begun, from London's concrete intensity, the man-made mentally and intensely constricting environment nowadays regarded as normal, to the mountains, the wide open spaces under the stars, where life is what one makes it, an opportunity for children and free spirits to enjoy and develop naturally.

As the sole member of the advance party, my first task was to attend the displenishment sale. This was held beside the outbuildings on a raw December afternoon. There was little I wanted, an exception being a fine gilt-framed wall mirror which hangs before me as I write. Whenever I had a winning bid the buyer was always referred to as 'I.T.'. This nomenclature, and another called "Procurator', aroused my curiosity until it was whispered in my ear by a local who, being secretly curious of the new owner had sidled close, that 'I.T.' stood for incoming tenant and the Procurator was not some form of undercover procurer, but the title given the monk who was bidding on behalf of the adjacent Benedictine Abbey. The mirror, a long eighteenth-century refectory table, eventually left behind and today valued at more than the whole of Ardachie estate was worth in 1952, this and assorted agricultural implements apart, my main discovery was that one of Dorothy's best university friends, Hetty Innes, was in the audience and living in the village. This vivacious Gaelic-speaking Hebridean girl, always full of fun, wildly outspoken and given to the occasional excessive enjoyment of alcohol, was married to Robert, the local forestry officer. Robert, a canny, quiet, reliable Aberdonian, became my best friend over the next fifty years until his death in 2002. We enjoyed many common interests, especially music and wildlife, but more important, a similar sense of the ridiculous and set of attitudes toward both the vicissitudes and pleasures of life.

Dorothy and baby Malcolm rejoined me in time for a very spartan Christmas. There followed, amid the daily mini-crises inevitable on any livestock farm, a succession of unlikely events which demanded all our attention over the next four years. These were in many ways the happiest days of my life, marred by the fact that for Dorothy these years were among the bleakest. For whatever reason, long since forgotten, the only diary I ever kept ended abruptly after only six months, on June 29th, 1953. A typical entry read 'March 12. A good weather day. Two chicks apparently chilled but recovered later. Dot and I weighed piglets and found weights above average. Planted early (Di Vernon) potatoes; Dot sowed a lot of seed. Raked the hen's deep litter and added lime. Find water trough deleterious, resolved to find a more satisfactory system. Soon we shall be able to tabulate a list of our errors. Still no electricity, forced to bed at 8.15 when the candles ran out (literally), notice growth in both Feona (a great joy and source of fun) and Malcolm (who begins to walk and play peekaboo). I wonder what returns the garden will produce and what seeds will succeed. A young cockerel eaten by Fluff. Nature!'

Part of our Ardachie inheritance included Jock Kirkpatrick, the shepherd. There was no keeper in the keeper's cottage so, spruced up a bit, it was used by my parents on their frequent visits. Jock had only one eye and in the early days acted as my stalking instructor. One had to be careful to remain on his 'good' side. On the very first stalk, on our way home Jock suddenly spied a fox and, wheeling round, in his enthusiasm narrowly missed both me and the equally startled fox.

Stalking deer aroused mixed feelings. Stalking on the estate was confined to stags in winter. On a crisp winter afternoon, with snow covering the ground, in total silence bar the breathing of the pony, being on the hill was a wonderful, life-enhancing experience. On the one hand, I came to recognise man's latent atavistic hunting instinct but on the other hand taking life away from these lovely creatures seemed obscene. After a year I abandoned the activity, allowing friends and, in our final year, a shooting tenant, to stalk stags, but only for culling purposes. But this was not before Ian Noble, my lawyer friend from University, by now a junior partner, found himself so absorbed in a stalk as to encroach on to the neighbouring Glendoe estate. For so punctilious a young man the thought of this infringement, Ian the poacher, was the source of much merriment. Happily he bagged nothing, but he returned to the lodge exhausted. Getting no response to a call for dinner, we found the fatigued young lawyer fast asleep in his bath.

One day James Robertson Justice drove up in his old Rolls seeking permission to fly his falcons, a request we felt unable to grant. As I have grown older a deep antipathy to shooting, killing creatures for fun in the name of sport, has grown. I see no excuse for the activity nor any good reason to regard the taking of life as sport. In the words of Bill Travers, a living animal is a treasure, a dead animal is a carcass. Reverence for life, as the great Albert Schweitzer taught, is a cornerstone of true civilisation.

Later that year Jock left us, unable to reconcile himself to a change in the sheep stock from Cheviot to Blackface. We were fortunate to find gentle Dan Scobie as his replacement. Dan stayed with us to the end, in 1955 his daughter having joined Feona as they faced their first day at school together.

Much effort was given in these early days to domestic repair and agricultural enhancement. While Mother was making the keeper's cottage bright and comfortable, Dadna decided to make a portable ark for the outdoor poultry. The joinery was done in an old wooden chapel desecrated by our predecessor and ourselves for use as a workshop. After many hours of sawing and hammering the ark was declared fit for purpose. Unfortunately, however, it had become imprisoned, too wide to get out of the door or through the chapel window. My father was duly chastened. Meanwhile, young Gordon, Dorothy's schoolboy brother, was busy fitting a new window in the roof of what was to be a deep litter loft for the hens. The work was excellent except that he had fitted the window frame upside down, a feature that can be seen to this day.

These joinerial infelicities were emulated a little later in my agricultural career, when, fencing a small enclosure intended for an isolation unit for sick swine, I proudly examined the finished product, only to find that there I was stuck inside the paddock with the tractor, with no gate through which to make an exit. There was no alternative but to tear down a section of fence I had taken such trouble to build, leaving it for the more expert hands of Ian McLean to erect a proper gate.

The McLean family were a treasure. Ian was the foreman lock keeper on the Caledonian Canal in Fort Augustus. In his spare time he helped us by converting stables into pig sties and a thousand other jobs as well as briefing us about the locals. His wife was a kindly, sensitive soul happy to look after the children on the rare occasions when Dorothy and I had dinner with the Inneses or travelled to Inverness. Their loquacious daughter, Jenny, became Malcolm's nanny, often accompanied by her younger brother Hamish.

On one trip to the cinema in Inverness with Gordon, a queue having developed, the gentleman behind us turned and whispered in slightly embarrassed tones "Excuse me sir, but I think you have a flea on your collar". On another occasion, before we had acquired our first car, I had gone to Inverness market with Peter Thomson, who having left Gairloch was now farming in Glen Garry, not far from Ardachie. After the sales Peter met up with two itinerant sheep dip salesmen. The four of us went to a local pub and, as is the habit with farming folk, Peter proceeded to order a round of neat double whiskies, the two salesmen then obliged by reciprocating, leaving me no choice but to order a fourth round. This was my introduction to the usquebough, and although I made it home and remained able to walk, from that day onward the taste of the liquid has remained anathema. I swore I was not drunk, but Dorothy knew otherwise. I have never been seven seas since, but what a horrible introduction.

In 1953, with another general election looming, Guy Senior and his wife visited us in the hope that I might be persuaded to stand again, but work in the farm made this quite impossible. Guy had grown even plumper than when we last saw him, so much so that he fell through our best armchair, damaging portions of his pride as well as his lower torso.

During our stewardship, apart from specific jobs, we had a succession of four very different stockmen, all of whom bar the first lived *en famille*, causing additional work for Dorothy who already had two young children and me to look after. First came the Wilsons, mother, son and a horse. They were not with us for long as the son seemed allergic to work, while the horse demanded more than its fair share of attention and space.

Then came John Cleeves. I see it clearly today in my mind's eye, waiting at the Ardachie road-end, wondering what sort of fellow would be turning up along the by-road that led to the lodge. I had not expected a tall, blond public schoolboy motoring along in a natty open yellow MG sports car. It seemed he had always wanted to be a pig farmer to which end his father had packed him off to Denmark for training. While there he had fallen off a hay lorry, damaging his head seriously enough to require a return to England where he found a job in the fashion department of Liberty's in London's Regent Street. Finding the rag trade, even at the fashion end, not really to his liking, and having sufficiently recovered from the fall but still unable to persuade his Dad to buy him his own farm, he came to us for further experience. By this time our pig population had grown, with a Danish-type piggery housing a hundred or more pigs at any one time, all in indoor pens with their own outdoor runs.

John was very good at the rough work, but was insensitive to animal well-being. Just as a good art dealer should have an 'eye' for a good painting so a good stockman should have an 'eye' for animal health and happiness. John stayed with us until he felt he had learned and saved enough to launch himself on to his own farm. This he eventually did, settling on the Gower peninsular in South Wales. Some years later, on the day of the Munich air disaster, John visited us in Ballater. When we last heard he was raising cabbages and cauliflowers rather than rearing pigs.

Looking back I suppose we were quite demanding since, in addition to tending the pigs and poultry, many other tasks came along as we tried to develop the steading. Thus, for example, my entry for May 10, 'Met Dadna in the village after two attempts, having first met the wrong bus. Coughing among some of the pigs suggests worms. A spate of visitors on a perfect afternoon: Peter and his hydro-electric friend McKenzie, his wife and daughter and McLean with son Hamish. John tried entertaining them alone but finds this harder work than laying concrete, which he returned to after tea with great vigour.'

Our third pigman, Nobby Clark, was in marked contrast to John. Slight of build, he found the heavier part of the work tough, but as a stockman he was outstanding. He had been manager of Oppenheimer's prize-winning herd of pigs in Southern Rhodesia. His knowledge was proven on the first day with us, when, inspecting our Large White boar, he said 'that must be a Field Marshal' which indeed it was. Nobby was a quiet, unobtrusive member of our family circle but after a few months we realised something was wrong. Occasionally he would appear with large bumps on his forehead, the result of frequent falls. Then we began finding him unconscious on one or other of the stone floors. When these incidents began to be allied to fever and behavioural changes, after first speaking with a medical friend, we consulted a psychiatrist at Craig Dunain Hospital just outside Inverness. Cerebral malaria was diagnosed. Although not certifiable he was advised to enter the hospital as a voluntary patient. We were very sad to see him go. Some years later he wrote to us from Canada enclosing a photo of himself in Canadian army uniform. It seems he had migrated to Canada where he had been passed fit for the armed services.

Many years later, in 2003, we had a sentimental visit from his Canadian widow and her two lovely adult daughters who had travelled over to Scotland specially to scatter their father's ashes and to erect a tombstone in his memory which they assembled on the banks of the River Tarff, our southern boundary. They told us he always remembered this spot as being so beautiful. It was a moving visit for all of us and I am delighted that we remain in touch.

Our fourth and final idiosyncratic pigman was Peter White. Peter was a professional commercial artist in London who had grown disenchanted with the demands of his calling and London life, and had broken up with his wife. With his red cravat and green beret he looked every inch either an artist or a Spanish onion seller. But happily he showed himself to be a practical artist. His principal legacy was the encouragement he gave Dorothy and I to paint. Each evening he disappeared into one of our large empty front rooms which he had converted into a studio, where he painted mainly portraits. Before long he persuaded us to buy canvases, paints and join him. Dorothy quickly became proficient, but for me, who cannot draw an apple, it took longer. It was certainly a cathartic exercise and time has never passed so quickly as when daubing away on a canvas.

Among his works were a small collection of oil paintings depicting various aspects of our farming life. When it was clear we would have to abandon Ardachie, as well as donating his iconic green beret he offered me these paintings, but finances did not allow us to make a suitable offer and it would have been unthinkable to accept them as a free gift when I knew Peter was returning to an uncertain future. Nevertheless, a lasting regret is that we have never discovered where the collection came to rest. We tried to renew contact through his ex-wife in London but she had no idea what had become of Peter except that he had been awarded a substantial contract with the Ministry of Defence. And so it was that Peter became another ship that passed in the night, of which there had recently been too many.

During these vicissitudes, there had been success as well as frustrating incidents with the pigs themselves. We had won first prize at the Royal Show at Windsor with one of our Wessex Saddlebacks but disappointment was in store when our hopes of repeating the achievement at the Royal Highland Show in Dumfries failed. We travelled in our ex-RAF open Hillman pickup with the heavily pregnant crated sow consigning poor Dorothy to the indignity of having to squeeze herself into the back, in which position the expedition arrived at the manse, raising the eyebrows of Dorothy's rather conventional mother. After Heather, that being the sow's pet name, had been placed surprisingly third, Nobby asked the judge the reason for this placement. He was told that Heather would have won had it not been for a blind teat. Our frustration intensified when back home we examined the lady's undercarriage to find all teats functioning perfectly.

On another occasion I escorted two young brother Landrace hogs on the long trail to London's Smithfield Show, the annual British livestock show for the benefit of breeders and butchers. In the parade ring, the two animals having been scrubbed and dusted down with sawdust, they looked a picture of health, with their proportions as prescribed, but I had forgotten one thing. We had failed to teach them ring craft. The buttons on my immaculate white coat scattered in every direction as the two wild brothers pulled me this way and that all around the ring, sawdust flying, causing much merriment from the assembled stalwart butchers and farmers. No prizes were won, but all was not lost for at the subsequent auction the hard-nosed conveyors of pork gave us the highest bid in the relevant class.

Another embarrassment occurred at the prestigious National Pig Breeders Association's autumn sale in distant Peterborough. Travelling on the train from Spean Bridge with two prize Landrace gilts, the important task on arrival was to produce them for the sale in spotless, shining condition. For this I was armed with talcum powder, brush and bucket. First to scrub and rinse, then to powder and preen. But unfortunately the bucket I had been given developed a large leak which left me scrambling twenty yards between tap and pig, water splashing everywhere, while the sources of my bewilderment continued slurping away without a care in the world. The life of a stockman is not always a happy one !

I loved my pigs dearly. Although most of our animals were bred for the pedigree market rather than for the abattoir, there was always a sadness when an animal not quite up to standard had to be sent away. Fortunately, we had a very successful herd, exporting to Canada and Kenya and gaining a variety of useful awards. My first experience of broadcasting was a talk on the BBC's weekly farming programme about breed assessment and the selection of appropriate animals for retention or disposal.

'Pigs are a race unjustly calumniated', wrote Dr Johnson, while Harry Truman once said that no-one should be president of the United States unless he understood pigs. Pigs, like wolves, attract many misconceptions as well as popular fantasy. Contrary to popular belief, they are very clean, intelligent animals. They are also enormously varied, the *World Dictionary of Livestock Breeds*[1] lists and describes several hundred breeds, while the *Handbook to the Breeds of the World*[2] illustrates 200 genetically differentiated types.

In an interesting, informative book,[3] Lyell Watson reflects that pigs 'Have a message for us that is there for the asking, because we share so much already. We are both products of an omnivorous upbringing, curious, dextrous and willing to explore new things. And, as a direct result of open-minded, open-mouthed enthusiasm, we are what we have eaten. Perhaps, even more importantly, pigs and humans find common cause in the fact that we are both the recently domesticated result of a long tradition of gregarious, playful, tuneful, caring, resourceful and generally reasonable beings. Pigs process thoughts. They understand 'if then' situations, they apply previous experience to novel circumstances, and they interact with their environment, and with each other as though they are conscious of the consequences'.[3]

* * * * * * * * *

One of the sacrifices consequent upon living in rural Inverness-shire was the absence of any opportunity to play cricket, the playing fields of Inverness being just too far away. But compensation one day arrived when a match was organised between a team I had managed to cobble together and the boys of the Abbey School, played on their picturesque, secluded tree-lined playing field in front of Fort Augustus Abbey.

Our XI was varied, with my friend Robert Innes, now on the verge of corpulence, behind the stumps, an athletic schoolmaster from nearby Spean Bridge who had once played for Scotland

---

[1] Mason, Ian L, *World Dictionary of Livestock Breeds*, London, CAB International, 1988

[2] Porter, Valerie, *Pigs: A Handbook to the breeds of the World*. Sussex, Helm Information, 1993.

[3] Lyall Watson, *The Whole Hog Exploring the Extraordinary Potential of Pigs*. Profile Books, London 2004, pp 248-9.

our star, with among others Gordon, my young brother-in-law. Having little idea of our communal skills, it seemed safer, having won the toss, to field first. After a few overs of comparative calm the moment seemed ripe to invite Gordon to bowl. I had no idea how skilled he was or even if he had ever played the game before, but the spirit of this unique occasion justified a trial. Gordon had passed the age of puberty and was by this time a serious-minded legal acolyte, tall, thin and slightly ministerial, with the wrinkled brow of raw experience. The first impression was favourable as, being asked where the keeper should take his stance, he suggested 'some way back'. 'He must be quite quick' I thought, little realising what lay in store. Running ferociously up to the wicket there came a savage windmilling of the arm but to no avail, nothing happened. No ball appeared. Muttering imprecations too quiet for the rest of us to hear, he returned to his starting point, the young batsman still on full alert. Onward came the second rush, but once again without any positive result. Gordon looked at the ball, at the ground, at his hand, and seemingly mystified at the devilish unhelpfulness of the sphere, he plodded back once more, albeit with less panache and careful elongated caution. By this time mirth had engulfed the fielders, one of whom was seen to escape rapidly behind the pavilion. The batsman struggled to restrain his glee in the interest of adolescent propriety, but finding this difficult fidgeted with his box, his braces and his shirt. The third attempt would surely bring the solution. This time Gordon adjusted his run-up, scrutinised anxiously his digits, fondly caressed the ball on his immaculate white trousers, and began again the run-up. Over came the twirling delinquent arm. The sphere fell limply to the ground. Now came Gordon's second big mistake for, instead of sharing in the hilarity which had engulfed the players, the umpires, and the spectators, he handled the denouement without any trace of aplomb. He stood his ground with an air of total and utter mystification, as if he had been inexplicably and unfairly offended by the law of gravity. There have been fewer funnier pantomimes on a cricket field, but I tell you this, Gordon has never spoken to me of cricket again, of rugby and tennis yes, of curling even, but of cricket never. The flaw was never assuaged nor the over ever completed, but for the rest of us it made a day never to forget.

Life on the estate had many more amusing divertissements as well as our share of mishaps and accidents. Recalling student life as an inveterate hitch-hiker I was always a sympathetic driver in these days when roads across the Highlands, especially around such tourist centres as Inverness, were littered with the impecunious young seeking free transport. One young lady, conveyed from Inverness to Fort Augustus, turned out to be an aspirant doctor from South Africa and her psychologist friend. The former's unusual initials 'GSD' stayed in my mind and this chance meeting led to her becoming a reviewer for me many years later.

An Italian holiday-maker once joined me from Glencoe, motoring to Dorothy's home at the manse in Dumfries-shire, and, having no place to stay, she was kindly given hospitality by my in-laws. My father, on the other hand, acted on some vague principle which forbade any offer of help, probably due to the old fashioned notion that nothing should come free. But on one occasion he relented. Motoring back with mother from Inverness he gave a lift to a young man en route to Fort Augustus. Several hours after depositing the traveller there came to our door two policemen. It appeared that my dear father had unwittingly assisted the escape of a convict from Inverness gaol. The fellow was soon recaptured and returned to prison, but I very much doubt if father ever gave another lift.

Malcolm was three when, in 1954, he fell in love with our new tractor. An early adventure nearly ended in tragedy. Dorothy was in Inverness, Malcolm was lifted on to the open-sided trailer conveying sacks of pig food down to the Danish piggery. I came out after unloading to find Malcolm on the ground having apparently fallen backwards off the trailer. A dash up to the house confirmed no serious damage. Dorothy on her return gave me the benefit of some severe advice on the responsibilities of parenthood. Malcolm's love has endured, his search for what has become of Massey Ferguson GST 743 continues to this day, fifty-four years later.

A more serious accident occurred a short time later. Driving home from Inverness with Ed Stevens, our part-time gardener beside me, with a trailer load of sawdust for the henhouse, as we rounded a sharp corner above the loch a man began to cross the road directly ahead. He failed to respond to an urgent blast on the horn, continuing to nonchalantly, slowly cross. In the split second available I had to choose between swerving to the left to avoid the bank above the cottage from whence the chap must have come or swerve to the right to avoid a sharp fall down to the loch. At that moment the pedestrian must have seen us out of the corner of his eye, because he hesitated, and having reached the middle of the road, turned to go back. Then the inevitable happened, a glancing blow to the side of the head from the swerving trailer, the victim falling to the ground. After the ambulance had left, a very shaken driver and his passenger travelled home. Investigation proceeded and I confess to a degree of fugacity as the police would unexpectedly visit when I was hoeing turnips in the rain or covered in pig manure. Eventually, after an interminable delay waiting to hear what the police and the Procurator Fiscal had decided, no charge was brought. It transpired that the poor man, who happily survived and returned to full health, was an elderly itinerant evangelist who was stone deaf. This fact, together with the advantage of having a witness and the brakes having been tested and cleared, ended the affair. But it taught me two lessons: a vital one; when driving always be prepared for the unexpected, and something of the mental agonies often felt by the innocent, as the decision whether or not to prosecute is held in abeyance.

In 1955, it became clear that it would be a great help to us all if Peter White learned to drive. On the eve of his test we decided to brighten proceedings by re-decorating the Hillman van with a coat of bright cream paint. Worried about the possibility of rain, not infrequent in Inverness-shire, the van was parked in a barn below the hen loft. The next morning, the dawning of the test, a quick check revealed a sorry sight, sawdust covered the chassis which was now carpeted with small star-like grains of contaminated sawdust. The ken-speckled vehicle had overnight become truly hen-spreckled. Having remembered to make a temporary repair of the passenger's internal door handle, and with the sawdust brushed off as far as possible, Peter set off, looking artistically cavalier with his scarlet cravat and green beret. During the course of the test, Peter thought to apologise for the state of the handle with its long nail replacement. 'Yes, I know' replied the examiner, with more than a hint of sarcasm 'its sticking through my trousers'. When Peter reversed back the way he had come rather than proceeding forward across the main road, the appropriate verdict was inevitable.

Many friends and other visitors arrived, some to stay for tea, some to stay for a week. Another example of lost opportunity about learning something interesting from ships that pass in the night came with the visit of Mr Le Poer Power, a name not easily forgotten. He was a tall, thin, mild-mannered man with the mien of a middle-aged cleric. A paying guest in London with my aunts, he spent most of his 'holiday' with us energetically scything bracken on the hill to make space for the pregnant sows, for it was good to have them free-ranging as much as possible. It took me forty years to discover that he was a close kinsman of Frank Le Poer Power, the monocled, sardonic Irish journalist, *The Times* war correspondent with Gordon at Khartoum and one of the last three remaining Britons left in the city. His famous interview with Gordon appeared in *The Times* on March 10th, 1884. After Gordon had resolutely but imprudently refused to surrender, he sent Power with the guileless Colonel J.D.H.Stewart down river in three steamers. Their purpose was to reach Dongola and to tell the world what would happen if Khartoum were captured. Stewart was ordered on no account to leave the river, should the engine fail he was to continue by sail. When only a hundred miles from Dongola where, though they didn't know it, Herbert Kitchener lay in wait disguised as a Bedouin, their boat *Abbas* entered the wrong channel and ran onto some rocks. In his book, *Imperial Vanities*,[4] Brian Thompson takes up the story, 'Just as Gordon had read it, Stewart accepted an invitation to go ashore to receive the help of a Sheikh who appeared bearing a white flag. He and Power left for the man's house unarmed. Only a short

---

[4]   Brian Thompson; *Imperial Vanities*, HarperCollins, London, 2002. See especially pp202-249.

while after sitting down and accepting the traditional hospitality which the Koran enforces on hosts, the two men were butchered. All the papers on board were sent to the Mahdi, together with Stewart's severed head'. How interesting it would have been if only I had known at the time to hear more of this fine journalist and scion of the Irish House of Power, of which the actor Tyrone Power was a member as well as the Countess of Poher, wife of the original Bluebeard.

A less illustrious, but more amusing visitor was our friend the saturnine radio actor Anthony Jacobs. One hot summer afternoon we set about distributing pig manure from the open trailer across one of the arable fields. The trick is to make sure the slurry disentangles itself from the fork when thrown.

Unhappily, this was a trick too far for Anthony's wild but amateur enthusiasm. As he lunged at the ground with his fork full of sludge he forgot to extricate himself from the load and the whole lot fell to the ground with a swish and a heavenly whiff. Anthony, the debonair Londoner, would not have been recognised by his friends at the BBC as he tottered with streaming eyes, voluted frame and a heady countenance back to the lodge and the promise of a redeeming bath.

Apart from crises which seemed to recur with increasing regularity, there were champagne moments, when the magic of our environment infiltrated one's activity. One such occasion was a late summer evening, a golden sun glowing across the hills and fields beyond, beneath a heavy bank of cloud. I was ploughing the top field when hit by a revelation: that to till the land is a deep and gratifying instinct in man's psyche, hidden until given the opportunity to experience it. This was an apocalyptic moment.

* * * * * * * *

A minor skill can easily be taken for granted, one that seems so easy if one only knows how. The required technique this day was how to persuade a reluctant pregnant sow to enter the cage of a weighing machine. The operator was my brother-in-law Howard, a humorous English vicar with a rich booming bass voice and enormous vitality but without the athleticism to prove it. Having somehow inveigled the young lady head first into the machine he hadn't time to snib the lock when the porcine mass propelled herself backwards. Seeing the door of the piggery open and not wanting to allow a complete escape, my brother-in-law just managed to catch on to the rapidly retreating tail. My first vision, working outside, was of a rampaging pig towing a billowing clergyman by the tail, Howard holding on grimly but to no avail. After a tortuous and demented dash around the paddock, my brother-in-law abandoned further pursuit, falling to the ground in defeated disarray. It was a case of the triumphant pulling the incumbent. I never knew if it was sarcasm when it was time for him to go and he said he had enjoyed his 'holiday'.

Colin Brown, who later changed his name to Colin Collin because he thought it sounded more professional, was a very good friend from student days, a vet with a photographic memory which helped to win the gold medal at Edinburgh's Royal 'Dick' Veterinary College. While still a student he suffered an inexplicable haemorrhage when boarding a tram. A visit to him in hospital was my first visit to such an institution. When I arrived I found Colin taking the nurse's temperature at the same time as his own was being taken. He was that sort of chap. In 1953 he was a lecturer at the Royal Veterinary College in London where among his pupils was a certain Professor Ivan Likar. Likar was an émigré from Yugoslavia who was required to pass a British examination before being allowed to practice in the UK. Likar persuaded Colin that he had successfully developed a process for extracting a hormone from stallions' urine used primarily in the production of ladies' cosmetics. We were given to understand that the potential economic advantages of this were considerable, given the much greater cost of the conventional alternative.

Persuaded by Colin, in spite of his known eccentricities – he once astonished a Yorkshire farmer by extracting by *coup de main*, a pair of ladies' bras from the nose of a cow, explaining them as the cause of the animals affliction – it was agreed to set up a company called Phabio, with Colin, his wife Celia, Likar and myself as co-directors. We would buy twelve stallions, engage a groom and the estate would receive a rental for the grazing rights.

A laboratory was set up in a large upstairs room, with pipettes, bunsen burners, glass distillation apparatus and a rich assortment of pipes arraigned on the un-carpeted floor.

Having converted an old stable block to accommodate them, for reasons of size we chose twelve lovely little Shetland ponies from various breeders around Scotland. Finding someone to undertake the work was more difficult, especially when it was pointed out that the duties included the collection and cooking of urine. After several applicants had left the interview suspecting that they had been the victim of a sick joke, we were fortunate enough to find Mary Grant. She was a saucy, fresh-faced, roughly spoken girl of about thirty, with a laugh like a rusty hinge, which she produced frequently. My parents vacated the keeper's cottage and Mary moved in, a large copper can bedecking her kitchen.

The next question was how to collect the precious liquid. Many trials were made until we eventually hit upon strips of mackintosh shaped like a Venetian cooking vessel and tied around the pony's rear end. The only problem was that when an animal lay down the pottage flowed out. This meant losing whatever may have been passed by day but embarking on a collection round as soon as the ponies returned to the stables at night, as well as rotating two or three of the animals kept in the stables all day. Likar visited us once a month to process the cooked spoils before sending his extraction to the perfumery. It was a joy to see the frisky young ponies roaming the hillside above the lodge, a pleasure much enjoyed by Feona and Malcolm, and I believe Mary was very happy in her work despite a brief unrequited love affair with the village milkman, a running commentary on the doomed affair being repeated to us nightly for several weeks.

But, alas, the extracts proved too limited to be economic. The ponies had to be sold, Mary had to leave, and a rather crestfallen board of directors closed down the operation. The next I heard of Colin was that he had migrated from a chair of Veterinary Science in Khartoum to a similar professorship in the Bahamas via a spell in Kenya during the Mau Mau rebellion, eventually settling down into a very lucrative private practice in British Columbia. Of Likar all we ever heard was that he too had moved to Canada, there falling foul of the veterinary authorities. There must have been a lesson to be learnt from this failed commercial enterprise but I never made out what it was, probably because I enjoyed the ponies too much and Mary was so much fun to have around.

Easter 1955 was a difficult time. Gentle Dan Scobie nursed a severely quinsied throat just before the lambing and, like most men who think little about illness until it strikes, believed he was going to die. This left us vulnerable, for the care of pigs is quite different to the care of sheep, especially at lambing time. Mountain sheep have their own preferred havens among the rocks and gullies where they often require neo-natal attention. I had no idea where, to use a golfing phrase, these preferred lies might be, and my midwifery skills were non-existent. However, the losses sustained were far less than might have been expected and the hirsel survived without undue deprivation.

Dan was an excellent tutor in how to judge the finer points that make a good ewe or breeding ram. Going with him to the sheep sales in Dingwall or Inverness with the markets' indefinably attractive sweet odour of wet wool and the earnest, coarse banter of the shepherds was always informative and never failed to be interesting. After a couple of years I was almost as comfortable assessing a Blackface sheep as a Landrace pig. The main difference between them and pigs in terms of stock improvement is, of course, that with pigs you can develop a specific programme, move towards one's chosen goal of conformation and type over the course of four or five generations, but to do the same with a flock of sheep because of the difference in the breeding cycle and the likely number of progeny takes three times as long.

Although there were always distractions and emergencies to threaten the even tenor of our days, there were moments of voluntary escape. Once such occurred in May 1955 shortly before another General Election.

Having come to realise that in a two-party system if one is to make any impact at all in politics one has to support, however reluctantly, one or other of the two major parties. I allowed my name to go forward to contest the Moray and Nairn seat for the Tories. James Stuart was the sitting member but word came through that he had lost popularity following his appointment as Secretary of State for Scotland. At a private tea party with members of the Fraser family at Beaufort Castle, where I had been taken by Neil McLean, the member for Inverness-shire, I had my first glimpse of the arrogance which permeated the upper reaches of the party. However, Lord Lovat's last word, as be bid me farewell on the castle steps was 'l'attaque!'. It was, I thought, mentioned merely to bolster my flagging ego although as a transmogrified Liberal I stood a good chance, always provided I told the selection committee what we knew they wanted to hear. Therein lay the rub. The Suez affair was bubbling as was trouble with the Unions. My views on both these matters ran counter to the party line and the fact I said so put a premature end to my nascent campaign. Stuart was duly re-selected, retained the seat with a reduced majority, in due course becoming Viscount Stuart of Findhorn.

But a taste for politics once acquired is hard to lose and at the next election I volunteered to help Neil McLean fight to retain his Inverness-shire seat. McLean, a charming if slightly bibulous ex-SAS officer, helped by his equally charming wife, Daska, 'the Pearl of Dubrovnik', made an attractive candidate face-to-face, but became rather wooden when addressing an audience and was almost tongue-tied when faced with an unexpected or difficult question. My job was to precede him on the campaign trail as often as work on the farm allowed and to remain beside him at question time. This worked very well until the last afternoon, at Dulnain Bridge, when the candidate, having been delayed in Inverness, failed to arrive. Although in retrospect enjoyable, the impromptu effort thus forced upon me was my last experience of active politicising. Without any feeling of sour grapes, in retrospect it seemed a lucky escape from a life of much humbug, hypocrisy and one devoid of any real home or family life.

There were other considerations. The campaign called to mind Graham Wallas's neglected but rewarding book *Human Nature in Politics*[5]. The political analyst and historian A. L. Rowse thought it the most original and important contribution to be made in political

---

[5]   Graham Wallas *Human Nature in Politics*, Constable & Co, London. 1948 edition.

thought by an Englishman in the twentieth century. The main thrust of the book is what Wallas called the rationalist fallacy, the assumption that human beings largely act in politics upon rational motives and trains of intelligent reasoning. 'No wonder', Rowse wrote in his Foreword 'that liberalism has been so ineffectual: it consigns itself to futility by clinging to what is so patently untrue of human behaviour in the mass. In short liberalism was digging its own grave by sticking blindly, against all the evidence, to a rationalist view of human nature, the intellectualist assumption'. As soon as one becomes embroiled in the political cauldron one is made aware that most political opinions of most men are the result, not of reasoning tempered by experience, but of unconscious or half-conscious inference fixed by habit.

Neil McLean, whose biography appeared a few years later, defeated the popular local farmer and former rugby international Henry Bannerman by a mere 966 votes.

All through these isolated events life on the farm carried on with seldom a day without the unexpected, the surging ebb and flow of the fluctuating tide of fortune. An entry from a sadly brief diary taken at random gives the flavour. 'May 19. An eventful day. Our effort to make an early start was thwarted on a wet day by Colleen's intransigence. Colleen, a Wessex Saddleback sow, would not go into the crate. Eventually we got her up with the help of a nearby loading bank and off we went to market. I bid for the champion gilt, lost her at 75 guineas but succeeded in getting the champion boar, the best animal there, for £59/17/0, and a gilt from the Midcoul herd with ten piglets for ninety guineas. A great thrill. Then with Dorothy to Achnasoul to deliver Colleen. Met the owner, Norman Christensen, who had been at the sale with his pig girl. (Norman was the brother of General Christensen, Commanding Officer, Scotland and was the only other pedigree breeder of Wessex Saddlebacks in the north). Then the fun began. Incident in Grant Street with the escaping boar. Eventually, and by great good fortune, Robertson our local agricultural haulier, helped us out as he had a load of sheep bound for Fort Augustus. Home in driving rain. Dorothy did the evening feed while John (Watson) and I spread another four loads of concrete for the new piggery. Trouble with chicks but all animals at last in bed. Colleen's ill son brought into the wash house and given an egg. Very pleased with purchases but worried over virus pneumonia. This life is worry and work.'

The next morning I wrote 'with a very heavy heart we bade farewell and bon voyage to the Watsons'. Little could we have guessed that we would never see each other again. My best University friend, so balanced, dependable, humorous and warm, died in Canada from stomach cancer two years later, aged just thirty.

Casual visitors came and went, among them mushroom gatherers, a couple from South Africa whose kinsmen they said had once owned the estate, a chap training for a spell in the Antarctic who asked if he could pitch his tent in the wettest, coldest place for a couple of nights, and then there was Father Morrice. Father Morrice had persuaded the Abbey to invest in a pair of porkers and, using the excuse of learning the trade, arrived on our doorstep on his tractor with increasing frequency, always just in time for tea. He was like a fish out of water, a man of the world rather than a monk, an impression not diminished when a short time later he was admonished and expelled to a 'safer' place, somewhere in England.

One of our village customers was the local hotelier, Mr Nelson of the great Scottish rugby team of the 1920s[6]. In the mid-summer of 1954 when his Caledonian hotel was full he asked if we could manage to take an overflow for bed and breakfast. Although Dorothy had more than enough to do running the home, looking after Feona and Malcolm plus our resident pigman and me, because mother happened to be with us at the time and she was always happy to meet a new face, we agreed. The spare room was quickly readjusted, the curtains shaken and unravelled, fresh towels introduced in the form of a coarse, mauve gimp I had myself hand-woven in Hampstead, where for a short time after we were married, having acquired a large Kentish hand loom,

---

[6] J B Nelson and Herbert Waddell of the Glasgow Academicals were the two celebrated half backs who together won nine of the eleven internationals they played in, alongside Bannerman and Smith.

Dot had been taught weaving by a pipe-smoking lady enthusiast. I never knew one could have such fun with a loom.

In due course there drove up to our door an elderly American couple, greeted at the front door by mother, quite excited in her expectation and new role. She welcomed them in, took possession of their bags and proceeded to mount the main staircase, our visitors dutifully following along behind.

Unfortunately, mother's knowledge of the rambling old lodge was severely limited and she had no idea where to find the guest bedroom. Up and along the top corridor went the procession until, finding no solution, the party descended a rear staircase, passed along the rear corridor until, somewhat breathless and flustered, mother and her touring party found themselves back at the front door. A loud 'coo-ee', mother's rallying call, aroused Dorothy in the kitchen and eventually under her guidance the troop hit base. The following morning, our American gentleman appeared at breakfast with a large stigma across his left cheek. We casually asked the cause to be told that the towel so proudly woven had been rather sharper than he was accustomed to or had expected. We vowed never to repeat the experiment although, as we will see, in time the guest room had other tricks to play.

Fathers and monks from the Abbey often passed by for an afternoon stroll and we came to recognise most of them. One winter afternoon in 1955 a Brother went missing. The police were called out, a search party from Gordonstoun School arrived, a band of Brothers combed the hill. The next afternoon there was still no sign of the missing walker, and the press arrived. The man from The Daily Mail interviewed me, asking if Brother X, I forget his name, was known to frequently stroll across our land. I reported that he was a Brother I could not recall ever having seen before. The next day the paper ran a story saying that Ardachie was one of his favourite walks. Such can be the ways of the press. If it is like this over a minor event what faith can we have about press accuracy anywhere? Remember Mark Twain's comment that if you don't read newspapers you are uninformed, if you do read them you are mis-informed. Sadly, the missing Brother was eventually found beside a stone dyke on the hill. It seemed he had lost his glasses, and with them all sense of direction, left to die on the hill of hypothermia.

Although life was always too full for us to play much part in the village community, tending animals is relentless, there was one vibrant annual exception: the summer dipping and shearing of the sheep. Farmers and shepherds from far around forgathered around the fank beside Dan's hillside cottage. The sheep having been collected from the hill, they were individually driven through a deep, narrow bath of sheep dip, their heads immersed by means of a special two-pronged fork before sometime later they were shorn. This event repeated many times among the local farms gave the shepherds an opportunity to help one another and to exchange gossip, news and banter whilst all the time carrying on the toil.

I have not mentioned any of our dogs. It was reputedly a woman[7] who first observed that 'the more I see of men the more I like dogs'. For my money, after family and home the dogs are the next most precious asset. One of life's sadnesses, as Lord Oaksey observed, is the comparative shortness of a dog's life. 'He is your friend, your partner, your defender, your dog. You are his life, his love, his leader. He will be yours, faithful and true, to the last beat of heart. You owe it to him to be worthy of such devotion.' First we had Lassie, an intelligent, eager, energetic little Border Collie who helped us herd the pigs; then we had Fern our first deerhound, the most graceful and gentle of creatures except of course when spying a moving quarry, especially deer. That has always been my one reservation, one overcome with our own hounds by allowing them to chase, without ever teaching them to kill. Most bitches need to be taught this by launching themselves at the neck of a moving prey, but if they are not taught it is possible to appreciate the thrill of the chase without the risk of damaging the deer. And, another thing, a deerhound released on the hill will always return to the point of departure, unlike Salukis and other hunting dogs, that can roam for days. During the war years, deerhounds survived thanks to the devotion of a very few owners. Today the

---

[7] The French revolutionary, Marie-Jeanne Philipson (1754–93).

Breed Society counts over 500 UK members, with more than 150 overseas members in Australia, Europe and North America.

Ben Fogle's father, Bruce, is a vet. In his recent book, *A Dog Abroad*, he expressed in a passage of profound beauty what it means to experience the moment that everyone who has ever owned and loved a dog fears most. Describing the loss of Macy, his retriever, he wrote 'Walking your dog is life-affirming, and its probably what I miss most now that she's no longer alive. Silence [walking together] . . is that not the true glue of love: the ability to be together, to do together, to understand each other without the need for words? The ability to feel love certainly predates language. Being with a dog, understanding her moods, her wants, her feelings, her emotions, without the need for words, returns you to the core of your being, to a time before words, when body language said everything.'

In the face of the manifold activities and demands we did our best to preserve one precious hour every day, immediately after lunch, when all the adults in the house enjoyed a touch of *dolce far niente*. Curiously, while this was preserved when we were still in our thirties and working on a busy farm, by the time we reached fifty and ever after, when we really needed it more, we have never been able to restore the practice.

Although, as I have said, we never had much time to participate in community affairs, there were a few local worthies whom we came to know quite well. There was the ubiquitous, bustling, ruddy Mr Leslie, the local grocer who boasted that he could provide anything from a pin to an elephant, a claim he proved many times over; his quieter competitor the postmaster Mr Macdonald, the ruby-faced, porky Tom Campbell who looked after our cars and, although failing with Peter White, successfully taught Dorothy to drive; two attractive Nelson daughters with whom we occasionally played tennis at the Abbey; and the mildly eccentric ex-SAS Brigadier Prendergast who lived at the end of the canal-side by Loch Ness and always slept on a camp bed to prevent himself, he said, 'from softening up'.

The single most memorable event during the four brief years we were at Ardachie occurred in 1953, but that is another story.

CHAPTER 4

The Unseen Guest

What beck'ning ghost, along the moonlight jade
Invites my step, and points to yonder glade?

[Alexander Pope]

It was not long before it became clear that Dorothy was going to need more help looking after the family and working occasionally outside than our casual daily, thickly bespectacled Mrs McKechnie, could provide. With this in mind my proactive mother decided to place a notice in her local London newsagent, advertising for a resident housekeeper. No address was given, only a box number. Among several replies my parents selected a Mr & Mrs Macdonald. Mrs Macdonald, half French and half Scottish, had been working as a housekeeper in London and wanted to get away from the city for, she said, health reasons, while her husband, in his late forties, was a trained millwright now working as a postman.

Accordingly, on August 17th, 1953 the Macdonalds travelled north by overnight train met by my father at our nearest station, Spean Bridge. Dorothy introduced them to the house and showed them to their bedroom which lay above their own private staircase at the far end of the lodge from ourselves. That evening, while Dorothy and I were sitting by the fire, the Macdonalds came bursting in saying that there was something 'wrong' about their room. It seemed that shortly after Bill, the husband, had fallen asleep, both of them being exhausted after their long journey, his wife Frances thought she heard footsteps approaching their room, then disappearing into an empty bedroom opposite their own. A few moments later the sequence was repeated although this time Bill thought the footsteps emanated from the wall next to their beds. All of us retreated to the kitchen where we tried to think of possible explanations, the generator, the dogs, the cat, a trip that Dorothy had made up and down another staircase thirty minutes earlier, but all could be eliminated.

In the course of a rather tired conversation it was clear that the couple were exhausted and Frances seemed a highly strung lady. She told us that immediately after they had arrived they took a stroll around the house and as soon as she entered what she called the rose garden, a small rather neglected area outside our study window, she felt compelled to enter through a small wicker gate but, overcome by an unpleasant sensation, withdrew almost as quickly. At the time this conveyed no particular message, its significance only came to our notice later. Cups of coffee having been dispensed, we returned to our respective rooms, my father to the keeper's cottage, the rest of us to opposite ends of the house.

Within twenty minutes the Macdonalds came hurrying back to our bedroom in great agitation. They said that as soon as they had got into bed and turned off the light, rapping were heard coming from the wall behind which Bill had first heard the footsteps. These ceased as soon as he turned on the light.

Now it so happened that as an interested psychology graduate I had joined the Society for Psychical Research. Hence my intrigue at the unfolding events. It was hard to believe that something odd was occurring in our own home. I suggested to Bill that the two of us should return to his room, leaving Frances to stay with Dorothy in the kitchen. We spent fifteen or so minutes in the unlit bedroom but heard nothing. On our return Frances asked if they might change their room. So it was that at around midnight Dorothy and I escorted the Macdonalds upstairs to the guest room, the room of the lethal towel. No sooner had we reached the door when Frances came to a sudden halt, staring at the far corner, apparently in a trance-like state, and began a beckoning motion with her right hand mumbling, "She's in here. There's a woman in this room". Dorothy went for the light switch but I asked her to wait as, seeing nothing myself (neither Dorothy nor Bill dared to look), it was interesting to observe what might happen next. Very gradually Frances reluctantly withdrew and once again we retreated to the sanctuary of the kitchen. Once there she told us in breathless tones, "I first listened at the wall and heard a sound like the rustling of wings. Then there appeared in the top corner of the room an old lady with a cap on her head, a shawl around her shoulders and a hand in front of, and hiding, her face, beckoning me to follow her. She had straggling grey hair, which looked as if it had been curly in her younger days".

This had me wondering whether the description could in any way relate to Lily Bruen from whose estate we had bought the house, but of whom we had never seen a photograph. The time was now past midnight and Frances, being quite distraught and over-fatigued, we led the two of them to yet another bedroom, this time adjacent to our own and to the children who had slept undisturbed throughout.

Once installed, we left the lights shining along the length of the upstairs passage as well as down the main staircase. Within a couple of minutes the Macdonalds were back again, having heard another succession of raps coming from above their bed head. Four of us gathered outside our rooms at the top of the main stairwell, facing the long corridor, all lights blazing. Frances turned to me and whispered in muted tones, "Come here Mr McEwan. There she is again. Can't you see her? Now she is crawling on her hands and knees with what looks like a candlestick in one hand. She is outside that room", pointing to a bathroom. I saw nothing, but in the hope that an audible message might produce some sort of reaction, I suggested Frances ask "What's troubling you ?". There was no reaction. But then Frances suddenly burst into a semi-hysterical running commentary as she followed the spectre who, she murmured, was now crawling towards us. With her voice rising to a crescendo we made a quick exit down the main staircase before the phantom arrived from the opposite direction to cut us off.

There was clearly nowhere in the lodge left for the Macdonalds to stay so we did the only possible thing and, at about four o'clock in the morning, I took them down to the keeper's cottage awakening my father who, although travelling to London later that day, abandoned his bed and joined us in the main house.

After breakfast, excited by the experience, although seeing nothing untoward myself, my interest in psychical research having been re-kindled, I made two resolves. First, to ring the Society in London to see if they could put me in touch with any nearby investigator. The second was to call upon our adjacent neighbour at Culachy, Mrs Beckett, who I knew had been friendly with Lily Bruen. What she told me was extraordinary. Although unable to produce a photograph of Lily, she said that toward the end of her life Mrs Bruen had become confused, paralysed, and eventually demented, accusing the servants of theft and crawling around the lodge by day and night searching for jewellery she imagined had been stolen by the staff. But that was not all. Mrs Beckett went on to say, without any prompting from me, that Lily Bruen always wore a hat, a red one, also a wrap around her shoulders which she said could easily be mistaken for a shawl. Her mental state had eventually become so bad that she was obliged to enter an Inverness private home where she died. There was a final revelation. One of Mrs Bruen's particular interests, Mrs Beckett told me, had been roses, much of her time being spent in the rose garden where once on a summer evening Mrs Beckett had had to rescue her, having found her friend crawling around on her hands and knees on the bare earth in the dark.

Nothing further untoward happened the next day and, their own kitchen seemingly the one 'safe' room, the Macdonalds elected to bed down therein, promising not to venture beyond the room during the hours of darkness. But at about 9.45pm Frances suddenly remembered she had forgotten to bring in the milk left by Dan Scobie on the hall table each evening. Even as she approached the door she alerted Bill to raps coming from just beyond the door and upon opening it she was faced with a spectre looking she said, particularly 'wraith' like. Nothing worthy of note occurred during the next three nights and on the 21st two investigators arrived from the Society.

They made an interesting contrast. J. D. Matheson was a young, rather dogmatic maths teacher, whose interest in the society seemed to be to seek non-psychical explanations in all cases. Mr R. Ross OBE, on the other hand, was an urbane ex-diplomat, prepared to accept psychic phenomena almost at face value. Although this pair were the only two members of the Society, apart from myself, within a radius of 200 miles, chance had produced two diametrically opposed attitudes, a happy circumstance, even though, as we shall see, none of us would be able to find any rational explanation for what had already occurred nor for what was to follow.

I left Matheson and Ross alone with the Macdonalds to discuss matters. They reported that, to their surprise, Frances seemed 'un-naturally' willing to co-operate. She told them that in spite of her aversion to the rose garden she had returned there and sat for ten minutes during the early evening. After dinner at about 10.30pm, with the children safely in bed and fast asleep, Bill came in to tell us that rappings had begun again and invited us all into their bedroom close to Frances' bed. The sound was similar to that made by knuckles on wood, but although I was nearest her, it was impossible to determine precisely from whence they came, especially as they were accompanied by loud sighs from Frances. I concluded that the most likely cause had to be Frances herself, but whether made consciously or unconsciously it was impossible to say.

There followed the most remarkable episode of all. The small room was in darkness save for a faint rosy glow from the Raeburn stove. Suddenly Frances shot up in the bed and in a dreamy far away voice mumbled, "Rose tree . . . neglected . . . it's coming to me now, someone has moved a rose tree". For everyone else in the room this made no sense but Dorothy and I immediately recognised its significance. In the walled garden there was a run-down greenhouse in which there grew a peach tree and a rose tree. In order to make room for tomatoes I had asked our part-time gardener to remove the rose tree and to re-plant it outside, an operation from which it never recovered. Within a week of this desecration Mrs Beckett, on one of her courtesy visits, remarked casually in conversation that the rose tree in the greenhouse should be tended with special care as it had been Lily Bruen's particular favourite, an early season variety with unusually splendid flowers. We never told Mrs Beckett what had been done nor could Frances have had any contact with the gardener who happened to be on holiday this particular week.

To the regret of both parties, in view of Frances' mental condition and Dorothy's growing concern, it was generally agreed that the Macdonalds would have to return to London, and on August 29th they bade the lodge farewell and returned to London.

In considering all these events one or two additional facts should be mentioned. We lived more than a mile from the village and, to the best of our knowledge, prior to the events described neither Bill nor Frances had been there and even supposing they had there was no one who could have known about the rose tree and it was most unlikely that the strange behaviour of Lily Bruen was generally known, still less recounted, to complete strangers. Another thing, Bill was most anxious that no report should be given to any newspaper, they were both very concerned to avoid any publicity. I found out the reason after they had left when, visited a month or so later by agents, I learned that the pair were not in fact married and Bill was being pursued for back payment of alimony.

At the psychological level, we were told that Frances had been brought up by a stepmother who 'hated' her. She had had two marriages and, although capable and reasonably intelligent, she was over-excitable and clearly had a disturbed personality. She told us that she had once worked for a London psychiatrist who said she was 'psychic'. Bill, although an extremely willing, able, mild mannered and seemingly honest person, was under her thumb.

In 1961, the BBC made an acclaimed film of the affair in the series *Leap in the Dark*. The producer had somehow managed to track down the Macdonalds. He asked them what they thought of the McEwans. "They let us down", replied Frances. "Why do you say that?", asked the producer, "Because," she replied, "they should have told us the place was haunted before we went".[1]

---

[1]   For a full account, written within days of the event, see my report *'The Ardachie Case'*, Journal of the Society for Psychical Research, Vol 38, No. 386. Dec 1955.

The nearest I can come to an explanation is that, while the noises all of us heard were probably caused by Frances herself, the phantom she reported was a result of Frances' turbulent personality, sensitised by travel fatigue, somehow tuning in to the psychic remnants of Lily Bruen. I cannot think of any way in which Frances could have had prior knowledge of the characteristics she described, nor can I conceive of any conscious or sub-conscious motivation for any dissembling or chicanery.

My report to the Society concluded: 'whether Mrs M actually experienced the vision she described and whether her trance-like states were genuine seemed to me matters of minor importance. The important question is surely not the form but the substance of the experiences. Why was it an old lady with a cap on her head and a shawl, why a crawling vision, why feel uneasy in the rose garden, why see a 'wraith' so suddenly on the back stairs and why allude to a rose tree that no one would notice and about its recent history (demise) almost no one knew?[2] The cumulative association with Mrs B is too great to allow an explanation in terms of pure coincidence. We have strong evidence for a neurosis. An additional explanation must, it would seem, be sought in terms of either (a) prior knowledge (which it is impossible to exclude conclusively), or (b) some paranormal activity, possibly evoked by the turbulent state of the sub-conscious mind of Mrs M. The latter hypothesis possesses the least number of inherent contradictions and accounts for the greatest number of facts with most economy.'

During the remaining three years we were at Ardachie there was only one other curious incident of a remotely similar kind. In 1955 we had staying with us a fellow Gafic Club member, now a London solicitor, Bingham Hobson. He was a thoroughgoing sceptic in matters paranormal. One evening as we sat chatting in the drawing room, we heard footsteps coming from the room above and the sound of something being dragged across the floor. This was the room which had housed Phabio's laboratory and was now completely empty, without even a carpet. Bingham,

---

[2]   In fact, only three people knew, Dorothy, our gardener, and myself.

certain we had an intruder, dashed upstairs but found nothing and checking the dogs on the way down found them both asleep in their beds. The incident left him bewildered and shaken.

Another curious experience occurred many years later, when we were living in Sussex. We had come to know quite well Michael Millar, a local antique dealer specialising in firearms. When shooting on the hill above Ardachie our friend had seen Dorothy walking along looking cold, wearing only a cardigan, and beside her an old lady. He greeted them with surprise, not expecting to see Dorothy in the north, but, in spite of a second greeting, there was no response as they slowly slid away – it seemed he had seen the ghost of a living person for when he related the incident back home in Sussex, sending a shiver down our spines, his incredulity was plain to see; he found it hard to believe that Dorothy had never left Sussex. "It was such a relief to know that you were still alive", he told us.

* * * * * * * * *

All good things have to come to an end. By the autumn of 1956 it had become increasingly clear our days at Ardachie were numbered. The problem was health. The asthma was getting worse, culminating in a visit to a consultant allergist in Inverness. After a variety of skin tests had revealed all he asked my occupation. "Farming," I told him, "Well", he said, with suitable professional sang-froid, "I'm afraid you are allergic to earth and trees". This fell like a death-knell upon my ears. Allied to the fact that Dorothy had herself become increasingly allergic as well as fatigued, this forced us to face up reality: we had to start a new life away from hens, pigs and country dust.

After Major Vernon, the owner of the adjacent Glendoe estate, had declined to make a bid, our stalking friend and vet, Mr Stuart, made an offer that equated with the original price. These being the days before inflation, we accepted. It was with a very heavy heart that the hens and pigs were shipped off to market, Dan Scobie agreeing to remain with the sheep until our successor reviewed his options. Mary stayed with us to the end, hoping to find a job on Deeside, but when nothing turned up our paths sadly never crossed again. Peter White packed up his paint box and his paintings, bequeathed to me his iconic beret as a lasting momento, and returned to London. Most of the furniture was included in the sale, among them the 17th century carved refectory table.

It was farewell to a dream, farewell to the lovely old lodge beside the cypress trees, to the front lawn with its encircling red rhododendrons, to the hill with all its crests and corries, to the sweet smell of the pigs, many of which I had come to know and love with their idiosyncratic mannerisms and the occasional louse behind the ear. No more collecting the daily milk pail from a nail posted on a tree in Culachy's woodland beyond the little bridge over the River Tarff, no more ploughing fields beneath the panoply of heaven. So many memories.

One lasting sadness was that whereas for me Ardachie had been in many ways the apotheosis of living, for Dorothy it had been the nadir. Now, as helped by my father, we drove our possessions across the spine of Scotland to rented accommodation in Ballater, Aberdeenshire, it would be Dorothy's turn to enjoy life.

After our departure the old house was never lived in again, we had been its last residents. Stuart never used the lodge but when visiting from his home in Conon Bridge, forty miles to the north, he stayed in a caravan parked on the front lawn. Aided by a substantial grant, he fenced the grazing area of the hill, called the 'Greens', replacing the sheep with cattle. After three winters shooting all the stags which annually sought refuge from our less sheltered but much larger neighbour, seriously threatening their 'sport', Stuart sold Ardachie to the Vernon family for a price rumoured to have been well in excess of what he had paid us three years earlier, certainly substantially more than Major Vernon had been willing to offer us previously.

The proprietors of Glendoe then committed an inexcusable act of vandalism, pulling down the old lodge, leaving not the vestige of a stone behind.

Then, in 1977, they sold off the keeper's cottage to an Englishman working with the forestry commission for £4,500. Some years later Dorothy and I were motoring home from

Sutherland when, stopping for lunch at a small hotel in Golspie we were astonished to see an illustrated advertisement which we immediately recognised as the old keeper's cottage, for offers over £45,000. Modernised and with the paddock transformed into a garden, it was available for a price that exceeded ninefold the price we had paid for the entire estate. Today the cottage is known simply as Ardachie. Much of the steading stands neglected and unkept, the old chapel razed to the ground, while the walled garden is now a woodland wilderness, the lawn an overgrown meadow.

CHAPTER 5

A Change of Direction

'Now this is not the end. It is not even the beginning of the end.
But it is, the end of the beginning.'

[Churchill]

The next two years, 1957-59, gave us an opportunity to recharge the batteries and to resolve what routes to follow in the journey through life. Our immediate base was the rather gloomy Osborne House, rented furnished accommodation in Ballater, while we searched for a place of our own. The Inneses came over from Fort Augustus to join us for New Year. Shortly afterwards we discovered Cornellan which was to be our home base for the next nineteen years. Early in July, Rhoderick ('Rhod') came into the world, the only one of our children to be born in Scotland. The following month Malcolm joined Feona, both of whom had first emerged in London, at the good local primary school, his first taste of external discipline.

At the beginning of May I was introduced to Crathie cricket club whose home ground at Balmoral Castle is a square originally laid down as a grass tennis court for the late Duke of Kent. Although this was the start of a lasting love affair, my introduction was not particularly auspicious as, at about half-past four, we were driven off the pitch by a blinding snow storm, but more of this later.

As well as having a new baby, we took delivery, as it were, of our first Deerhound brood of pedigree pups, one of whom, Calum, was destined to become a champion when in the ownership of one of the breed's staunchest patrons, Norah Hartley, sister of the playwright Rex Hartley.

In collaboration with Tony Colclough, Aberdeen's chief planning officer, a friend we had met through the Inneses, I developed a passing interest in motor rallying. The plan was to learn something about the basic procedures by joining Aberdeen Motor Club. This was in days when rallying on public roads was still permitted. Armed with all the weaponry available, maps, mileage tables, and mathematical aids of every description, the plan was to drive my elderly Standard Vanguard in local rallies, Tony acting as navigator and co-driver, while for the RAC Scottish Rally the roles would be reversed in Tony's open Hillman tourer. The first all-night jamboree round the hinterland of rural Aberdeenshire saw us in a lucky drive-off. Lucky, because in the middle of the night my navigator suddenly shouted 'turn left' causing me to brake sharply in order to take an abrupt left angle turn, but the competitor following behind, perhaps too closely, charged into us, smashing all his lights and destroying their any further interest as, undamaged, we proceeded on our apologetic way. When it came to the RAC event, we acquitted ourselves poorly, largely because on the various road tests of manoeuvrability Tony rather lost his competitive nerve, but we sped through some beautiful places, particularly the glorious coastal road between Stoer and Drumbeg beyond Lochinver, with its hidden bays of golden sand that emerged dramatically around almost every scenic corner.

But in the autumn the family narrowly avoided disaster. Dorothy, her physical resources drained by farming life and further reduced by a recent pregnancy, developed pneumonia and acute asthma. Our local GP at the time was prescribing drugs of only limited value and had failed to make the correct diagnosis quickly enough. Dorothy's life was saved by the fact that Dr Duthie, Aberdeen's leading chest consultant, happened to be in residence at his holiday home in nearby Crathie. He immediately ordered an ambulance and changed the medication to relieve the asthma. Dorothy's mother came north to help me look after the children. After stabilisation and a spell of convalescence Dorothy travelled south to stay with my parents in London while baby Rhod also went south to be looked after by his aunt Helen in

Southampton. The reason for all this movement was that whilst all these worries were still upon us, I had applied and been accepted for an academic appointment in Central Africa which meant sailing with the old Union Castle line from Southampton.

For the two years we were in Cornellan, very slowly becoming accepted by the local community, we had been fortunate in obtaining the services of Donald and Agnes Davidson, the latter known to everyone in the neighbourhood as 'Nessie'. Donald spent hours with Dadna repairing everything mechanical, from cars to garden shears, while Mrs D, as we called her, was an absolute godsend, helping us through Dorothy's illness and then, at the end of our first Ballater stint, packing the family and assorted personal belongings into the Vanguard. Inside the car were Feona and all our luggage, on top of which rested a large mattress upon which lay Malcolm and our cat, a grey moggie that had been dumped outside the Ardachie steading by an unseen hand shortly before we left Fort Augustus and who, because of an eczema, had an amputated tail. She was to be fostered by the Inneses in a quiet part of Inverness following Robert's promotion to the position of Conservator of Forests for the North of Scotland. The journey to Inverness through deep snow was marred only by a skid into a fence somewhere in Strathdon, and Greypuss, as we called her, disgracing herself somewhere near Dulnain Bridge. After a night with our friends we sped south in glorious winter sunshine through Glencoe and Glen Fillan, Loch Tulla ethereally majestic in the stillness of a freezing day, beneath a cloudless blue sky.

With the family once again united it was a case of hail and farewell on the S.S. *Pendennis Castle* as we set sail for whatever lay in store in our new life in distant Northern Rhodesia (Zambia). The customary heart wrenching moments as the liner slid slowly and inexorably away from the quay, the last hand waves disappearing as we steamed slowly out into the bay, en route to the unknown seas and lands beyond.

I was fortunate in having obtained a good degree in psychology and sociology, enabling me to enter the portals of academia. My application to become a research fellow in Northern Rhodesia led to an interview in London and eventual acceptance. We were bound for the outskirts of Lusaka in Northern Rhodesia, to the Rhodes Livingstone Institute[1], an anthropology-based African outpost of Manchester University. My remit was to investigate, analyse and report on the increasingly troubled labour relations in Northern Rhodesia's so-called Copper Belt, centred around Ndola and Kitwe.

Our two weeks as passengers with the *Pendennis Castle*, on only her second voyage, was a time of much appreciated relaxation, especially for Dorothy who was gaining strength every day following her illness, in spite of the asthma which – alas – had become a permanent legacy. The fact that it was a two class boat was irksome, but in all other respects the journey was a civilised pleasure, Norman Wisdom among the passengers. I managed to win the chess prize, a victory rather tarnished by the fact that in the final I most stupidly left my queen *en prise*, a lapse that astonishingly passed unnoticed by my equally unobservant opponent.

Disembarking at Cape Town we were painlessly transferred to the famed Blue Train which travels daily from the Cape to Bulawayo, taking two days across the arid Great Karoo, via Kimberley. To anyone familiar with the Boer War the evocative names of Pretoria, Krugersdorp, Mafeking, Ramatlabma, Gaborone flashed past, followed by a quick change in Bulawayo to a smaller train preceded rather dramatically by an armoured engine carrying armed gunmen aloft.

The Institute consisted of a number of bungalows surrounding a small office block and library with an adjacent hard tennis court, all cut out of the African bush. Occupying the bungalows were the Director, Henry Fosbrooke, several anthropologists touching base from their field studies; a visiting Rhodes scholar; and one bungalow held in reserve for visiting authors and itinerant researchers.

Fosbrooke, a retired Tanganyikan[2] district commissioner, although having little academic pretence was an able administrator, while in sharp contrast to each other were the two anthropologists then in residence, Raymond Apthorpe, an ascetic, brilliant,

---

[1] After Federation it was incorporated into the new University of Zambia.
[2] Country names are those used at the time.

eccentric, homosexual, immersed in tribal language and culture, later to establish a significant niche for himself among fellow anthropologists in Cambridge before settling in Australia, and David Bettison, a big burly Australian extrovert always in bush-whacking khaki shorts, with a hearty laugh to match. David and family eventually emigrated to Canada where he became Dean of the Faculty of Arts at Simon Fraser University in British Columbia. The visiting Rhodes scholar was Harvard and Oxford educated American historian, Bob Rotberg, a hard working, highly cultivated, amusing and intelligent young man whose Political History of Tropical Africa established for the author an international reputation. The inhabitant of the guest bungalow when we arrived was Bob Sutcliffe, a clever young fellow from Buxton who had elected to spend his summer pre-university break, nowadays called a gap year, as a research assistant working with Voluntary Service Overseas, an organisation then in its first operational year.

Absent on field work during our stay was one lady researcher, Ann Tweedie, a serious blue-stockinged economist. Part of her remit was the study of market forces among the women of four Bemba villages. At the outset she reported two unanticipated problems. The ladies asked Ann to please teach them how to knit. The first problem was how a research worker, required to always adopt a neutral stance when faced with local issues, should respond to such a request. The second problem was that Ann did not know herself how to knit.

Fortunately for us, with a family of five there was no available accommodation at the Institute so we were billeted a mile away along a rutted dirt track in a modest but pleasant newly built colonial house owned by the country's British transport commissioner, currently on leave. An old Land Rover covered in African dust was placed at our disposal. Many roads across central Africa are rutted in red dust reminiscent of ribbed sand at the seaside when the tide ebbs, leaving deep rippled scars. The secret of driving along these rutted, dusty roads, is to go fast enough to aquaplane across the ridges, a method that works as long as you are not behind another vehicle when the dust obscures everything, or if there is the serious likelihood of sudden braking.

Along with the house we inherited Abraham and Isaac, two African stalwarts only a little educated but both natural gentlemen. Abraham helped Dorothy in the house, including doing most of the cooking, while Isaac tended the garden, recently reclaimed from the surrounding scrub. Isaac quickly won the affection and admiration of Feona and Malcolm by killing a dangerous puff adder in the garden, very close to the house.

The heat was considerable. I found it so completely enervating that after a light lunch I had difficulty in holding my head up, having to lie flat on a cool stone floor for half an hour before regaining enough energy to see me through the rest of the day. Apart from getting to know my colleagues and being briefed about the work ahead, the most memorable moment was a visit to the Lusaka dog sanctuary where we found faithful Sally, a lovable short-coated sable mongrel bitch who remained with us throughout our stay in the country. And then there was the adventure with David Bettison.

David offered to show us a new part of the country in the untamed African bush, so one Sunday we set off for a picnic beside the Kafue river. Never one to enjoy a meal *en plein air*, on this occasion it was an offer we could not honourably refuse. As a newcomer I could not possibly rebuff a valued colleague, one so intimately acquainted with bush life and local African culture.

We encamped in a small clearing about fifteen yards above the river, with a party of hippos gently transporting themselves in the wide, slow flowing dirty looking water. David proceeded to light a bush fire and took from the boot of his old Land Rover a rusty spade. Balancing the spade above the fire he next produced five juicy red beef steaks. As they fizzled over the heat, a host of large flies, each the size of a British bluebottle, settled upon the spade and the fizzling steaks which David then proceeded to nonchalantly remove one by dirty one. For Feona and I this marked the end of all barbecues; I swear to this day I have never gone to another although Feona did relent by the time she was thirty. But Dorothy was more worried about upsetting David than upsetting her stomach and fed on, but even now, flies and food eaten outside in the relaxing warmth of a British afternoon or evening represents an activity to be avoided at all costs.

After a couple of weeks my luck held, although at the time we didn't fully appreciate how fortunate we had been. The situation on the Copper Belt had become so inflammatory and unstable as to make useful work too difficult and in any case too unsafe. In view of this development Fosbrooke asked me to produce an alternative proposal. After discussion with colleagues and an exploration of the literature, I drew up a plan to study white migration in the south (Southern Rhodesia). This having been accepted, the first step was for me to embark on a reconnaissance of the country, settling on the capital Salisbury (Harare) as base. It was near the middle of the colony and adjacent to the University with its library and facilities for data processing, as well as being the centre of the most likely population from which to find suitable research assistants.

In Salisbury I stayed at the renowned Meikles Hotel in the centre of town. Bearing in mind the free and easy lifestyle enjoyed at this time by the whites, I was surprised, on entering the restaurant for breakfast, to be politely asked by the African head waiter if I would please retire and put on a tie. It seemed nineteenth century etiquette had not completely died out.

Travelling east to the Vumba mountains I came upon the lovely unspoilt little town of Umtali (Mutare). Then into the hills to a most beautiful small hotel: Leopard Rock. In 1932 a prospector and gold miner called Seymour-Smith arrived in the area intending to start a fruit farm. Having built a home for his wife and himself, World War II intervened and Seymour-Smith joined the Rhodesian army, leaving his wife and daughter to run the farm. With time on their hands and, to augment their threatened income, they decided to invite paying guests. After being invalided out of the army, Seymour-Smith thought that running a hotel would be a better bet than developing a fruit farm. In two years a hotel was built, named after a leopard that had once been seen sunning itself on a rock nearby.

This most imposing and tranquil building was opened in 1946 by Sir Godfrey Huggins, then the Prime Minister. The late Queen Mother and the present Queen spent several days there in 1953. Her Majesty wrote 'there is nowhere more beautiful in Africa and it is clearly one of the special places in the world'. Later the hotel was severely damaged during the upheavals of the 1970s before eventually having to close down due to a fuel shortage. It is now owned by a tobacco merchant who renovated the building prior to its re-opening in 1993, together with a golf course built on the side of an adjoining hillside, with the property's own game reserve close by. It was a truly magical place although one hates to think of what must be its present plight.

The family bid farewell to our short-lived friends in the north, migrating to a house kindly found near the University in Salisbury by Bob Rotberg who was himself now living and working in the capital. After a short spell there we moved first to the lovely Spanish-style home of Mr Howe-Ely, the Clerk to Parliament, with a large garden full of pompelmoose and avocado trees, and beyond them a fine swimming pool.

Although I never learned to swim – some have said that one of the legacies of bronchial asthma is negative buoyancy – we had wonderful times in and around the pool, a favourite place not only for the family but for all our assistants, especially when the temperature was at its height. The pompelmoose trees were another source of family pleasure. Known also as the shaddock, after a Captain Shaddock who introduced the fruit to the West Indies early in the 18th century from its native Polynesia, the tree grows to thirty or more feet and carries large orange-like fruit that can weigh as much as fifteen pounds. Although less tasty than its near relative the grapefruit, it made a splendid football, exploding with a generous array of seeds and heavy pith if booted too hard or too often. The screams of delight whenever Malcolm or Bob caused such an explosion must have been heard for miles around.

Mr Howe-Ely, whom we never met, was on leave and in his home we spent one memorable Christmas. Bob Rotberg lived with us for a time and I was lucky to welcome back to Africa Bob Sutcliffe who had agreed to join us as a temporary resident researcher. With his effervescent good humour, balanced upon legs like trunks of oak, and oodles of *savoir faire*, he had agreed to return to Africa to spend the long summer vacation from Oxford with our team.

Our final home in Rhodesia was a nearly new but empty house owned by the de Giacomos, an absentee Italian family. The main attraction of this homestead in a quiet street well away from the hubbub of the town was that instead of a swimming pool there was a tennis court, so that every Sunday afternoon we hosted a tennis party and, being in an almost hidden cul-de-sac, we could invite African and Indian friends without fear of a police presence or of arousing public suspicion, such then being the state of this glorious but benighted country. The disadvantage was that being completely unfurnished it required weekly visits to the local auction room to purchase beds, chairs, a couple of tables, some linen and cutlery, all of which had to be sold before leaving except for a small opium table, an electric floor polisher and a sewing machine which travelled with us back to Scotland where they still survive. There were also ants and fleas. Living in the crevasses of the virtually new parquet flooring were millions of ants, while settling on our two dogs, Sally and the macho Rhodesian Ridgeback 'Rhodes', were an army of fleas that required regular removal by bathing the dogs every fortnight in a strong insecticide. Watching the dead siphonopteras come floating to the surface not only proved the need for the procedure but provided very visible satisfaction that the labour had been successfully accomplished. We were told that ants helped to reduce fleas by devouring their eggs but this was a theory we never had the motivation to properly test.

* * * * * * * * *

At the height of Imperial expansion in Africa during the end of the 19th century, there had developed a fixed stereotype of the African, which was extremely unfavourable, based in large measure on Victorian middle class presumptions. The white settler, as he was known, was at the same time idealised in the popular mind as the representative of civilisation and private enterprise. From the end of the First World War there was a gradual shift of opinion; the conventional image of the African was slowly transformed in response to a number of ideological, economic and social factors while a more positive view began to be taken of African social institutions. Simultaneously, the white settler's stock began to fall. Both these processes were accelerated after the Second World War during the subsequent 'decolonisation'. A fresh set of stereotypes was created of the white settler, a term by this time used pejoratively. Both stereotypes were as inaccurate as the Victorian image and in spite of the difficulty of achieving balance at the current time of rampant political correctness, these images demand further analysis.

The pattern of European migration to Southern Rhodesia showed a steady increase from the time of the first settlement in 1860, when the first farmers and representatives of the London Missionary Society arrived, until the successful conclusion of the Matabele war, when the number of whites exceeded ten thousand. Thereafter the white population expanded ever more rapidly until, in 1961, it had reached 225,000, by which time 85% of the white population were immigrants, probably a higher proportion than for any other country in the world. Furthermore, it was a very youthful society, the average white male was 28.5 years old and the white female 29.1. This meant that 77% of the white female population were of child-bearing age, a fact largely responsible for the high average net reproduction rate.

It was also, within its own confines, a very open society. When, for example, I first visited Roy Wilensky, Prime Minister of the Federation, he saw me in his braces without a security guard in sight. Although it has to be said that Sir Edgar Whitehead, for a short time First Minister of Southern Rhodesia, was less extroverted; being monaural, with a profoundly deaf right ear, he invariably inclined his right side toward any interviewer he wished to ignore or whose questions he found difficulty in answering.

In the late 50s and early 60s, with the breakdown of the Central African Federation[3] and impending independence, the task I had set myself was an analysis of the absorption and assimilation of

---

[3]   Southern Rhodesia, Northern Rhodesia and Nyasaland (Malawi).

the white population. Absorption was the degree to which, and the social processes by which, multi-cultural Rhodesia accepted white immigrants. Assimilation was the degree to which, and the psycho-social processes by which, individuals changed, and the nature and extent of the change as they accepted or rejected the prevailing attitudes and mores of the country. This is a topic of particular relevance to contemporary Britain, one that has been researched in greatest depth, for obvious reasons, by Israeli social scientists.

While the results of the research can be found elsewhere, it may be of interest to note, bearing in mind what has befallen the country in the meantime, two quite separate sets of conclusions. The first may be summarised as eleven fundamental aspects of white cultural values. Because these had never been incorporated in any national social integration, Southern Rhodesia as a society was no more than a social aggregate held together by a convergence of dominating social interests rather than a close-knit, increasingly ethnocentric culture in the process of forming a nation. When hostility is directed to a common out-group (then the black African, now the white man), at times of mounting personal insecurity, it is understandable that hostility escalates.

The eleven dominant characteristics of white culture in the country can be described as follows:

1   Active mastery of the physical and social environment. This implied a stress on power and manipulation allied to a low threshold of tolerance or frustration.

2   Reliance on independent effort rather than on government interference. This naturally carried over into hostility and suspicion toward any external authority or individual who criticised the territory's internal affairs.

3   A greater interest in extrovert activities such as open-air physical pursuits rather than introvert activities. This led to a condition described by a local historian as 'the featureless quality of the social landscape'.[4]

4   An ethic based more on expediency than on universality.

---

[4]   L H Gann and P Duignan *White Settlers in Tropical Africa*, Penguin 1962

5   A belief, firmly entrenched, in the basic superiority of white culture, associated with the principle of universal equality of condition, each requiring continuous conscious effort to sustain, the former by practical endorsement, the latter by reiterated articulation.

6   Basic allegiance and patriotic sentiment towards the British crown.

7   Related to the first point was the gratification of desire, especially the provision of a high degree of physical comfort and tolerance of divorce.

8   The quality of casual friendliness without the concomitant encouragement of profound inter-personal relationships.

9   An emphasis on individuality rather than group identity, although with tolerance of socially organised white minority groups. Hence there was no compulsion to assimilate, nor any socially significant distinction made between the old pioneer families, some of whom had been resident for three or more generations, and even the newest arrivals.

10 A high value attached to political solidarity so far as political ends were concerned.

11 A tendency toward the secularisation of fundamental values.

Today, to a very large extent, these values have been reversed by the prevailing black culture, dominated by an extreme dictatorial style of government. But it can be easily understood how the notion of superiority among the past white population, allied to their abject failure to encourage a basic black infrastructure, contributed, although it certainly does not excuse, the present apodictic racist repression and socio-economic collapse.

Apportioning blame for the appalling Mugabe regime is perhaps a sterile exercise, particularly when in historical terms standards of morality differed from today's. But a brief examination of its historical antecedents is necessary in reaching a balanced assessment, without which plans for the long term future of this wonderful but benighted country cannot be sensibly considered.

When the white man first arrived he brought with him a grasp of material exploitation allied to the dogma of Christianity.

While agents of the former confiscated the land the latter sought to extinguish traditional beliefs and customs so that together they achieved the annihilation of native subsistence and culture. The ruthless confiscation of land and the breakdown of tribal value systems and beliefs led inevitably to alienation and the loss of natural dignity, with passive antagonism. The white man sought to accentuate and perpetuate his dominance by denying the black man access to the very attributes that had created the incomer's material success – education, training and any meaningful role in self-government. In the enforced collapse of their culture intelligent blacks harboured passive hostility while their less intelligent brethren became cowed and subservient. There was no incipient black organisational infrastructure of any kind, all roads to personal accomplishment were barred, so that when the whites were eventually overthrown there was the combustible mix of anger and ignorance.

The other side of the coin recognises the benefits introduced by the invaders: better health care, relief from inter-tribal conflict, the immense commercial advantages of western agricultural procedures, and the exploitation for the common good of the country's vast natural resources.

The terrible tragedy is that the white man, when he had the opportunity and indeed the responsibility, to educate, to promote commercial *savoir faire*, and to provide a share in local as well as national government, totally failed to do so. He not only failed but actively encouraged unquestioning obedience and general subservience, thus reducing self-respect still further. This was not just a lost opportunity but a recipe for disaster of immense and awful proportions. The great sadness is that the disastrous legacy of ignorance and hatred has been borne not just by the whites who have remained but by large numbers of the indigenous blacks in gruesome internecine conflict.

Restoring order and prosperity will obviously take time but, if any lessons from the past are learned at all, after the provision of food and the basics of life there must be the introduction of a broad based educational system, encouragement for all to share the fruits of their labour, respect for the rule of a just and tribally impartial law, and, now that so many western ways are entrenched, there must be the introduction of genuine democracy allied to the gradual introduction of meaningful local government. This will involve western consultation but the advisers must be servants of the state, not self-promoting entrepreneurs.

* * * * * * * * *

The second quite disparate but exciting set of conclusions we found related to climate and intelligence. For the purpose of this study intelligence was viewed as whatever is measured by standardised I.Q. tests.

As a person unusually sensitive to the effects of climate (real or imaginary) and professionally interested in the comparative diffusion of intelligence among a white tropical population, I was keen to discover how intelligence varied, if at all, according to class, nationality and/or length of stay, both individually and generationally, in Southern Africa. The challenge was considerable as indicated by the fact that none of the major works on intelligence mention climate, except for an occasional cursory reference among the bibliographies.

There are three ways in which the hypothesis of a relationship might be assessed. The first is by examining intelligence in conjunction with month of birth. A number of studies have produced statistically significant results. In the United States, for example, significantly more subnormals are born in the first three months of the year than at other times. In England, also working with subnormals, there has been some support for the notion that winter births, and to a lesser extent those in spring, are related to poorer mental ability.

The second way to examine the hypothesis, by comparing intelligence among peoples living in contrasting extremes of climate, remains impracticable until satisfactory measuring instruments become available that conclusively overcome the problem of cultural differences. Nevertheless, a recent controversial book[5] lists what purports to be the average intelligence (mean I.Q. score) in

---

[5]   Lynn & Vaitenon, *I.Q. and the Wealth of Nations*, Praeger Publishers, New York, 2002.

185 different countries. Even allowing for probable approximation and a multitude of causational factors, when considered against national climate what emerges is at least suggestive of a strong climatic factor. The top fifteen countries all lie in the temperate zone, Hong Kong being the only exception. The bottom fifteen countries are all in tropical Africa except Jamaica.

The third method, the one we adopted, was to examine an intergenerational study of migrants from one climatalogical environment to another. To do this we examined all the white children in the country born in 1949, using a test standardised in South Africa, from where comparative results were available. In addition to test scores, details were obtained regarding place of birth, year of arrival in Southern Rhodesia, the language of each parent, the first language of the child, any physical defect likely to affect the scores, and the socio-economic status of the child's residential area.

This mass of data, involving 1,696 children, travelled home with me to Ballater where several weeks were spent undertaking a rewarding and surprising analysis.

A few years earlier the Rhodesian Teachers' Association had found that when children were differentiated according to their parentage, interesting results emerged.

Mean I.Q.

Group I	Children born outside Southern Rhodesia	99.87
Group II	Children born in Southern Rhodesia – both parents outside	98.70
Group III	Children born in Southern Rhodesia – one parent outside	97.36
Group IV	Children born in Southern Rhodesia – both parents inside	95.05

In another study, using non-verbal test material in Northern Rhodesia, Good[6] found that English-speaking children born in

---

[6]   R Good, *Intelligence and Attainment in Rhodesia*, Oversea Education, London, 1956.

the UK had a mean I.Q. of 102.23, English-speaking children born elsewhere had a mean score of 97.66, while Afrikaans-speaking children born in Africa and with almost certainly a longer ancestral span in the tropics, scored only 90.79.

To my considerable surprise I found a statistically significant difference among the 1,696 children we had tested when relating birthplace to mean intelligence. Children born in the UK had a mean score of 107.04 whereas those born in Southern Rhodesia scored 106.17 and those born in South Africa 104.49.

There were three possible explanations for these variations. The first could have been selective migration: were white Rhodesian immigrants of superior social class and intelligence ? To answer this an analysis was made of the South African-born population in Southern Rhodesia by occupational scale. It was found that their place was in almost exact proportion to their total in the population.

The second explanation might have been the possible test-sophistication of children coming from Britain. But the high scores achieved by children from Britain within the preceding two years was equalled by those coming from South Africa, a result which could hardly be ascribed to greater test-sophistication. Furthermore, children coming from other countries, including other parts of Africa, Asia, Europe, and North America, all produced a similar high mean.

The third consideration to be examined was the possible influence of socio-economic differentials. However, when children were divided into three socio-economic categories based on income, occupation level of parents, and parental education, the same differences between the South African and UK-born emerged.

It was reasonable to conclude that climate may have been a factor in determining degrees of intelligence among children in the Rhodesias. If confirmed, and to the best of my knowledge no one has developed similar research elsewhere,[7] such an influence does become apparent, but may not operate, until about the third generation. This offers the most feasible explanation for the lower

---

[7] Although for unexplained variation see Lynn and Vaitenon.

performance of South African-born children irrespective of sex, language, type and location of school, length of residence in the country, or socio-economic class.

* * * * * * * * *

During our time in Southern Rhodesia, we managed to bring together a fine team of research assistants. The linchpin was Bob Sutcliffe, who, as already mentioned, had been persuaded to join us for the three most critical months of data collection. He lived with us *en famille*, a fund of good humour, hard work, musical entertainment and prudence. Another valued friend who lived with us for several months, although undertaking his own historical research and never part of our team, was the other Bob from the Institute, Bob Rotberg. He kindly came with me in the Institute's Land Rover to Lourenço Marques (rechristened Maputo in 1976) to collect a new red Hillman Estate car. We returned in convoy via the Kruger National Park, an iconic experience, with elephant, giraffe, lion, acacia and baobab trees, and everywhere thick red dust. In many ways, as landward travel goes, this was the trip of a lifetime.

On the secretarial front, I learnt for the first time what was to be repeated many times in the future, the important but often undervalued role of a really good secretary. In Southern Rhodesia I was fortunate to have had two, a brave girl of unfailing cheerfulness, daughter of an English MP and who, although confined to a wheelchair, was intensely independent, always insisting on propelling herself in and out of her specially designed car without assistance. The other lady, one of refined middle age, long afterwards produced another one of life's little frustratingly unanswered questions. Her name was Mrs Kekewich and it wasn't until many years later that I learned of the existence of Major-General Robert George Kekewich, surely a kinsman of her husband. Kekewich joined the army in 1874, was immediately catapulted into the Perak expedition in Malaysia, then moved to the Sudan where he was promoted to brevet major. During the Second Boer War he commanded the 1st Loyal North Lancashire Regiment, defended Kimberley in 1899 alongside Baden-Powell, and at the outbreak of the Great War was appointed to command the 13th (Western) Division. He eventually shot himself in 1914 when ill-health put an end to the military career which seems to have been the prime motif of his life. What tales he might have told !

On the domestic front, Feona and Malcolm were now old enough to benefit from the overseas experience, Feona especially enjoying ballet lessons with a Rhodesian ballerina who had once danced with the famous Merle Park, while Malcolm most enjoyed learning to ride a horse and being airborne with his friend Peter Cowan, whose father owned the local flying school. When baby Rhod was not with Dorothy or fast asleep in his pram, he was looked after by Hilda, our devoted young African nanny.

Dorothy was still being troubled by occasional attacks of asthma although these were substantially relieved by an Indian Swami with whom she practised yoga and by more conventional ministration from Dr Maurice Gelfand, the distinguished senior consultant, accomplished amateur anthropologist, and historian of African medical care. She also applied herself again to painting which Peter White had so encouraged her to pursue at Ardachie, becoming fascinated by the portraiture of young black children. One of her portraits was accepted for inclusion in the inaugural Annual Art exhibition at the newly established Rhodesian National Gallery, whilst another work was purchased by the Ghanaian Ambassador in London.

I had a brief interlude in March 1960 to attend an international seminar on migration studies, organised by Professor Eisenstadt, the doyen of immigrant scholars, at the Hebrew University in Jerusalem. Amid the arid, desiccated, depressing landscape, the most rewarding experience was meeting Ron Taft, a cheery outgoing Australian psychologist who specialised in assimilation studies. Unhappily, although remaining in touch for several years, we have never had an opportunity to meet again.

Before returning to Salisbury I dashed north to Ballater where Dadna was waiting to greet me on the steps of Cornellan. The deep snow, an extreme and most welcome contrast to Rhodesia, was falling fast and for the whole of the following day Ballater was cut off by the heaviest snowfall in living memory. Ballater has never seen its like again.

During our time in Africa it was clear that the white population was sitting on a powder keg of its own making. Black Rhodesians had no power, inferior educational opportunities, and very little hope of personal advancement in a land dominated by racist whites. The gradually deteriorating situation seemed not to be understood and certainly not accurately assessed by the staff of the British High Commission. They mixed, like diplomats the world over, with their foreign counterparts rather than with either the white or black communities. The messages reaching the government at home must have been frighteningly misleading.

In a minor and modest attempt to breach the chasm five of us launched a multi-racial discussion society christened The Sixty Group, in recognition of the year of its birth.

Nathan Shamuyariwa was at the time the African editor of the one national multi-racial newspaper, *The Rhodesia Herald*; Victor Tarica was a Jewish South African chemistry lecturer at the University who also owned, with his wife, the capital's main bookshop; Philip Laundy was the Librarian to Parliament, a jolly rotund figure, author of the definitive *Encyclopedia of Parliament*; and Mrs Izod, a liberal housewife, brought us charm and feminine insight. In order to remain in as relaxed a mode as possible we elected no office bearers and adumbrated no constitution. The five of us worked as an informal committee, deciding the topics for discussion, with the moderator for each fortnightly session rotating among us. There was a perceived threat that meetings might be overwhelmed by white liberals, a possibility avoided by ensuring that African nationalists like the late Reverend Sithole were invited as well as a few more typical representatives of the white community. Meetings, each with an advertised theme and an opening speaker, were open to all, irrespective of age, gender, race or religion and took place in houses large enough to accommodate a throng of thirty or more. Although familiar with J.K. Galbraith's cynical dictum 'Faced with choice between changing one's mind and proving that there is no need to do so, almost everyone gets busy with the proof', in the interests of racial harmony and less prejudiced discrimination, we were determined to try.

Two meetings stood out. One was an enthralling exchange opened on the one hand by Lewis Gann, a right-wing historian of reasonably balanced views, author of *The History of Northern Rhodesia* and much else, who was the country's archivist, and on the other hand by Terry Ranger, a strident left-wing academic historian. The topic encapsulated social divisions: did the beneficial influences of the white population exceed their adverse effects ? In a society so charged with emotion, the two main speakers had scarcely ever spoken to each other. Their conflicting opinions and attitudes, although calmly presented, were unrehearsed, un-scripted and uninhibited but were certainly provocative. The discussion confirmed an anomaly I had often noticed, a disparity between practical action and professed belief. Many *soi-disant* liberals treated their black servants with less dignity and understanding than many entrenched right-wingers. The former found it hard to accept inferior education or intelligence, the latter recognised the innate dignity of the Africans in spite of regarding them as somehow inferior.

The second notable meeting was held in the main African township attended by, among others, the Chief Justice. This seemed such a remarkable event to the authorities that we found the meeting-place ringed with white police and patrol cars.

It was gratifying to know that the Sixty Group continued for a number of years after we had left, indeed in 1970 the survivors kindly sent me a telegram on the occasion of their tenth anniversary. Unfortunately, not long afterwards, when Laundy had migrated to Ottawa to become Librarian to the Canadian Parliament and Victor had gone home to South Africa, the Group came to an end. Subsequently, Nathan Shamuyariwa, who had been such a balanced, moderate, multi-racial journalist became, with the arrival of African government, a prime example of the corrupting influence of power, growing increasingly extreme, eventually becoming a senior minister and spokesman in Mugabe's Government. The equally extreme Ranger, until his retirement the second Rhodes Professor of Race Relations at Oxford, returned to Zimbabwe as a visiting professor.

There was an occasion when, permission having been granted for me to enter the main prison in order to interview some of the immigrant whites, I was ushered into the governor's office. After describing in broad outline the daily routine he introduced me to the white-coated inmate who was to be my escort as we travelled from cell to cell. The man was a pharmacist by profession, in charge of the prison's medical supplies. When I asked the reason for his incarceration the governor told me that he had murdered his wife. But what seemed so extraordinary was that, before leaving, my guide conducted me round the prison garden in which was being cultivated, cannabis – a drug which the Government was doing its utmost to eradicate.

Zimbabwe is a wonderful corner of the world with an ideal, predictable climate, a varied and beautiful terrain, an abundance of rich wildlife, but flawed by a threefold schism between the powerful Shona tribe of Mashonaland who comprise over three-quarters of the black population, the more aggressive Ndebeles of Matabeleland and the now fast dwindling whites.

* * * * * * * * *

We were sad to leave this beautiful country as it stood on the brink of independence and subsequent chaos. For the journey home we planned to sail via the Red Sea on the SS *Stirling Castle* but inspecting her on arrival at Durban she was so shabby and old compared to the glistening *SS Pendennis Castle*, with its dark, heavy mahogany bunks in a faded cabin, that Dorothy and I decided we couldn't bear to travel with her. Fortune favoured us as the *SS Rhodesia Castle*, a one-class ship, happened to be in Durban at the same time, about to sail to England on the eastern route, via Walvis Bay. We were able to transfer ship with no more than a steamy walk up the main Durban hill to transfer our tickets at the local Union Castle office. There followed a happy journey home with Feona and Malcolm old enough to enjoy the experience. Dorothy and I enjoyed post-prandial bridge most evenings with two contrasting grandees, the under-bidding svelte English Archdeacon of Malawi and the plump, over-bidding Goanese state pathologist of Kenya.

The one distressing affair was that, imported on to the ship by a medical family, Rhod contracted impetigo. The treatment prescribed was to cover his face in unsightly gentian violet. The only favourable consequence was that it needed little imagination to prepare the young fellow for the ship's fancy dress parade. He joined the procession not as a human at all, but as a gentian violet, in which capacity he carried off first prize. I doubt if he has ever forgiven us.

The following two years were spent back in Cornellan. Malcolm began his school life two years below Feona at the local primary school. The red Hillman had been sold before leaving Rhodesia to be replaced by a sleek green Singer Gazelle that awaited our disembarkation at Tilbury. Sally and Rhodes, our Rhodesian Ridgeback, had both been found good homes and as much as we were sad to have to say goodbye there was the compensation of being reunited with Greypuss, the Ardachie foundling who had been fostered by Robert & Hetty Innes in Inverness, and Fern, our original deerhound who had been well looked after by an English family used to the ways and needs of the breed.

Dorothy spent these years running an antique business in Braemar with Margaret King, Ballater's unusual minister's wife, which they christened The Snuff Box. Margaret's involvement in trade was anathema to many of the traditional locals who regarded a minister's wife as someone with an accent on matters spiritual rather than a soul tainted by trade. But feisty Margaret, being the character she was, remained quite unfazed. Their stock of fine porcelain and paintings was occasionally strengthened by the results of my mother's forays among the antique malls of London. Although mother had a sophisticated eye, she knew little, and cared less, about market value, so the Snuff Box sometimes found itself hosting Meissen porcelain and Georgian silver of considerable worth but at prices few tourists understood or could afford.

At the beginning of these interim years, many days were spent analysing the deluge of data brought home, preparing a final report as well as my doctoral thesis which Edinburgh had permitted me to do once again *in absentia*. My advisor, with whom I had spoken just once when in the UK, after the Israeli symposium, was none other than a graduate from my own year who had remained in Edinburgh, winning his academic laurels as a junior lecturer when I was earning my agricultural spurs at Ardachie. This led to a bizarre but very fraternal consultation.

When neither writing, walking the dogs nor helping Dorothy organise the family, weekends were spent playing cricket in the superb setting of Balmoral. The game of cricket first came to Upper Deeside in 1881 when a match was played at Abergeldie, at the time leased to Queen Victoria, between the tenants and residents of Abergeldie and the staff of Balmoral, a match painted by George Simpson, of Boer War fame and a frequent illustrator with *The London Illustrated News*. This was played in a field adjacent to the castle, a grass tennis court having been laid for the benefit of George, Duke of York. When no longer used for this purpose, a cricket team calling itself the Royal Household XI played there for several years during the visit of the sovereign. After World War II, the field no longer being used for sport, Bud Fraser, the estate's head ghillie, a jovial, streetwise, canny war veteran who was already coaching cricket to youngsters on a hand-mown single wicket at Abergeldie, asked the Duke of Edinburgh if the cricket square might be restored for the use of a local team. The Duke having graciously agreed, Bud suggested to a couple of friends that they form a club. These were the late Harry Wright, exciseman at the local Lochnagar distillery, a Yorkshireman and schoolmate of the former English skipper Norman Yardley, and dependable Frank Banks, the royal upholsterer and former member of St Ronald's C.C. in Aberdeen. So it was that Crathie Cricket Club came into being – unable to call itself Balmoral because a club of this name (now dissolved) already existed in Aberdeen. Frank became the first President, Bud the Captain and Harry the Secretary. From the beginning the club was fortunate in having as resident factor the late Major Andrew Haig, who was both a charming man and a good cricketer. Haig[8] was one of only

---

[8] Andrew Haig achieved an unusual honour being one of very few royal servants ever to voluntarily resign and then return to royal service several years later. He left Balmoral to manage Col Whitbread's Letterewe Estate in Wester Ross before rejoining the royal staff as Deputy Keeper of Windsor Great Park.

two cricketing factors in the club's history. Apart from becoming a regular all-round member of the team, specialising in bowling so slowly as to be reminiscent of J M Barrie's comment about his own bowling that if he didn't like a delivery he could always run after it and bring it back. Haig was elected President 1952-55, kindly allowing annual meetings to be held in the castle, the only years this has happened.

Haig's presidency established a precedent whereby the resident factor for the next fifty-two years became president virtually ex officio[9]. The precedent was broken when the former English opening batsman John Edrich came to live in Ballater and kindly agreed to support the club.

My initiation took place on the occasion of the club's AGM in March 1957. The meeting was held in the tiny heather-thatched pavilion by the light of a single bulb connected to Harry Wright's car battery, the car parked on the grass beyond the pavilion door. It was there that I first met a delightful bunch of country lads. We enjoyed our village cricket in a manner alien to most contemporary players. All were residents of either Crathie or Ballater, the majority being employees of the royal estate. Mr Dear, the local liquorish Hebridean dominie, played once but failed to score, thereafter his pride was upheld by acting as a self-appointed, rather partial, umpire. One day a member of a visiting team, having previously experienced Mr Dear's partiality, erected a sign beyond the boundary rope 'Beware of the Dear'.

Because of the glorious setting almost every game was played at home, and all matches, except for two cup competitions, were friendlies. The club played all three services, naval teams from Rosyth, the Highland Brigade from their barracks in Aberdeen, the Royal Guard from Ballater, the RAF from Lossiemouth, Kinloss and Boddam; also schools and universities, with a leavening of teams from all grades in the Aberdeen league, as well as, on occasion, Aberdeenshire itself.

Every year we seemed to lose a player or two through migration and retirement, and every year someone new would

---

[9] 'Virtually' because until 2003 the club had no written constitution.

arrive to replace them. Among occasional players whose names appear in the old score books are the Earl Spencer, Duncan Todd – a royal pastrycook who had played for Northants when working for the Gloucesters – and the late Alan Stewart, headmaster at Aboyne who, it has to be said, when keeping wicket, which he did well, was not averse to kicking or otherwise nudging the ball back on to the stumps claiming that the poor, unobservant batsman had been bowled.

Among regulars of note were Douglas Franks, an ex-Lancashire League fast bowler and novice hotelier, who took the game to a higher level of seriousness, requesting the pitch be rolled between innings, the sight-screen wheeled into the right position, while he himself liked to sink a steak or two before a match (so he told me), and always cantered twice around the boundary to loosen up before the umpire's call of 'Play !'

During the whole time we were in Africa, the late Bob Fraser, one of Bud's three cricketing sons, kept me regularly informed of all the games, a thoughtfulness very much appreciated.

Among the many happy hours, some blisteringly sunfilled, but more often spent shivering in wintry squalls, a few poignant memories stand out.

The second cricketing factor we were fortunate enough to enjoy was the late Colonel Charlie McHardy, a veteran of Alamein, who had played for the army before the war. The first time he agreed to turn out, the match being fixed to start as usual at 2.30 pm, he arrived on the ground at 2.15 pm and was sorely relieved to find the rest of the team and the visitors eventually rolling up at 2.45 pm. Later, when invited to bowl, he stopped in the middle of his run up, telling the skipper (me) that he couldn't bowl without a cover point, the fielder in question standing with a lit cigarette drooping from his fretful lips. Thereafter, whenever I was captain, I made a deal with our two inveterate smokers that if they were touched before a cigarette had been lit they would desist, that is until the fall of the next wicket which always seemed to be lighting-up time, when the pantomime had to begin all over again. I found myself spending many exhausting moments dashing from one side of the field to the other since the two culprits invariably fielded at opposite ends of the wicket. An onlooker must have been bemused by such manic, seemingly pointless, activity.

On another occasion, returning from a victory in Edinburgh, our most garrulous and well-lubricated stalwart became so intensely loquacious as to loose his lower false teeth over the Forth Road Bridge when they were last observed in the rear mirror rolling mischievously over the parapet into the Firth.

There was one demeaning episode after my retirement which should never have been allowed on a variety of counts. My fellow umpire, now deceased, was a newcomer to the club, reputedly very well-to-do, with a son, he told us, who was being coached at Lord's. I was standing at square-leg when the visiting batsman took two paces forward, was hit on the pads and, to my astonishment, an appeal from our bowler was upheld. The next thing I knew was the visiting captain and another of his team come storming out of the pavilion, demanding to take over the two white umpiring jackets. In the first place the bowler should never have appealed; secondly, our umpire was blinded either by ignorance, eyesight, or prejudice; thirdly, the two visitors, one of whom I later discovered was none other than the President of the Aberdeenshire Cricket Association himself, had no right to intervene without first consulting the fielding captain. All this left me feeling very aggrieved at being coerced to abandon my post through no fault of my own. Faced with either extending the drama that was already developing dangerously or quietly retiring from the scene, I chose the latter course. Such can be the machinations of village cricket.

In the history of Crathie cricket there have been many memorable moments when cups have been won or promotion achieved, but one event towers above them all. Saturday, July 31st, 1999 at Balmoral was a glorious sun-soaked day. Beside white marquees glistening in the sunshine, the largest crowd ever seen for a cricket match at Balmoral had gathered to welcome the Lord's Taverners, guests at the club's Jubilee celebrations. The Taverners were fielding a team of celebrities including two ex-captains of England, Mike Denness and Brian Close, an opening England batsman Chris Broad, four British rugby Lions: Gavin Hastings, Roger Uttley, Colin Deans and Douglas Morgan, an international badminton champion: Mike Tredgett; while from show business there came Bob Bevan, David Essex, Nicholas Parsons and Robert Powell. Leading out Crathie for what was almost certainly the very last match he would play in his distinguished career, was the club's President, the former English captain and gritty opening bat, John Edrich. Included in his team was one former Crathie skipper who had flown over from Hong Kong specially for the match.

Having won the toss Crathie decided to bat, even though the 10.30 start was the earliest wake-up call the team had ever experienced. How they rose to the occasion, making 312 for 6 declared, the highest score ever reached in the team's fifty-year history. After a suitably bibulous lunch, the chairman of the Jubilee committee, my old friend and opening partner the late Gillespie Munro, read a message of greetings from Prince Philip (the Patron of both teams), followed by an appropriately witty response from Nicholas Parsons on behalf of the visitors, and it was left to elderly Harry Wright, the club's surviving father, recomposing himself after an awkward trip over a chair leg on his enthusiastic trot to the ritual cake, to duly cut it.

As was only to be expected, the Taverners responded with an equally buccaneering innings. The end could not have been better stage managed for, with one ball left to be bowled, Tredgett and Denness at the crease, the visitors needed a boundary to win, the home team required a wicket. Neither happened, two runs were scored, the match therefore ending in a most honourable draw, the Taverners having reached 311 for 9. Standing with the late Andy Kemp as one of the umpires, my legs no longer fit for purpose, I had been invited to judge the Man of the Match award. With his team's best bowling average and hitting 40 runs with the bat, the magnum of malt whisky, generously donated by Lochnagar Distillery, went to David Essex.

This had been a wonderful day, a game of high achievement, played beneath summer skies in the friendliest spirit before an appreciative crowd. The day demonstrated how the great game of cricket can, and should be, enjoyed by young and not-so-young alike, bringing to mind the words of Harold Pinter 'I tend to believe that cricket is the greatest thing God ever created on earth'.

The last photo of Gaga Rose, with Feona

Gaga McEwan, the centenarian

In 1943 my father volunteered for the RAF

*One of the two grandfathers I never knew,
Grandpa Rose*

*An Edwardian wedding - my parents on
their happy day in 1923*

*My parents in Berlin, 1948, at the time of the
Airlift*

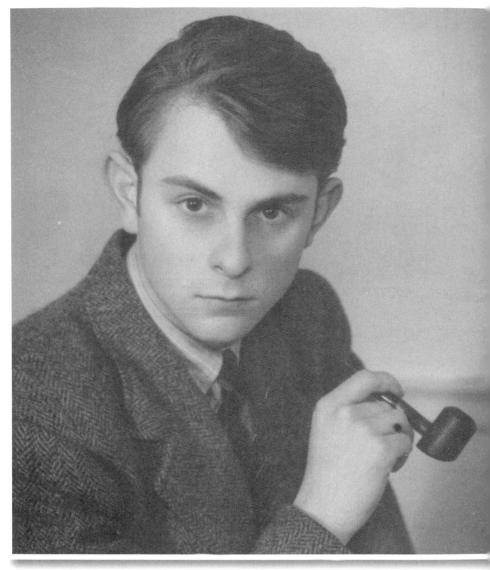

Twenty-one

The first photo

With cousin Peggy in our Hampstead garden in 1930

The Gafic Club at play. L to R, Doug Smith, John Fuller, Ken Lindford, Christopher Floris, Christopher Morahan, John Wurr, Rodney Tucker, Bingham Hobson and Ken Shaw

d Hall. We sledged down the brae on VJ day

Aune, my longest standing friend. But I only remember her as a teenager!

Theodore Mallinson, ('TGM'), the soul of Highgate School, in his 100th year

In 1949, I accompanied Princess Elizabeth on her visit to E Suffolk Rd hostels

The Pleiades outside Cown House, from L to R: myself, an interloper, Tom Batho, Peter Weigall, Ted Whitley, Ian Noble, Mansell Prothero, Jim Batho and John Watson (on bicycle)

In 1949 Alastair Sim delivers his rectoral address in the McEwan Hall, Edinburgh

John Hick, theologian and prolific author, whos Philosophy of Religion became a best seller in Ch

The view from the front door at Ardachie, Dorothy and the two children, Loch Ness beyond

Watson and Ian Noble, with Dorothy, Feona and Malcolm

Ardachie House with the old Hillman van

Betty with some of the ponies, Fort Augustus

Dorothy's father and Nobby Clark in holiday gear on top of Eilean Horisdale

Feona enjoys a ride on Heather, watched by grandmother and Dorothy

Peter White, artist and pigman

Dadna with a Large White, Feona and Malcolm 1954

Below the hen house steps, mother, father, Auntie Lal, Malcolm and a friend

Dan Scobie and I review lambing season

Le Poer Power cutting bracken on the hill

Dorothy learns to drive the tractor watched by my father 1954

board the SS Pendennis Castle to South Africa

On the SS Pendennis Castle

anny Hilda with Rhod amid the bougainvillea

Malcolm and Dot

Mary Harris (a research assistant),
Bob Sutcliffe and the children with
some of Sally's pups, guarded by
Rhodes

*Laundy, librarian to the
sian and Canadian Parliaments

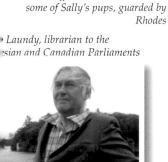

Abraham and a cheeky helper (Rhod) in the garden at Mossville, 1959

Dorothy, Susan and Rhod

Silas, our cook, with his family

Bob Rotberg

The site of David's barbecue on the banks of the Kafue river

Opening the Denmark conference, watched by Professor Gelhorn and Dr Mathiesen

Robin Simmons at Dean's Mill, with Kirsty

Dorothy at Harlingen on our way home from a Social Science & Medicine Conference

In Finland with Warren Kinston and Louis Lemkow (Mai Zetterling's son)

At the World
Health
Organisation
headquarters
in Geneva,
1964

Bill Gannon

International Studies
team at New Paltz,
USA. Dot on far left,
Sari and Ivy Nasir
on extreme right

A pensive Colin Parkes

Peebles 1998, Manny Eppel toasting the
haggis, Raymond Illsley
admiringly approves

The great Arnold Goodman

*Prince Philip receiving a Crathie CC tie from Gillespie Munro
on the occasion of an Old Timer's match 2002, at Balmoral*

Prince Philip leaves the Gallery after opening the James Renny Exhibition in 1985

The Gallery Stand at the NEC Antique Fair in 1985

The drawing room at Glengarden during Exhibition time

Springtime at Glengarden 2007

The Diplomats. Back row: John Berger, Colin Hamilton, Ian Preston, me, Rhod, front row: Malcolm and Glen Barclay

A Private View

...rling: the national sport of Scotland. Our family team, Rhod, myself, Dorothy and Robert Innes

Malcolm & Glynis on their wedding day, 1983

The view from Eileen Horisdale towards Badachro

With Scott Sheret & friends at the summit

Feona, Rhod and Malk

With Dorothy outside Doune Castle

Inke and Dot inspecting the duck

The family in 2008

ona's wedding to John in 2006, on a shivering day - an occasion I sadly missed due to breaking my arm a week prior. Stuart, Rhod, Feona, Andrew, Dorothy and Malcolm

Chenko, the Russian Blue

A recumbent Bisket with her favourite toy

Cricket at Balmoral

Glengarden snowed in

Glengarden in Highland summertime

*August 1 2009, a wee tipple on our
Diamond Wedding Anniversary*

*John Petersen & Dorothy enjoying our Diamond
Wedding dinner in the gallery*

1. Robert Gemmell
   Hutchison RSA *Wash Day*

2. Joan Eardley RSA
   Street Urchin, Glasgow

3. Sir Edwin Landseer RA
   Scottish Deerhound 'Maida'
   1890

4. William Alfred Gibson
   Washerwomen on the Canal

John Maclauchlan Milne RSA
Corrie Harbour, Arran

Abraham Hulk *Calm Evening*

*Picasso presented this drawing to his friend Frank McEwen.
Although no relation, we also knew Frank during his time in
Southern Rhodesia as Curator of the National Art Gallery.*

Sir Robin J Philipson RA PRSA *Altarpiece*

Allan Ramsay (1713-1784)
Francis Piggott of Pelling Place

1. George Melvin Rennie *Ballater*

2. Joseph Farquharson RA *Coming Home*

3. Thomas Gainsborough *The Gainsborough Boy*

CHAPTER 6

Serious Business

Nothing in education is so astonishing as the amount of ignorance it accumulates in the form of inert facts.

[Henry Brooks Adams]

An application for a visiting professorship in African studies at the State University of New York having been successful, the next footsteps along the pathway of life took us to the United States.

After a pleasant crossing on the old *SS Mauritania*, sharing a restaurant table with an English musician and his wife on their way to conduct a symphony orchestra in California, we drove our unheated Gazelle to a small village in upstate New York. Motoring through the city and on to the State Highway on a muggy, wet autumnal evening was my first introduction to driving on the right. The greatest difficulties were caused by knowing how to process the tolls (knowing the correct coinage to throw into a shute – without having the right change caused great embarrassment as a long queue of impatient, horn-blaring drivers closed up behind); and taking care to observe the traffic lights which operated at a higher level of sight than at home.

New Paltz is about ninety miles north of New York, nestling on the banks of the Walkill river, beneath the Catskill Mountains. The village has an interesting history, taking its name from the Rhein Pfalz in Germany, from whence it was founded in 1678 by French Huguenots who had first escaped to Germany before crossing the Atlantic to America. Some of the old stone houses in Huguenot Street are among the first stone buildings erected by Europeans in North America. The village boasts the departments of Arts and International Studies, part of the dispersed State University of New York, whose main campus is in the state capital, Albany.

I had signed an annually renewable contract in the Afro-Asia programme to which – reminiscent of my time at Wood Hall – was added responsibility to teach criminology, a subject I had never previously studied nor for which I had any particular enthusiasm. It was necessary to learn and learn fast.

Every student in the Arts faculty was required to participate in the international programme during their final year. In addition to Professor Haas, a mild-mannered, equable native American psychologist, my colleagues for the course were an engaging mix: Dr King was a quietly spoken, elegant, slightly haughty Ghanaian whom it was said came from chieftainly stock, Ahmad Haffar was an unassuming, pro-American, western educated Egyptian; Vimla Patel, the only lady in the group, was an elegant, excitable slightly birdlike Indian, a gazelle among bullocks; Mulu Wodajo, a young beguiling, handsome American-educated Ethiopian economist; and Sari Nasir, a conspiratorial, swarthy, excitable Palestinian who, although educated at Harvard, was quietly pro-Arab and distinctly anti-American, author of *The Arabs and the English*. Sari and I got along very well, helped by the fact that his elegant American wife Ivy and Dorothy found themselves on similar wave-lengths.

Several aspects of American undergraduate culture quickly became apparent. At the start of a new university year parents accompanied their disoriented offspring just as British parents do at the beginning of a child's first year at school. This, after all, would be for most Americans a student's first venture away from home, while young males especially were younger and surprisingly less streetwise than their British counterparts of similar age. What Sari and I found difficult to accept was the requirement laid down by the Dean at the first staff assembly, that the top 75% of every class had to be passed, irrespective of quality. This appeared to us quite unreasonable and contrary to legitimate educational standards. It was a demand over which several others of my colleagues found compliance difficult.

As the year progressed one implication became clear: in the States, undergraduates generally began at the academic level of a British sixth form, the two systems broadly equating at the graduate stage.

In more general terms, our introduction to American culture excited a number of strongly favourable reactions, offset by a number of negatives. On the plus side, the comparative classlessness, except among the very wealthy, was refreshing, as was the dominant ethos that welcomed any new hypothesis, idea, plan or proposal until it was proved faulty, in sharp contrast to characteristic British reserve and scepticism. In America an idea is good unless proven bad, in Britain an idea is suspect unless proven good. There was, however, one significant exception. Nothing was tolerated that threatened the prevailing ideology, whether political, racial or religious. In these matters conformity was expected, nourished and rewarded.

We were very pleasantly surprised when at the end of their first week at school Malcolm came proudly off the school bus clutching a large shiny brass trumpet and Feona flourishing a clarinet. All the children had been given the opportunity of selecting an instrument of their choice. One wonders how many state schools in Britain, given the chance, might follow ?[1]

At the casual level people were very friendly, making transitory acquaintances without any initial suspicion or hesitancy. Less attractive was the strong current of commercialism that runs through most aspects of life, and an underlying violence exemplified in the gun culture, the death penalty and gangsterdom. Conformity in attitudes, beliefs and behaviour was depressingly everywhere.

Dorothy had resurrected her violin, enrolled in the college symphony orchestra, culminating in a fine concert featuring Howard Hansen's seldom heard 5th Symphony. It is said that Hansen, once dubbed 'the American Sibelius', was inspired when composing this elegiac work by the story of the resurrection as described in St John's Gospel.

---

[1] Since writing, I have heard that the cellist Julian Lloyd Webber is spearheading a goverment scheme to provide free musical instruments and expert tuition to underprivileged children in England.

Compromise, we noted, was a pejorative term, one was expected to either ban or promote. Several decades later the tendency to conformity reached its apotheosis with the notion of political correctness and, to a lesser degree, in the rise of evangelical Christianity and Christian fundamentalism.

Another feature of American culture which quickly became apparent was that of scale, the distances between places, the size of the population as well as the size of people, places and material objects. This, allied to constant immigration – USA is a society of migrants – renders genuine sentiment of belonging to a unified country or nationalism difficult to inculcate, hence the frequency with which the national anthem is heard and the American flag unfurled. This makes it difficult for an observer of the national scene to keep track of events so that only true aficionados can become informed of national trends and performances. As Simon Barnes has reminded us 'America is an island culture and its sporting culture expresses its insular nature. Sure, we live in an American world. American 'food' dominates the high streets of the world. But America doesn't import. It is a selling nation, not a buying one. It is not receptive to outside influences. In sport America is the nation which plays with itself'.[2]

Because of the great distances between centres of excellence there is a need for a multitude of conferences fragmenting information into many self-contained compartments of knowledge and news. Another disappointment was that, beneath the hale exteriors of the confident, outgoing personalities, there was often the absence of any core. Crude, insular vulgarity was commonplace, which made the exceptions especially cherished.

During our stay we again enjoyed the occasional company of the two Bob's. Bob Rotberg, living with his English wife Joanna in Boston, was now teaching African history at Harvard and hoping desperately to be granted tenure, the invariable ambition of every young academic in the States, especially those teaching at one of the Ivy League centres of excellence. Bob Sutcliffe was also in Boston

---

[2]   Simon Barnes, *The Times*, Sept 19, 2008.

having won a Harkness Fellowship to undertake postgraduate studies at Harvard's department of economics. Earlier, Bob, who by this time had acquired strong Marxist leanings, had spent the final (Easter) term of his honours course at Oxford alone on our island croft swotting so successfully that he gained a first-class honours degree before being appointed a junior don at Worcester College. He had been happily undeterred when one day on the island he received a postcard for all to read informing him, with total falsity, that uncle Richard was due to be released from jail the following week. As expected, this discreditable news circulated around the coastal community for many weeks.

When the international programme's teaching group came together to decide what texts to use it became clear that there were no obvious choices, a lacuna Bob Sutcliffe and I decided to fill. The result was *The Study of Africa*, published by Methuen, re-christened for the American market *Modern Africa*.

Among the peripatetic academics there was a clear division between those like Ahmed Haffar and Vimla Patel who were fully acculturated and committed to the American way of life, and others like Mulu, Sari and me who had every intention of returning to our own country. These contrasting viewpoints added piquancy to the social mix.

As the only British family on campus we were a source of amusement and curiosity, views probably enhanced by the fact that we travelled in a small right-hand drive car, without heating. This meant that in the cold midwinter its every use had to be preceded by twenty minutes spent thawing the frost encrusted windows, using a cover never having occurred to us. Motoring into New York city along Interstate Thruway 87, sometimes with our German Shepherd upright in the passenger seat where Americans expected to see the driver, caused much amusement and occasional consternation.

It had been an interesting year, introducing me to undergraduate teaching, making some good new friends and opening up a vista on the American way of life, but at the end of the last semester all essays and exams having been marked, I decided against renewing my contract. We were happy to be going home again, this time travelling on the old *Queen Mary*, having been driven to the New York docks by Bob Sutcliffe.

The question then was: where next? The croft on Eilean Horrisdale was still there, the water would still be gently lapping on the sides of the old mahogany dinghy, and the Torridon hills – among the oldest rocks in the world – would still be towering over all, Cornellan in Ballater awaited us, heralding a happy reunion with our deerhound, with Greypuss and, of course, cricket. For Dorothy, The Snuff Box beckoned.

The boys were happy to be home again and back in the good village primary school. For me there was the attempt to construct a book on the human condition with a title already chosen: *The Human Element*. Many references were pored over, notes taken and a draft begun, but in the face of many interruptions the project has never been finished.

Enquiries were renewed to find the next academic resting place. At first it seemed a desperately difficult choice between the offer of a chair in Addis Ababa or one in St. John's, Newfoundland, a position eventually filled by my old friend Bob Paine who proceded to become Dean. Bob was now an anthropologist, having done his fieldwork helping to herd reindeer among the itinerant Lapps in northern Lapland, one of whom he married.

Neither of these appointments held much attraction, hours were spent tramping over the hills of home with the dogs, agonising over what to do. Realising that neither option represented a really attractive opportunity I was on the point of having to take a reluctant plunge when a totally unexpected telephone call came through from the States offering me a post at Harvard. With Feona now thirteen and happily placed at St Leonard's School for Girls in St Andrews, this was as easy to accept as Ethiopia and Newfoundland had been difficult. So it was that after a fallow year, having compiled and proofread three volumes of *The History of Africa* for Oxford University Press, the family prepared once again to cross the Atlantic.

Before leaving Ballater and home we committed an act of most enjoyable folly, purchasing a new cream ('old English white') Austin Healey Mark III sports car, the most exciting vehicle I have ever had the pleasure of owning. After a number of teething problems in London, including the embarrassment of coming to a standstill approaching Hyde Park Corner and again outside Scotland Yard, both caused by a faulty fuel pump, Dadna and I drove north, passing through a violent thunderstorm in the Midlands which certainly tested the quality of the hood's waterproofing. A short time later the whole family motored to York where Dorothy's brother Gordon was getting married, quite a squash for the three children in the back, huddled like sardines in the dicky seats. My oldest brother-in-law, Howard, vicar of St. Austell, surprised us all by leaving the wedding dinner at 10 pm. It appeared this was his unswerving custom, one from which he never deviated not even when his bishop came to dine.

Bob Rotberg had kindly organised our first house in Cambridge, the home of an economic professor on leave as a Presidential advisor. I had been hired to replace another English academic as Director of the Family Research Unit in the Department of Community Psychiatry at the School of Public Health. My brief was twofold: (a) to develop ongoing research on mental health within the family or to obtain finance to fund an alternative, and (b) to teach social science to graduate psychiatrists in the department's programme of community psychiatry.

Contact was made very quickly with three Brits on the staff, two psychiatrist colleagues, Colin Parkes and Alan Sheldon, and Dorothy Roberts, the secretary I had inherited. Colin is a tall rather gangling enthusiast with a warm balance and prudence whose speciality is the study of bereavement, an experience about which he has devoted a lifetime of research, becoming a senior adviser in the aftermath of the Abervan disaster and an international authority on the subject; Alan is a will o'-the-wisp, a friendly man with broad interests from who flowed a constant stream of ideas, open to suggestions and proposals from every source. With Dorothy Roberts I was fortunate in having the most generally efficient secretary that it has been my good fortune ever to work with, a quietly spoken, unassuming English lady, highly organised, with rapid shorthand and typing skills and a willingness to engage whatever new imposition landed on her desk. She had been the cabinet secretary in Uganda, coming to Boston with her American librarian husband. Another lesser piece of good fortune, was that very soon after my arrival the Unit's offices were moved from the main building to a house further along the same street, offering greater freedom and reduced threat of interruption.

In my second year among the fresh arrivals was a young fuzzy-haired Scottish psychiatrist. During one winter's day he joined Malcolm and the rest of the family on a weekend expedition to the nearest ski slope. On arrival, seeking the hiring of equipment, the manager took our party to one side. On being told that Bruce, our guest, was from Scotland, the manager disappeared with a conspiratorial air to return with what he said was his best pair of racing skis. Bruce hid his embarrassment beneath a cloak of overt enthusiasm. It was with eager anticipation that he was watched by us all bearing, as it were, the ensign of Scotland. All buckled up and ready to race away he unsteadily arose only to immediately come crashing down on his backside. With a helping hand under each Scottish arm, we eventually hobbled along to the nearest and shortest slope, but before the first lift appeared, our support having been withdrawn, dear Bruce again fell to earth. The confused mirth of the assembled throng and the embarrassment of our young psychiatrist was hard to reconcile. Sad to relate Bruce never did make the hill that day but luckily the manager had already retired to his office, obviously recognising that not all Scotsmen are skiers and our man was certainly not among those who were. It did not require genius to conclude that Bruce had never set foot on a ski before and as far as I know has not done so since.

Community psychiatry intervenes and deals with characteristic traumas that affect communities, both at the individual and social level. The main examples of the former are birth (eg post-natal psychosis), marriage, divorce (eg counselling), loss of employment, and bereavement. The principal focal points in society are the family, the community, schools, the workplace, and hospitals.

The departmental chairman, the doyen of the discipline, was another Englishman, Gerald Caplan, a Jewish Mancunian, particularly able at selling his discipline and quietly administering a *mélange* of very different people, leaving us to our own devices, always providing that we produced the goods. The mature graduate students, all qualified psychiatrists, were limited to around fifteen a year, representing a challenging and exciting mix of highly talented, highly motivated men, mostly American, with a garniture of Australians and the occasional Brit, carefully selected and all destined for senior positions in their chosen field.[3]

Another curious example of the practical distinction often found between knowledge and action was that Caplan, an authority on community relations, hosted the most socially stultifying parties imaginable, his guests being invited to sit around the perimeter of a large rather bland drawing room expected to speak in turn. Furthermore, the department itself had no meeting place for staff/student discussion or relaxation until Alan and I succeeded in persuading Caplan of the desirability of having a staff common room.

Rather than developing the work of my predecessor who had been following married couples through childbirth and beyond, I preferred to pursue a new line of research. In consultation with Alan, who was also searching for a new challenge, we hit upon the comparatively neglected field of retirement. This meant preparing a research plan, building upon earlier studies, writing up and costing a research proposal, then to await a site visit from representatives of the National Institute of Mental Health in Washington.

During this process and the regular lecture seminars, I was invited by the World Health Organisation to participate in what turned out to be two group consultations on statistical aspects of the family as a necessary base for indepth studies of family health. In addition to the convenor, WHO's resident Austrian demographer, Harald Hansluwka, there were Dr Lothar Herberger, a German statistician; John Deeble, an Australian economist; an English physician Fred Walker; and myself representing the social sciences. Harald is a dapper, gold-toothed, charming,

---

[3]   During the three years I was there, there had not been a single woman among the post-graduate students

patient academic turned bureaucrat, Lothar an open-minded highly competent mathematician, John a burly bushwhacking economist who found it hard to get his head round the notion of family health, the very concept that had brought us together. Fred, now deceased, was a wise, silver haired paediatrician, director of a well-known, highly respected Newcastle study that had been following the health of a hundred families all the way through the life cycle from birth to death.

Our brief was to examine five principal areas: (1) possible sources of information for developing a socio-psychological approach to the study of health and disease; (2) implications of recent developments in statistical methods and techniques which facilitate and improve the gathering of information relevant to a family-based approach to the study of health problems; (3) the formulation of guidelines and recommendations for the revision of standard vital and medical records, so as to include information relating these events to the family; (4) discussion of various types of statistical studies and surveys required for expanding knowledge of the family as regards health status and patterns; and (5) the identification of major gaps in statistical techniques and information needed for the development and formation of an epidemiology of family disorders and diseases.

The notion of family health is, of course, ambiguous. It may denote the health (i.e. absence or presence of disease) of family members or it may denote the condition of the family itself. In each case the criteria of 'health' differ, for only individuals have diseases. Although the notion of a healthy family, meaning an effectively functioning unit, implying the possibility of its opposite, is yet little used, it is growing in currency and therefore cannot be neglected. The notion of the healthy family refers specifically to the social functioning of a group so that the use of the term 'healthy' is misleading. A social group can be effective and functional or ineffective/dysfunctional. We had to decide whether the phrase 'healthy family' should be encouraged and promoted on the grounds that it is already in common usage or whether a more accurate substitute should be agreed in the interest of clarity.

The complexities before us will be apparent. The family is the only social institution other than organised religion which is formally developed in all societies. It is the principal mediating agent between the individual and society. The family unit of socialisation is the family of orientation as distinct from the family of procreation, the reproductive family unit. While varying from one culture to another, there are four basic forms of family. The nuclear, consisting of a husband, wife and children; the extended form, consisting of several generations living together; the stem, common in parts of the United States and Japan, wherein only one child, usually the eldest son, inherits property and title; and the joint family of India, comprising people sharing property rights within the family, generally all the brothers in each generation in a direct line, so long as the family unit remains cohesive.

In relation to health, the most common social factors in the causation of disease concern the family, ethnic background, socio-economic status, and religion. Each involve characteristic patterns of socially determined behaviour and because the family is the prime unit of socialisation it can be said that the family is the single most important single factor in the social aetiology of organic disease. The relationship between family variables and family disease can take many forms. These include, for example, practices of child rearing, genetic transference (at least one in every two hundred births carries a serious genetic defect), a reciprocity between disease and social factors, type of residence, and parental management.

The nuclear family passes through four natural stages of development, each presenting characteristics, opportunities and strains. These are periods of expansion, dispersion, independence and replacement. As the family proceeds through these stages, crises may be experienced with implications for physical and/or mental health. In addition to transitional crises (marriage, birth of first child, retirement, bereavement), there are many potential non-transitional danger points, such as dismemberment (e.g. war separation), accession (e.g. unwanted pregnancy), demoralisation (e.g. alcoholism), and any or all of these in combination (e.g. divorce, imprisonment, desertion). To complicate matters further, severe disruption of lifestyle may be encountered: sudden impoverishment, prolonged unemployment, sudden wealth or fame, refugee migration, natural disaster, wartime deprivation, or political declassing.

The whole, equally complex, question besetting the measurement of family function was also on our agenda. In the event, the group left WHO's headquarters in Geneva, each of us with a chapter or two to write before returning several months later in the hope that we would bring together a final report.

In the midst of these activities in Boston and Geneva two other significant developments were taking place. Dorothy, with Feona settled at school in St Andrews, Malcolm at Loretto in Edinburgh, and Rhod happy in Franklin High School in Lexington, had time on her hands. Playing the violin in a classical quartet run by our neighbour, although enjoyable, was not enough. The spirit had to soar by day as well as at eventide. The lure of antiques, the endless, exciting search for treasures, nourished by the Snuff Box, needed to find an outlet. A chance meeting with the English wife of a Polish engineer solved the problem. Sylvia shared Dorothy's enthusiasm for antiques of all kinds and with time on her hands, a little spare capital, and sound business nous, she made an ideal partner. Together, they opened a shop, Balmoral Antiques. Charles Street, the throbbing heart of Boston's antiquarian trade, found them dealing in ceramics, small furniture, paintings and silver. The business prospered, with many interesting clients and stimulating forays to the main auctions in New York and Massachusetts, a step up from The Snuff Box. The most memorable deals were a set of silver-appointed bagpipes for an American psychiatrist with distant Scottish connections, and the lease of several objects for use in the film *The Thomas Crown Affair*. Dorothy faced the hazards of Bostonian traffic each day, travelling to work in a large, reliable but not very comfortable old grey Ford Rambler.

Before the year was out Sylvia was forced to withdraw to join her husband who had taken a job in California. After a lot of heart-searching and encouraged by a helpful accountant, Dorothy decided to continue on her own. Incidentally, my main memory of Sylvia's Polish husband is of a driver who resolutely refused to break the speed limit when driving on the thruways. In the face of continuous honking of horns and the occasional gesture of impatient contempt, he drove imperiously along the fast lane never exceeding the legal limit which it seemed every other motorist in Boston ignored. Being his passenger was always an embarrassment.

One of our greatest regrets when leaving Boston was having to terminate the business. As one grizzled old trader remarked to Dorothy 'congratulations, you know you might have fallen flat on your face'.

Early in 1965, our six-month lease in Barberry Road having expired, we migrated further out of town to the quieter suburb of Lexington. It was at this time that, just as in New Paltz, when a gap had to be filled in teaching African studies, the teaching of the social sciences to medical graduates highlighted the absence of an appropriate medium with which, to aid teaching or through which to engage with other social scientists working in the medical field.

It had become increasingly clear that the medical and social sciences had grown more closely interwoven in many areas, a fact not adequately reflected in any publication. Not only did the inter-relationship require a vehicle of expression but there was also a growing need to sensitise the relevant disciplines to recognise and develop the importance and extent of their interactions. In the field of psychiatry the relevance of the social sciences for a more complete understanding of many problems and processes was obvious, although even here there were associations that sophistication on both sides needed to recognise and understand. Again, there was the problem of language, different disciplines spoke in different tongues. A new journal would need to encompass preventive public and social medicine, epidemiology, and psychiatry as well as anthropology, economics, psychology, sociology, and moral philosophy while all the time seeking to cross national boundaries. Many topics and their treatment were contentious making peer review more than usually important and the selection of reviewers correspondingly delicate.

There was an important and unusual tactic that I sought to introduce from the beginning. The journal would occasionally publish material around a predetermined topic. Such issues, because they were contentious or of growing significance and because they had been pre-selected, demanded equable treatment. There had to be no question of editorial influence in the treatment of content and only occasionally in its selection. To this extent the journal would be proactive. Two examples in the early days were the contribution of the social sciences to some of the ethical problems that were coming to increasingly preoccupy the medical profession, and an examination of the need for detailed socio-economic planning in the medical arena, allied to a discussion of the major factors relevant in the determination of ends and the assessment of means. This policy laid an additional but worthwhile burden on editorial time. Later examples were the concept and significance of 'heresy', and research into whether there might be a causal relationship between psychological stress and some types of cancer. Co-ordinating the former was an erudite lady anthropologist in Istanbul, the latter by an oncologist at the Royal Marsden Hospital in London.

For all these reasons it seemed an exciting opportunity to launch a new international and multi-disciplinary journal devoted to all aspects of the social sciences relating to health and health care.

One of the substantial advantages of living in Boston is that whatever one's interest there is always at least one resident expert and generally several. And, of course, Harvard has an especial cachet so that any new idea emanating therefrom carries an added valency.

I invited my colleague Alan Sheldon to join the venture and, always ready for a fresh challenge, he agreed to become an Associate Editor. An esteemed anthropologist friend, Don Kennedy of Brandeis University, my favourite American academic, agreed to join the team as research editor and the late John Kosa, an Hungarian sociologist currently working at Harvard Medical School, would be responsible for book reviews. Thus we had a medical man, a sociologist, an anthropologist and a social psychologist. Invitations were then circulated to medical and social scientists in Australia, Canada, France, Germany,

Japan, Latin America, Poland and the United Kingdom. The only recipient who questioned the legal implications of being an editor in the unlikely event of there being litigation, then or at any other time in the subsequent history of the journal, was my old bush whacking colleague from Zambia, David Bettison, now a professor in Canada.

Armed with a formidable array of international scholars prepared to participate, I wrote to Robert Maxwell. Maxwell had been a colleague of my father's in the British Military Government in Berlin and at the end of the war had launched the Pergamon Press, specialising in the publication of learned journals. Maxwell had in fact asked Dadna to join him in the venture, but my father already knew enough about Maxwell's probity to decline. This, however, seemed no reason for me not to make an approach. Maxwell replied positively, inviting me to contact his agent in New York. After a couple of meetings and detailed correspondence the proposal was approved. It was agreed the journal would appear quarterly, published by Pergamon who would be responsible for all aspects of marketing and financing my expenses but nothing more. With the approval of Gerald Caplan, who saw it as a free advertisement for his enterprise (called officially a Laboratory), Alan and I set about planning the details with Dorothy Roberts as the journal's first highly efficient secretary.

I visited an English professor of chemistry across the river, the editor of a quarterly Pergamon journal, in the hope of learning more about the review process and the demands involved. He reassured me that, with a good secretary familiar with the names of an extensive panel of reviewers, his commitment was the equivalent of only about one day a month. Although momentarily encouraged by this information I soon found that it failed to take into account the fact that whereas he was dealing with a single discipline, with readily identifiable departments around the world, we would be working with many different disciplines from anthropology to the many branches of medicine, often with no identifiable department involved, sometimes dealing with contentious topics where it was necessary to select reviewers most carefully to ensure balanced assessments.

The next major decision was to agree a title. *Acta Sociomedica* was the initial front runner but this seemed pedantic and insufficiently succinct, so the *International Journal of Social Science and Medicine*, to give it its full name, was born in April, 1967. The next question, apart of course from the content of the first issue which was by invitation, was to chose the colour of its cover. The Countway Medical Library, just across the road from my office, is one of the finest medical libraries in the world, so Alan and I repaired to their journal section reviewing the colours of the periodicals likely to be seen in any major medical library adjacent to our own. The final choice was turquoise, a colour that in due course was changed permanently to red.

Editors were not involved in any aspect of finance, including the fixing of subscription rates, nor did we receive any remuneration other than expenses but, equally, Pergamon exercised no editorial control whatsoever, either in content or in editorial appointments. Regional editors were appointed in Australia, Chile, France, Germany, India, Israel, Japan, Poland, Sweden, UK and USA. Added to these were forty-eight advisory editors, two of whom were from Britain.

Within three years the arrival of good material merited an increase in output to six issues per annum until, in 1973, the journal became monthly. In 1977, 18 issues began to appear annually and in 1981 this number rose to 24, a burden supported by 87 editors from 31 different countries. In response to appeals from distressed librarians, beginning with volume 18 in 1984, two volumes have been published annually. At the time of my retirement in 1995 there were 107 editors from 36 countries. Marking the ineluctable passage of time, it is sad to reflect that after forty-two years, of the 65 original editors I am the only one still associated with the journal.

During the first 29 years, 501 issues appeared, approximately 7,500 papers were published and more than 15,000 manuscripts declined.

When after two years John Kosa unexpectedly died, the journal commemorated his memory by instituting a Kosa Award. In addition to the prestige afforded the winner, there was a rather grand certificate, a modest cash sum donated by the publisher, and as much publicity as the journal and publisher could muster. The award went to the author of the paper which, in the opinion of an international panel of judges, made the most important contribution in any language to any branch of the social sciences relating to medicine. This involved a panel of nominating judges with the task of drawing up a list of six or more nominations which were then assessed by a separate, independent panel. Given the international nature of the process it can be appreciated what a complex operation this became. Unhappily, though perhaps inevitably, as the journal appeared more frequently, administering the Kosa Award became increasingly difficult to handle and eventually it had to be discontinued. Perhaps one day, now that many more journal administrators are involved, it might be resurrected.

There was an experiment in the 70s with issues being segregated according to disciplinary content, but the confusion this caused libraries, subscribers, and the trend it encouraged toward compartmentalisation, led to a quick return to the status quo.

As the journal became increasingly well known, with a continuously mounting volume of submissions, senior editors replaced regional editors. Senior editors had primary responsibility for processing respectively anthropological, economic, geographic and ethical material. I retained primary responsibility for psychology and medical sociology, and for final decisions overall. Social epidemiology and health policy were added later. After my retirement my successor added a 'managing editor' to the team and recently two of the senior editors each acquired their own 'assistant editor'. Changed days!

In addition to the expected duties, surprising requests were occasionally received. An invitation once arrived inviting me to act as a referee for a Nobel Prize nominee, and quite often senior appointments would be refereed, for both universities and the main funding agencies.

The legal ownership of the journal was unclear. On two occasions I received approaches for a take-over. The first came in 1970 when by this time I was at the University of Sussex. An Indian market analyst, an employee of Pergamon, came to visit me producing the most detailed subscriber list I had ever been allowed to see, and proceeded to make a proposal based on the presumption that as it was 'my' journal it could be taken wheresoever I wished. The proposal he placed before me was that he would be responsible for production and marketing and we would share the substantial profit. Since by this time the journal was already appearing every second week, for which I received only a very modest honorarium, the invitation was tempting. But a combination of loyalty, the project's uncertain legitimacy, and a lack of confidence in the unfamiliar proposer persuaded me to decline the opportunity. Several years later, when I was now editing virtually full-time and Pergamon was going through one of its recurring crises, overtures were received from a leading London academic publisher. We reached the stage of having a dinner in Aberdeenshire and a luncheon in London before I again declined the offer in spite of the fact that by this time the legitimacy of a transfer had been confirmed by lawyers.

Apart from several visits to Maxwell at Headington Hall, his capacious house and headquarters in Oxford, with each of the guest bedrooms named after an Oxford college, fitted with their own self-catering facilities and basic foodstuffs, I had two significant encounters with the man. The first was sometime in the 70s, before his right to exercise proper stewardship of a publicly quoted company had been questioned. A surprising invitation arrived asking me to prepare a report directly to himself on ways in which, from an editorial point of view, the company might be improved. Although the purpose of this request never became precisely clear, its motivation remaining as obscure as it was unexpected, my report was duly delivered, the main thrust of which was the need to establish a clear chain of command in order to leave the company in sound shape whenever Maxwell retired or withdrew. Needless to say, I never heard anything more beyond a formal acknowledgement from Maxwell's hard-pressed managing director.

The second encounter was more significant. At the height of his second battle to retain Pergamon, following the Leasco debacle, Maxwell publicly announced that an enquiry among his editors had produced overwhelming support for the retention of his stewardship. As I for one had not been consulted I wondered how many editors had indeed been approached. There was one other editor of a Pergamon journal on the faculty of Sussex University where I then was. A phone call quickly confirmed that he too had not been among those allegedly canvassed. When further enquiries found none of those contacted had been asked it was clear that Maxwell's claim was just another of his ruses. I forwarded details of my disclosures to *The Financial Times* which they duly published. To his credit – unless of course he never saw the piece – Maxwell never responded, neither by letter nor in any more threatening way.

At about this time *Social Science and Medicine* achieved an accolade sufficiently meritorious to overcome the publisher's normal reticence in reporting good news to its editors. The journal topped WHO's citation list for non-clinical medicine, ahead of such illustrious publications as the *New England Journal of Medicine* and the *British Medical Journal*, as well as being among the top six for clinical subjects.

Tact and diplomacy were always necessary in dealing with authors and editors, some of whom were prima donnas and some with extreme views likely to excite irrational hostility when being themselves subject to criticism, an inflammatory mix. During my thirty-eight years of editorship I can only recall two fires which threatened to burn out of hand although each was eventually extinguished without lasting damage.

The first occurred in the 1980s during a period when editors were invited to contribute in rotation an 'editorial', a topic or treatment close to their heart. It was made clear that these invited contributions although not submitted for normal peer review would be subject to any revision I might suggest. One of our number, a very bright but slightly obsessive Marxist medical chap, objected to the proposed deletion of a paragraph. At first he was so disinclined to comply that, without telling me, he wrote to the publisher demanding my removal, a letter I was shown, and when this produced no effect he travelled with his family to Denmark where our next editorial meeting was to be held, presumably intending to propose a vote of censure and to get my decision reversed. The gentleman had his case demolished by his fellow editors and departed without, I believe, attending any sessions of the conference itself.

The second commotion took place in 1989. That summer we had published a paper by a Canadian psychologist, John Philippe Rushton, analysing certain aspects of race. The paper inhabited the highly sensitive field of racial variations. Part of the author's arguments, based on r/K selection theory, which relates to the selection of traits that promote success in particular environments, was that East Asians have on average a larger brain, have greater intelligence, show more sexual constraint, slower maturation and greater social skills, including law-abidingness, than Europeans, who in turn scored higher than Africans and their descendants. This was a classic example of an extreme polemic weakening its case with arguments beyond the limitations of any supporting data, with critics allowing their conventional outrage of the whole thesis to occlude their judgement about some of its parts.

At the International Conference that year, organised by the Journal, the opening address was to be delivered by Charles Leslie, our highly respected senior medical anthropology editor. He later told me that it was not until boarding the plane that he had decided the subject of his talk. In retrospect, it reminded me of Churchill's comment about Lord George Beresford, 'He is one of those orators of whom it was well said, before they get up they do not know what they are going to say; when they are speaking, they do not know what they are saying; and when they have sat down, they do not know what they have said'. His Address became a diatribe against the Rushton paper. For the first (and only) time at these meetings loud acclamation erupted at its close, especially from the younger conferees. Personally, I found the nature of the Address surprising, its reception unfortunate, the degree of passion involved disappointing. It was surprising because as chairman (as well as editor-in-chief) I had been given no forewarning and, at another conference in Edinburgh a week earlier, a similar paper by the same author had received only objective rational debate. It was unfortunate because it was difficult to restore rationality to the meeting and it was disappointing because it demonstrated how, in the States particularly, free speech in certain areas is seriously compromised, a fact recently confirmed by the enforced resignation of Harvard's last President, the distinguished economist, Professor Laurence Summers. This was brought about by his suggestion, not please note an assertion, that one of the reasons why women are under-represented in American faculties of engineering and science is that there might be an innate difference between the way female and male brains function.

An American Professor, Max Bauerlein, has identified three elements among academics in his country that provide a bias toward self-reinforcing group-think. He has called them the common assumption, the false consensus, and the law of group polarisation. Together, he argues, they are transforming American Universities into 'intellectually homogeneous, left-wing reinforcement parade grounds'.

There has long been evidence of an incipient fascism among the higher echelons of American society generally, evinced on an earlier occasion by the treatment Bertrand Russell received at the hands of the College of the City of New York in 1940.

James Watson, who shared a Nobel Prize, was banned from delivering a lecture at the Science Museum in London because he had expressed doubts about prospects in Africa since 'all our social policies are based on the fact that their intelligence is the same as ours – whereas all the testing says not really'. The censorship did not end there. Cold Spring Harbor Laboratory, where Watson was the director and president, recalled him home and relieved him of his duties. The issue, of course, was not over the truth or falsity of the opinions expressed, but the fact that he dared express them at all.

There is another incipient evil by no means confined to the States but which is becoming endemic throughout the western world. Artistic censorship. I offer two examples, one in America, the other in Britain. On August 12th 2008 the large American publisher Random House was due to publish *The Jewel of Medina*, an historical novel about the wife of the prophet Muhammad. In what has been described as 'another wave of self-censorship and cultural cowardice sweeping Western art circles', the book was written off. In England, the BBC, having spent several months researching for a documentary *The London Bombers*, decided to scrap the programme as being Islamophobic and offensive.[4]

These facts raise a number of issues. The first is censorship, for intolerance is as reprehensible as overt racism. The cancer of censorship is the product of political correctness without the will to transgress, and fear, the fear of terrrorist reprisal. If it is allowed to grow unchallenged it will destroy freedom and annihilate creativity.

The second issue is the need to examine genetic variations in an objective way. Blasphemy was once the dominant heresy, now it is the Rushtonian belief that race differences exist. It has been pointed out that in an Olympic 100 metres final all the contenders will be black and that the Japanese, with minimal body hair, find human odours on the London Underground far more unpleasant than do their European counterparts. Racial differences exist and need to be explained without any qualitative undertones or irrelevant moralising.

The third issue is the question of racism itself. Correctly used, racism is belief in a racial difference or characteristic based on prejudice alone. When arguments from any specific genetic variation according to race are based upon legitimate evidence objectively examined according to scientific principles, this is not racism but, more accurately, racialism. Unfortunately, the ability to adopt a genuinely objective approach is extremely rare, very often the degree of passion is proportionate to the absence of the possibility of an objective test.

Earlier there was another example of the powerful emotions involved over quite a different matter. At our 1974 conference a group of women participants, most but not all Americans, convened a private meeting, myself and one other man being the only males invited, for the purpose of considering why it was

---

[4]   For details of these cases, and others, vide 'It's a festival of grovelling to terrorists' Mick Hume, *The Times*, 12 Aug 08.

that there were so few women in academics generally and on our editorial panel in particular, and what could be done about it. This seemed a valid criticism and one in need of correction. However, when reporting this the following evening to the conference's steering committee, I was astonished by the virulent and passionate reaction of several prominent colleagues, medical men and a professor of divinity among them. They found even the promulgation of the question intensely threatening.

Harvard songbirds are expected to sing for their supper. Hence, blazing the conference trail across the country, Alan Sheldon and I found the notes frequently flat and often repetitive. It seemed to us that a kind of conference was needed that would break the mould while preserving the implicit intent: individual enlightenment and social benefit. In 1967 hostility and suspicion between the social sciences and the medical profession remained a potent obstacle to co-operation and progress. With the launching of the journal the time seemed ripe to plan an international meeting that would enable medical and social scientists to discuss common problems together but within a format different to the conventional. The formal delivery of prepared papers would be excluded, initiating instead an informal exchange of experience, attitudes, ideas and opinions. The aim was to foster convergence out of divergence.

Although, to avoid extramural diversions, a rural location would have been preferred, my contacts in Aberdeen and the facilities they were able to offer persuaded us to go there, and on the 4th September, 1968 the first International Conference on the Social Sciences and Medicine opened at Aberdeen University. This lasted three days with four themes being discussed simultaneously under the guidance of discussion leaders carefully chosen in advance. No papers were prepared, the group meetings being conducted on a seminar-type basis. The experiment, for that is what it was, produced one of the most constructive and useful groups we ever had. The topic was 'death and dying'. Among others, there was a psychiatrist, a theologian with experience of working among terminally ill patients, a hospice nurse, a social psychologist and a surgeon. They quickly recognised that their approaches, although professionally so different and thinking in almost different languages, had much to offer each other and, most important, the meeting had given them an unique opportunity to make common ground and to enhance their work in significant ways for the common good. An abundance of information which we call specialization forms a barrier between one man and the next for each believes that his subject and its language cannot be understood by others. The prime aim of these meetings, as reflected in their format, was aimed at breaking down these barriers.

An administrative pattern emerged, whereby a planning committee held a two-day meeting in January of the preceding year prior to a conference convened every second year. The most important, exciting and time-consuming item on the committee's agenda was the selection of prospective themes. These were then distributed to all our editors inviting their comments and ranked preferences. A small executive group then met to design the content of the final programme.

Administration and a working budget were in the hands of a locally based executive secretary. As was only to be expected, the effectiveness of the eight executive secretaries we had over the years varied enormously. Their's was a demanding role for as well as organising the various sections and locating them in their most suitable rooms, he/she was responsible for finance, for administering the rosters for meeting and returning conferees to/from their points of arrival and departure, as well as tending to all the daily irritants and requests registered by people from many different backgrounds and countries. Four of them stood out for their unfailing good humour, administrative skills and fiscal dexterity: Derek Gill, a chain-smoking rufous, ex-RAF mature Ph.D. student who managed the two inaugural meetings in Aberdeen; Jan Matse, a jolly, imperturbable Dutch sociologist with the chuckle of a choirboy, who was persuaded to undertake the task four times, the last after he had officially retired; Louis Lemkow, professorial son of the actress and author Mai Zetterling, who guided us through the Spanish jungle with impeccable English and sardonic retraint; and the glamorous but very firm Danish anthropologist, Anne Reeler, who did the job twice, once in my absence in Hungary when she also chaired the steering committee, and again at the last and largest meeting, in Peebles.

On the eve of the conference a steering committee came into existence consisting of the planning committee, discussion leaders, and the executive secretary, a group which continued to meet daily throughout the week to review progress and to prepare provisional agendas for all the sessions meeting on the following day so that participants could decide which group they wished to attend. An appreciated and important feature was that all participants coming by air or rail were met on arrival and transported to the conference site. We found that the logistic problems presented by this procedure, and there were many, were amply justified by the appreciation of overseas participants inducing the tone of friendly co-operation it was so important to establish.

Each section had a background paper published in an advance copy of the journal although it was made explicitly clear that there was no obligation to pursue any of the lines indicated. The interests of those present, often in the light of a group momentum and cohesion already achieved, was paramount.

In 1968 for the first and only time, participation was by invitation only. The first major development, apart from abandoning invitations, opening the door to all who wished to apply, was the introduction in 1972 of an opening address, an edited version being subsequently published with commentaries from others, with a final rejoinder from the original author.

It soon became clear that funds were needed to cover the mounting administrative costs incurred during the planning cycle as well as the meeting itself. A registration fee of £5 was initially introduced, a figure that has gradually increased. It is interesting to note that the degree of financial aid from outside sources ranged from zero in 1977 to £132,000 in 1996.

Another important procedure, with financial implications, was our co-ordination with simultaneous or sequential gatherings under other auspices as, for example, in 1987 when a WHO-sponsored group met in the same Spanish town during the first two days, enabling their participants to join our conference thereafter. In 1992 the London School of Hygiene facilitated the attendance of a number of post-graduate students from third world countries, a procedure replicated by Harvard University in 1996.

In keeping with the *esprit de corps* we tried so hard to foster and maintain, each planning committee included at least one member unconnected with the journal and there was always at least one representative from one or other branch of the medical profession.

A perusal of the themes through the years makes interesting reading, illuminating professional fashion and preoccupations.

The success of the format largely depended upon the skills of the discussion leaders. They had to be perceptive, firm, flexible, open-minded, with an ability to keep the main gaol in sight while recognising worthwhile diversions. The demands were so onerous that, when someone excelled, the temptation to keep inviting him/her became hard to resist. An account of these meetings would not be complete without mentioning two quite outstanding examples.

Harmon Smith, professor of Divinity at Duke University, had spent a large part of his professional life dealing with the moral and spiritual aspects of the terminally ill; his toleration and the wisdom born of experience merged to make him irreplaceable when considering the delicate issues that surround this area.

The second paragon was the late Philip Wood, a leading British rheumatologist with a mind open and sensitive to many subjects other than his own. He had the innate ability, given to only a few, of being able to draw forth pearls from the most hermetic souls whilst at the same time being able to patiently silence the empty vessels. There is a little used word 'maieutic', an adaptation of the Greek term for a midwife, which describes this process precisely 'serving to bring a person's latent ideas into clear consciousness'.

An invaluable innovation in 1985 was for a carefully chosen member of the steering committee to circulate among the groups, monitoring how things were going. Adjustments were sometimes required, either to the discussion leader's methods or, in serious cases, to a change of leadership. One example when a change was badly needed was a German discussion leader who had organised positions around the table hierarchically, according to seniority. Such observation and correction, however, required judgement and sensitivity of the highest order so that when at one conference our specialist monitorist, Warren Kinston (a psychiatrist), was unable to attend, his successor, another psychiatrist, was soon forced to abandon the task, the tactical skill required being beyond him.

Possible outcomes of these meetings came in several forms. Probably the most important has been the intangible influence of the meetings upon individuals, benefiting from the opportunity to exchange ideas and experience with a multitude of caring colleagues from differing cultural and professional backgrounds, in an informal and friendly atmosphere. Among more tangible outcomes it would be invidious to provide examples when many remain unknown to me, but one can mention the evolution of similar regional conferences, networks and international associations, some conceived directly during one or other of our events, and the planning of collaborative cross-cultural research into comparative systems of health care. It has been a great privilege to have worked with so many caring and dedicated colleagues many of whom I would otherwise have had no opportunity of meeting.

Organizing international conferences illuminates the diversity and extremes of human character. Far from home and keen to make an impact on one's fellows seems to bring out basic characteristics of the human psyche. A few participants enlarged petty problems such as finding themselves in a room with a window facing the wrong direction, into an uproar of complaint; but for every one of these there were always several who went out of their way to help and encourage others. There were bombasts who sought to control discussion and there were the silent ones who often had much to contribute but who needed to be drawn, like a splinter from an injured finger. There were a few who sought sexual conquest but the vast majority came to enrich their thinking through the genuine exchange of ideas and perceptions. It was a gratifying experience to find Iraqis sitting down with Iranians (this at the time of war between their countries), Jordanian Arabs deep in professional debate with Israeli Jews, Russians sharing ideas with their American and British counterparts. When, after a span of thirty years and with 52 countries represented at the last meeting, the series came to an end, I cannot deny that it was disappointing no-one could be found willing and able to take up the cudgels. It had been a profound and enjoyable privilege which I would not have missed for the world and which I believe made a lasting and solid contribution to the many subjects involved.

A source of great appreciation and pride was the honour done me by a leading American medical sociologist, Professor Andrew Twaddle. In addition to dedicating to me his book *Health Care Reform Around the World* he kindly referred in his Preface to the value of these conferences. 'It would be interesting to know', he wrote, 'how many collaborations began in these meetings and how much knowledge was generated because of them. This is something we will never know, but it is certain that Dr McEwan has had an enormous impact on the state of social science and medicine'.

Many are the warm memories of participants who, on arrival, volunteered their help without even being asked. Then there were the administrative assistants, young post-graduate men and women chosen by recommendation from around the world for their intelligence, dedication and temperamental stability, many of whom now adorn their respective professions across the globe.

No series such of this could have been without its moments of drama and joy. Three times there came a gentleman from Eastern Europe who spoke no English, had no money, and always insisted on kissing every member of the admin team, male as well as female. Three golden moments were the late Dr Jansen's presentation of flowers at the first meeting in Aberdeen, a small task but done with such dramatic aplomb as held the audience momentarily spellbound; the late David Maddison and Peter Schweifel playing piano duets at Leeuwenhorst,[5] whilst on the

---

[5] As a very young man in Australia David had been a concert pianist before training as a psychiatrist, later becoming Dean of his medical school before succumbing prematurely to a massive heart attack.

dance floor Hezekiah Adesina from Ghana captured the mood as he cavorted to western rhythms in colourful tribal costume; and the inimitable late much lamented Manny Eppel addressing the haggis at Peebles in 1996 in true Glaswegian brogue.

In 1995 the time had come to relinquish the reins, retiring at the same time as Val, my last splendid full-time secretary. I had to find an editorial successor. Although a number of senior Americans and others had expressed interest, the publisher agreed that we should find a suitable British successor if possible. This makes close liaison between editor-in-chief and publisher much easier as well as retaining within Britain the journal's eminence.

Our British editor from the early days had been awarded a CBE and although he too had retired, Sally McIntyre, subsequently to earn an OBE, had been chosen to succeed him in Aberdeen, before taking part of the team with her to Glasgow where she had been offered a chair of medical sociology. Sally accepted the invitation to take over the journal but on condition that she could employ a 'managing editor' to handle all routine affairs, thus inaugurating a position retained and expanded to this day.

Throughout my time at Harvard a principal source of pleasure was the daily visit to the open-air paper stall in the middle of Cambridge Square there to buy the airmail edition of the *The Times*. When this invaluable facility was first mooted it had given rise to considerable debate. Argument was joined by the President of Harvard himself occasioning the immortal headline in a local paper 'HARVARD PRESIDENT FIGHTS ERECTION IN CAMBRIDGE SQUARE'.

One project that never really got off the ground was a book Alan Sheldon and I wanted to write about eccentricity, a notion so alien in North America. Every Tuesday evening for a year we met and took notes on the concept, but fruition escaped us mainly because shortly after my return to the UK an interesting book on the subject had appeared, written by two Edinburgh clinical psychologists. Unfortunately, the issue of eccentricity in art was not covered although Thomas Hess wrote an important introduction to a comparatively neglected subject, inviting

148 • McEwan

analysis from many different angles.[6] All we had to show for our labours was a luncheon I had with an eccentric English aristocrat and a pop article I wrote for a glossy magazine.

During our time in Boston many friends came to visit, Hetty Innes and the late, effervescent Professor Hilde Himmelweit from London among them. One whose stay occasioned subsequent sadness was the publisher, Rex Collings. Rex had been the editor at Oxford University Press who guided my books on African History through to publication. We had become friends and at the time of his visit he had just launched his own one-man publishing firm. A lovely person, keen on wildlife, perceptive and unassuming it was only after his death, in 1996, that I learned so much more about him that had never even been hinted in our chats together. Although I knew that Rex had struck gold with his brave publishing of *Watership Down* it was not until his obituary[7] appeared that I learned that he had stood twice for parliament (winning 16,000 votes in Plymouth), was chairman of the Liberal Party's committee on Africa, a founder member of the Middle East Committee and vice-chairman of the Africa Educational Trust which grants many millions of pounds to deserving students. As Quigley wrote 'his personality was like no-one else's . . . its main characteristic an unswerving integrity that refused to budge. An immensely likeable man, his irony and dryness were salutary, he loved the old virtues, he disliked hypocrisy and liked to puncture the accepted respectabilities and startle the trendies'. The sadness borne upon me was of yet another passsing ship laden with treasures too hidden to be appreciated until the vessel had been lost beneath the restless waves of life.

My chronic disenchantment with the American way of life, the New England climate, and the stiffness in the neck from having it always beamed toward home, persuaded us to return to Britain. This was not without problems, for Dorothy it meant giving up her business and for me deserting the research upon which almost as many dollars has been lavished as would fund

[6] Thomas B Hess (ed) *The Grand Eccentrics; Five centuries of artists outside the main currents of art history*, Art News Annual, xxxii, MacMillan Co. New York, 1966
[7] Isabel Quigley: Obituary, *The Independent*, June 8 1996.

a British University for a year, also Rhod had to leave the school into which he had happily assimilated. Needless to say, our friends and colleagues in American thought we were mad. My place in the research team was taken by Dr Carol Ryser and in 1975 *Retirement; Patterns and Predictions* appeared. Another phase was over.

CHAPTER 7

Home Again!

In research the horizon recedes as we advance..research is always incomplete.

[Mark Pattison]

Mid pleasures and palaces though we may roam,
Be it ever so humble, there's no place like home.

[J.H. Payne]

During our stay in Boston Dadna had died, leaving my distraught mother widowed and alone in Bexhill. I cannot put into words all that I owe to my father, his honesty, his loyalty and above all his balanced wisdom. He was the best and most loved male friend I ever had, the type of man people naturally turned to in moments of trouble and doubt. His passing was another potent reason for returning home.

After a short stay in Cornellan and a welcome bout of cricket, meeting again all one's flannelled friends, we motored overnight south to Lewes to a rented house. It was to be a case of learning the idiosyncrasies of Sussex University and launching the family on an exciting search for a new permanent home in the beautiful East Sussex countryside.

As soon as we came upon Deans Mill outside Lindfield we knew we had found the treasure we had been looking for. To achieve it there were two obstacles. The house was further from the university than was normally allowed, and the asking price was more than three times my annual salary, exceeding the ratio allowed by conventional mortgage companies and we were without sufficient private means to fill the deficit. The first obstacle the University authorities waived on appeal, partly I suspect, because at least one member of faculty lived in the village already. The second problem was resolved almost as quickly when we found a lady broker who managed to obtain a 100% mortgage, with no commission payable to her by ourselves.

Strictly speaking the name is a misnomer for it was the miller's house beside a watermill. Deans Mill had existed from before 1066, having been rebuilt in 1761 and again in 1881. Although when we arrived the mill was still working, when we departed, four years later, economic realities had taken their toll and the mill had become an empty shell. Our cosy half-timbered house, with its oak beams and low ceilings, hidden behind a bank of towering *Gunnera manicata*, the evocative smell of wood smoke pervading all the public rooms, a vinery in the garden beyond a rose-encircled lawn, large and smooth enough for croquet, made an exciting home of which we were justly proud.

Sussex University received its Royal Charter in 1961. It is the only English University located entirely within a designated area of outstanding natural beauty. The buildings, which were still pristinely white and clean, stand at the heart of the campus, designed by Sir Basil Spence. The University prides itself on an innovative teaching style with greater emphasis on ongoing written work than on formal examinations, and with small tutorials rather than large lectures. Although more labour-intensive and therefore expensive, the method has several significant advantages. Teaching is more personal, giving the process of learning increased salience. It identifies the student who, while able to give lip service to a subject, fails to comprehend the underlying meaning, and it is fairer for those students who find immediate recall within the confines of a formal examination room difficult, often knowing the answers but failing to find them under pressure. Underlying this style there is a commitment, particularly in the Arts and Social Sciences, to an interdisciplinary approach, students being expected to study ancillary subjects in addition to their chosen speciality.

My responsibility was to develop the embryo of a Centre for Social Research. Over the next five years, as well as providing a research resource for members of the arts faculty, the Centre developed its own various projects of applied social research, conducted under the direction of an interesting variety of research fellows. John Powles, a brilliant, slightly hesitant Australian medical man, led a team examining possible improvements to the National Health Service, producing a lengthy report and a long list of detailed recommendations last heard of reclining in some Parliamentary pigeon hole. David Richards, a hard working, slightly neurotic, saturnine asthmatic psychologist led a team collaborating with a group from the Department of Health, examining the efficacy of various preventive procedures relating to female health.

David was musically quite knowledgeable, sharing my enthusiasm for making discoveries among lesser known composers. Several winter evenings were spent with him attempting to identify our most recent acquisitions. When unable to identify the composer he was nearly always able to guess the nationality and the period. Chris Bagley had come to academia from journalism with the invaluable facility of shorthand, and was involved in research into migrancy.

The most ambitious programme was a study seeking to demonstrate the predictive value of 'A' levels for university performance, the subject of prolonged public debate which still resonates. The number of intervening variables made the study extremely complex and the volume of data great. My chief assistant in this endeavour was a young Irish Oxford classical scholar, Robin Simmons. As Robin lived with us at the mill until finding suitable accommodation nearer the University our family grew to know him well. Unfortunately, he had one severe problem that I was never able to help him overcome. He was a stubborn perfectionist, resolutely refusing to allow data out of his sight until his analysis was complete. Thus, when the time came for me to leave Sussex, with the project still unfinished, Robin remained sitting on swards of data which he was quietly determined to transport back to Ireland. In spite of many attempts to locate his Irish whereabouts I never heard from him again, all attempts to locate him having failed. I blame myself for failing to apply harsher discipline, but the young man was such a bright, charming but insecure young fellow, I hadn't the heart. Every time debate on the predictive value of school leaving exams and other University entrance techniques are raised in the press, I wince.

Of others just mentioned, John Powles, after returning to Australia for sixteen years, since 1991 has followed a distinguished career at Cambridge, researching topics of broad public health interest in general and the dietary determinants of vascular mortality in particular. Poor David Richards, after becoming a University Dean, died very prematurely when his heart was no longer able to withstand the ravages of bronchial asthma and severe allergies. Chris Bagley migrated to Canada, returned to a professorship in England, eventually retiring after surviving a salacious court case involving child pornography. Adrienne Mead, another member of the team, abandoned academics to open a book shop in Lewes, but after a few years found the going tougher than she had supposed and, having forged links with an elderly francophone, migrated to France.

Academics are on the whole a queer set of people. They pursue whatever their principal professional interest with mental resolve, for the life of the mind is their domain and other pursuits are considered inferior. Judgement of personal merit is based on the amount of published work, assessed by one's peers, hence the modern proliferation of journals. Since most influential people in society are involved in the pursuit of power and/or wealth while the proletariat aim to improve or retain their current status, the few who teach and research inhabit a different universe. This can lead to arrogance and pretentiousness, heightened when the workplace, the lecture theatre, is inhabited by those who, by definition, have less knowledge and can therefore be seen as at least temporarily deficient. Academic life, like golf, is essentially selfish for, apart from the comparatively few gifted members of research teams, academic work is performed alone, reading, writing, teaching, and marking. In his provocative book *The House of Intellect* Jacques Barzun distinguished between intellect and intelligence. 'Intellect', he wrote, 'is mankind's intelligence caught and compounded. Intelligence is the superior in adaptability and scope, but intellect proves itself in steadiness and speed. Intelligence comes first and does painfully and at length what intellect, the second-born, does easily and at once'.

Life in Sussex was very pleasant. We had a lovely home, Dorothy had recovered from the loss of her antique business in Boston and was building an enterprise specialising in the graphic arts. Feona was doing well with her studies at Edinburgh University, Malcolm had also elected to go to Edinburgh, where he was reading psychology and captaining the cricket first XI, and Rhod was enjoying Loretto, especially on the sporting fields. His final year at prep school (Lathallan) had coincided with an outstanding rugby season when their first XV, of which he was skipper, not only won all their games, but did so without having a single point scored against them.

Socially, in addition to university friends, I organised a social bridge group among friends, playing in each other's homes in rotation. The most consistent pair was John Ball, a post-graduate maths student, and his schoolmaster friend Kevin Cobb. Thirty-five years later I decided to see if the internet could tell me what might have happened to these gentlemen. Kevin had become a housemaster at Oundle school; John is now Professor Sir John Ball FRS, Sedleian Professor of Natural Philosophy at Oxford, President of the International Mathematics Union 2003-6.

For most of these Sussex days we enjoyed three family pets, Weaver, an elegant Deerhound from Anastasia Noble's Ardkinglas kennels in Argyll, cuddly Kirsty, a Bearded Collie, and Koko our Burmese cat. Sadly, at the time of the 1972 conference held in Denmark, both dogs had to be kennelled and the day we returned we were told that Weaver had died, having succumbed to bloat. He was our last Deerhound but Kirsty lived on, producing a healthy brood and coming with us to our final two homes, in the second of which she lies buried.

That year Dorothy was exhibiting at the Inverness Antique Fair, which coincided with the start of the university vacation. In the Volvo station wagon was packed, in addition to the four of us,

Kirsty with two of her puppies, our cat, paintings and assorted antiques, among them a Georgian table and, neatly folded inside a tin box, General Gordon's dress uniform. One doubts if a more varied load has ever motored up the A1. At another time Dorothy and I travelled up to Scotland by sleeper with thirty-four paintings, dispersed under the beds, on the racks, in the luggage van and on one of the bunks. The taxi driver who took us to Kings Cross asked if we were moving house.

Later that year Dorothy decided to exhibit at the Perth Antique Fair. After the fair was over, rather than drive home late at night with a carload of paintings and the two dogs that I had brought south rather than leaving them at home or in an alien kennel, we retired to the luxury of an early bed in a Perth hotel. At about eleven o'clock we were no sooner asleep when we were aroused by a loud hammering on the door to be told that our car had been ransacked and that two dogs had been seen running off in the direction of the city. Quickly donning a sweater and trousers I dashed down to the car park to find the rear window smashed by a fire extinguisher, with broken glass strewn everywhere. Kirsty and Xanda, for it was them, soon returned and to our great relief all our valuable paintings remained intact. What appeared to have happened is that some football enthusiasts (St. Johnstone had been playing at home that day) having hurled a fire extinguisher into the boot of the car on their way home, did not expect two large fierce looking dogs to jump out, persuading them to run off as fast as their beer-sodden legs could carry them.

Back at Sussex for the start of a new term in 1968, a pleasing innovation was the introduction of a weekly seminar devoted to the subject of 'love'. This is surely one of the most important and complex human emotions, one which can take many forms yet appears only most rarely in any university syllabus. There are courses in cookery, marketing, woodwork, tourism, but seldom if ever, love. The students who enrolled in the course for the one term it was held, came from a variety of disciplines but mostly from one or other of the natural and social sciences. Because of time constraints the course had to be limited to discussions about the forms of relationships between people which makes sense when used in conjunction with the phrases 'falling in love' or 'being in love with'. Other forms such as the love of God, the love of art, of money, of pets, had to be excluded, but agape (spiritual love) and eros (carnal love) were of course incorporated. Romantics believe, with Sir Walter Scott,

> *Love rules the court, the camp, the grove,*
> *And men below, and saints above;*
> *For love is heaven, and heaven is love.*

Others, like H L Mencken, regard love as merely 'a state of perceptual anaesthesia'. Among my students it was good to have both romantics and cynics represented. Unfortunately, to the best of my knowledge, no one on the staff offered, nor was asked, to take up this unconventional but worthy baton after I left, although it is pleasing to note that a regular course has since been established at another university.

My most enjoyable and important venture at Sussex began when Asa Briggs, the Vice-Chancellor, asked me to establish a liaison group with the medical profession. Asa Briggs, now Lord Briggs, was a remarkable man and an inspiring Vice-Chancellor. In addition to running a new university, still finding its feet as it struggled to cope with pervasive innovation, Asa wrote the definitive history of broadcasting as well as science fiction and being involved with countless committees. Whenever I visited his capacious office the large desk had not a scrap of paper on it, just a gently lit green library lamp, a dictating machine and a blotter, evidence of an orderly mind, a capacity to delegate, and three good secretaries.

The first task was to assemble a small nucleus of medically oriented colleagues. Keith Taylor is a medically qualified bio-chemist and Martin Black was a medical physicist involved in a variety of innovative projects including the design of a new type of heart valve. We brought together a body that became known as the Medical Consultative Group. In addition to the three of us plus Manny Eppel, the Pickwickian avuncular Director of the University's adult education programme, and John Maynard-Smith, an internationally recognised evolutionary biologist, after discrete researching among the local medical fraternity we persuaded seven interesting and contrasting distinguished medical men and women to join the group.

There were seven of them, Mr Reid, a taciturn, precise general surgeon, Dr Williams, a friendly anaesthetist, Sol Jacobsen, a learned, streetwise psychiatrist, Tony Trafford, politically attuned and dynamically astute consultant physician, Joanna Sheldon, a quiet, warm general physician, Bob Gibson-Smith,* an ebullient plump, genial consultant dermatologist, and William Reid[1], a slim, pragmatic pathologist whose delicate dissection of a Dover sole was beautiful to behold.

Various projects and joint hospital/university courses were introduced but the main aim came to be the establishment of a Sussex medical research centre. I first raised the idea of a centre because it seemed clear that any serious relationship between the medical fraternity and the university required a nucleus around which appropriate developments could focus and expand. It was quickly appreciated that the initial challenge, on the outcome of which depended the viability of the enterprise, was money. Many thousands would be needed for the erection of a building and inaugural staffing. The university kindly offered a suitable site but the rest was up to us. Then into our orbit there swam a white knight.

Bill Gannon was an Irish entrepreneur, the part-owner of Business Computers. He lived in nearby Littlehampton and was seriously interested in medical research. More important at this stage was that he got on very well with the group. After meetings with his lawyer he agreed to put up a significant sum provided we could match it from other sources. This led us to examine a wide variety of possibilities. Fund-raising experts were consulted but proved too expensive; the possibility of launching a local football pool led us to Cardiff to meet the man who was successfully organising such an operation in aid of Tenovus, a Welsh charity devoted to cancer research. But without a millionaire to underwrite such a project we felt unable to follow suit.

---

[1] Pseudonyms

Asa Briggs joined us in consultations with a London-based charity who agreed to provide limited support. We decided to make a formal approach to the University's Chancellor, Sir Hartley, later Lord, Shawcross. Sir Hartley, who lived near Ringmer, not far from the campus, had been involved with the University since it's foundation. It was arranged that I should visit the great man in his home, shortly after the tragic death of his wife in a riding accident. Ushered into a small book-lined parlour, a butler proffered an elegant silver coffee pot and tray. I expected to be directed into some magnificent study or drawing room but not a bit of it, Sir Hartley joined me in the parlour. One of the ploys this suave, gracious elderly lawyer proposed was to visit the Marquis of Abergavenny, Earl of Lewes, and sometime Master of the Queen's Horse. The Marquis was Sussex county's most senior figure and, Shawross thought, in addition to having a few spare pennies himself, he might allow his name to appear on the Appeal's stationery as well as pointing us in the direction of other sources of support.

Meeting Sir Hartley's Rolls at the gates, the wily old chap suggested we leave his car out of sight, driving up to the impressive portico instead in my old Volvo, for otherwise Abergavenny might think there was more wealth already at our disposal than was indeed the case. My recollection of the vast interior was of cut flowers on every side and in every corner. The coffee brought us by the Marchioness was impeccably well sugared. Abergavenny, although sympathetic, was unable to offer anything concrete. Later meetings with Shawcross in his palatial room at the rear of the merchant bank where he held court in the City produced more lasting prospects.

One of our ideas was to call upon the help of celebrities with Sussex connections One such person was the tennis player Virginia Wade, a maths graduate of the University. I met the young lady in London where we enjoyed a good lunch at the late lamented Royal Commonwealth Society of which we both happened to be members. Virginia embarrassed me by conversing with our foreign waiter in fluent French, obviously expecting me to follow. Although she had not yet won Wimbledon, she was already well known and agreed to help whenever her busy schedule allowed. But in the end logistic realities made it impossible to call upon her, or any other celebs, for useful promotional support.

When the time came to leave Sussex, a Medical Centre was close to fruition. But unforeseen events had overtaken many of us. By the time the Centre was inaugurated in 1974 I had retired from University life and was living in the Highlands, Keith Taylor had departed to a Chair in Australia, Martin Black was preoccupied building an empire from a Chair in Leeds, Bill Gannon's company had unexpectedly passed into receivership, Joanna Sheldon had died, and Tony Trafford, having been elected an MP and been awarded a life peerage for his work with victims of the Brighton bomb attack, had succumbed to cancer. But, large oaks from tiny acorns grow and the centre we had worked and dined so hard to conceive eventually came to life, christened the Trafford Centre of Medical Education and Research. I believe that at the opening ceremony, of those who had worked so hard for its fulfilment, only my old friends Manny Eppel and John Maynard-Smith were invited, both of them and Martin, alas, now no longer with us. Lord Briggs left the university and returned to Oxford in 1976.

By 1973, with the journal and conferences demanding an increasing amount of time, and thinking how nice it would be to enjoy more private space, to leave academic politics behind, and encouraged by a surprisingly high valuation for the house, we decided to throw another hostage to fortune, leave Sussex and, with the limited capital accruing from the sale of Deans Mill, open a small painting gallery in premises already promised in Braemar by Francie Farquharson, the dynamic American wife of the laird of Invercauld. We took with us, as well as Kirsty and Xanda, our very handsome first German Shepherd, the flourishing journal. Xanda was rather special being litter brother to a Crufts supreme champion. The only reason the breeder had released him to a normal home was that he had two floppy ears which refused to assume their correct erect shape, thus rendering him totally unshow-worthy.

* * * * * * * * *

After an emotional farewell to my staff, other university and extra-mural friends, and to Susan Lewis my dependable, efficient secretary, we returned once again to the Highlands.

Ballochlaggan is a small well-appointed comfortable home, at the time the only inhabited house in Glen Feardar, with magnificent views across to Lochnagar, without a road or any human habitation in sight. With Cornellan now on the market this became our permanent home.

Dorothy opened a small gallery in Braemar, helped by John Inglis, a budding young artist who lived with us over the first summer. The problem was finding secretarial support to deal with the journal and conferences. This was unexpectedly solved by the good fortune of finding Joan Fox and Theresa Watson. By one of those happy conjunctions that can only be found in rural communities, it happened that Theresa, the wife of an atypical gamekeeper on a nearby estate, lived along the same postal run as ourselves. I taped my journal correspondence which was delivered the same morning to Theresa whose work on it would then come back to me per the same postman two days later. I often thought how inexplicably odd it would seem to subscribers in some urban university anywhere in the world if only they knew this procedure for conducting journal business, and could see the unassuming isolated hillside base from which the work emerged.

Joan Fox lived at Abergeldie and the arrangement with her was to exchange tapes and correspondence in a small wooden box on the main road below Crathie Church which thirty years later is still in place, used, I am told, by the local milkman.

My years of editing had seen a revolution in mass-communication and the recording of data. In the very early days records of MSS received were kept in specially printed large multi-columned sheets upon which were recorded the full history of each MS as it passed through the hands of reviewers and then, if accepted, the date sent to the printer and the proposed date of publication and issue number. This very soon became unwieldy as well as making it difficult to monitor the performance of the growing multitude of referees. We perfected a system which saw my time through almost to the end. Each paper was given its own file with its own detailed label, provided by the publisher, which the secretaries had to remember to complete every time a related event needed to be recorded. Files were housed in three separate four-drawer cabinets, one for accepted material, one for the rejects (periodically archived), and two for those still pending. The performance of reviewers had to be continuously monitored and recorded in a separate ledger, although with the gradual increase of material being received it became increasingly difficult to find appropriate new names to invite.

As the conferences were expanding *pari passu*, one secretary had responsibility for processing MSS, leaving her colleague to deal with general journal correspondence (other than processing), filing, and all conference matters.

Eventually, although the era of the email had only just begun to enthral and consume us, the age of the computer arrived. The immediate affect was to lose a first class secretary who felt too old to change her ways. But with the arrival of a computer literate replacement and two state-of-the-art machines the office eventually succumbed, although when the time came shortly afterwards to hand over to my successor we still had many drawers full of written material to pass on.

Looking back on these changes, and the developments of printing which have done away with the need for reams of page proofs, I still feel that some very important personal matters have been lost, the machines have taken over and with them the operators (euphemistically called managing editors) have taken things, in the name of efficiency, one remove further away from personality toward robotism.

* * * * * * * * *

After only eighteen months, the inconvenient isolation worried Dorothy and, with Cornellan almost sold, there was wind of a house where Dorothy had once had tea, coming on the market at the foot of Glengairn, a mile west of Ballater. Unfortunately, our move to Glengarden coincided with the resignation of Theresa's husband who had decided to revert to his original career as a photographer. On her last Saturday morning with me, the first week in our new home, Theresa typed forty-six letters, all without error. That is how good she was.

Our new house, Glengarden, now a listed building, has an interesting history. Built of warm coloured stone and timber, it was designed by the Swiss artist Rudolphe Christen in 1902, modelled in a Swiss manner to remind him of his home village, St Imier, after which he named the house. Sadly, he enjoyed the property for only four years before cancer killed him in 1906. There were no children and his wife survived until 1920, having written a biography of her husband entitled *Rodolphe Christen, The Story of an Artist's Life,* which included several interesting illustrations of the property in its very early days. One of Madame Christen's lasting legacies was the donation of an annual prize, chosen by the children themselves, for the most popular child in the local school. The winner came to the house to be presented with the prize by the grand old dame herself.

After Madame Christen's death in the early 1920s, the property, which includes a small pond and an acre of woodland, was purchased by Colonel Arthur Stewart, recently retired from the 3-10th Baluch Regiment, Indian Army. He was the author of a book *Tiger and other Game,* popular among big game marksmen. As this first appeared in 1927, it must have been written in Glengarden. After his death in 1957, his widow remained here until she too passed away in 1975.

Stewart had bequeathed Glengarden, as it had come to be known, 'garden' being an anglicized version of the adjacent river Gairn, to his wife for her lifetime and, having no children, then to his best friend and cousin, Lord Lyle of Westbourne. But Lyle had himself died and his son, having no desire to live in the Highlands, disposed of the fine Indian artefacts and furniture to Sotheby's before placing the property on the market. The following year the son died which meant that for the second time in fifty years the title had become extinct.

* * * * * * * *

Our first visitors arrived unannounced when we were still sitting on tea chests. Two gentlemen in proverbial raincoats asked to see me. They came quickly to the point. Could I please give them my confidential opinion about two people they believed I knew who were being considered for sensitive positions. John Miller, my successor as senior president of Edinburgh's Student Council and best man at our wedding, was in line for an important business appointment with access to secret defence matters, while one of the younger secretaries in my Centre at Sussex had applied for a position in the Commonwealth Office. Though it was tempting to fabricate a tale with a Marxist tinge about John this would have been a gross and unkind misrepresentation for he is an upright pillar, a solid, reliable 'right of centre' Scotsman of strict principle. But the young lady presented more of a problem as I was aware of her reputation as a chartered libertine. I had to be honest and report that while, to the best of my knowledge (she had never done work for me personally) the applicant was a girl of good professional competence, she was emotionally unstable. John was duly appointed but of the young lady I heard no more.

Further up the glen there lies the tiny church of Glen Gairn. Dedicated to St.Mungo, the church was built after the Disruption of 1843, celebrating its jubilee in 1913. It seats just one hundred souls. Here it was, in this cosy kirk in the heartland of upland Aberdeenshire, that Malcolm and Glynis became man and wife in September, 1983. Glynis is an attractive, down-to-earth young lady from a medical family who the Scots would describe as 'couthy'. She provides Malcolm with the firm sense of direction he sometimes requires. The reception was an intimate, happy occasion held in Glengarden.

The house, now a listed building, is well suited as a gallery, with its large central high-ceilinged room below a minstrel gallery. Being here allowed Dorothy to close the Braemar outlet, concentrating her resources in our new home.

The main challenge we faced was lack of sufficient capital. After several years had passed when it might be said our spurs had been won, we went in search of venture capital. After all, we thought, even the best known galleries in London have backers, whether it be a Rothschild, a Glasgow financier or an ordinary commercial bank. To our mild surprise, we were successful in attracting help from the first merchant bank we approached.

The art business suffers in high capital intensity more than what it gains in low labour intensity. Constantly seeing items we coveted but could not afford was so frustrating that we decided to approach Grossart & Noble, a leading Edinburgh merchant bank. By this time Sir Iain Noble, the nephew of our deerhound friend, Anastasia Noble, had left the bank to become a proselytizing Gaelic speaking landowner on the Isle of Skye, but Angus Grossart having responded positively, we were invited to Edinburgh to discuss possibilities. Angus Grossart is a highly successful art-loving, urbane, tough financial entrepreneur. The proposal involved the gallery being granted a substantial loan for purchasing paintings forming a discrete portfolio. The conditions were severe for we had to pay not only one half of the net profit on every sale but also fixed interest paid quarterly on the existing loan. For a time this worked well, enabling us to add paintings to our stock which we could not have afforded otherwise but after a few years both parties began to lose their enthusiasm. The bank became increasingly dissatisfied with their return while, on our side, the feeling of having a critic and a very demanding one on one's back and constantly leaning over one's shoulder became increasingly irksome. We therefore reached an amicable agreement whereby hands were shaken and the current portfolio of paintings reverted to the bank. Looking back, it had been a useful experience, the higher quality stock had enhanced our reputation in the formative years while the tough negotiations had improved our commercial sophistication.

As the business gradually expanded we made many new acquaintances and a handful of close friends. Three of the latter we especially cherished. Norman Wise was a leading London barrister specialising in planning matters, a devoted man of the hills. After his tramps we spent many delightful hours reviewing the state of the world, receiving his counsel over our business problems, and counselling him over his own familial woes. His languid, mellifluous tones and balanced views were sadly missed when the pig's heart valves he had had to endure eventually wore out. Being no longer able to look forward to his visits and quiet, cultured dinners, was a sad, sad blow.

Mary and Ron Braga and Tim McDowell each suffered tragedies in the early days of our friendship. Mary Braga lost her gracious, unpretentious husband and Tim McDowell lost his lovely, sensitive wife. During the brief time we had enjoyed the privilege of knowing him, Ronald Braga featured in one of the most amusing episodes in the life of the gallery.

It was the day of the opening of our summer exhibition, there was much murmuration around us as Ron asked in confidential tones for the whereabouts of the rest room. On his return he began speaking to me in his silken tones about Thorburn's woodcock paintings, comparing them, so I thought, with those of our gallery artist, James Renny, visible in the gallery above us. I ventured the opinion that there was indeed an interesting difference in their work, especially in their treatment of woodcocks. 'No', he said, rather quietly, 'I was trying to tell you that your ball cock needs attention.'

Mary is one of life's enhancers, brave in the face of all kinds of adversity, a person of piercing perceptivity, quiet, benevolent and informed, warm in her concern for others, with an overall enthusiasm for art and life in general. Now in her mid-eighties, badly arthritic and surviving a stroke she still crosses the Atlantic to stay in her Scottish home at least once a year and seldom misses a visit to a major art exhibition in New York, London or Edinburgh. A captivating, wise and wonderful life-enhancing lady.

Each August the Gallery holds what we call our annual exhibition, with a private view, to which are invited our best clients plus a smattering of local worthies who Dorothy would find it embarrassing to exclude. One one such day we were told the American Ambassador might be coming. It seemed he was surveying the route for a walking tour he was planning from John O'Groats to Land's End and, if he did come, we were asked to keep his visit low key and confidential. At about a quarter to five, when only a few remnants were still with us, the Ambassador arrived in an open-necked shirt, khaki shorts and walking shoes.

Our neighbour and friend the late Scott Sheret had grown rather deaf and prone to grasping the wrong end of any stick that came his way. Not having heard the request for reticence, Scott rushed up to the Ambassador, tail wagging profusely, 'Ah', he stammered, 'it is so nice to meet you High Commissioner (Scott had mis-heard and thought our visitor represented Australia) I have a cousin in Wollagong, a place I'm sure you must know'. Before we could whisper the error of his ways, Scott dashed next door to find his atlas to confirm the precise position of Wollagong. But before his return, the atlas duly found and carried under his deferential arm, the Ambassador had seen the red light and had quickly and quietly withdrawn.

Tim MacDowell is a wise man of the world, a former chairman of *The Irish Times*, with a wide compass of friends and acquaintances, a gentleman who shares my outlook on many things. When the time came to retire from the editorship of *Social Science and Medicine* it was Tim who gave me more than invaluable advice, he introduced me to the inimitable, great Lord Goodman. Thus it was that in negotiations with the publisher to agree appropriate departure arrangements, I became Lord Goodman's last case. Bearing in mind that the publication I had founded had been a substantial commercial success, netting many tens of thousands of pounds for the company annually, and that years had been spent without remuneration beyond working expenses, he was horrified by the story, fighting my corner while refusing any financial reward. In spite of his seriously ailing health, confined in his living room to a large upright chair reminiscent of Jeremy Bentham, he pursued the cause with extraordinary vigour and for that, as well as for Tim's advice, I shall always be deeply grateful. Anyone reading Lord Goodman's biography will know that throughout his long life he fought worthy causes without thought of publicity or recompense. A truly great man, a noble champion of the arts and underdog the like of which it is unlikely we shall ever see again.

A couple of vignettes we found amusing were provided by the gentleman who asked if he might use our toilet. Minutes later he reappeared, rejoicing, 'Argh, that was good', and promptly left. Then there was the visitor who asked the name of the larger of our two German Shepherds, 'Bisket', we told him. This caused him much merriment so Dorothy asked the man what his German Shepherd was called, 'Chloe', said the man.

* * * * * * * * *

In 1980, after suffering a painless but mentally precarious old age, mother died. She had spent all her long adult life in perpetual fear of cancer but died of natural causes when her frail body finally gave up. She was a wonderfully warm-hearted, caring mother and if at times I found her excitable temperament difficult, I will always cherish her affection and be for ever grateful for everything she did for me and the quality of integrity she sought to instil.

* * * * * * * * *

The procedures involved in successfully acquiring a painting for stock have been described in detail by Malcolm Innes in his privately printed autobiography *Going North, Going Orff.* Our visitors are unlikely to be aware, or even to give a thought, to the expense of effort and time involved in purchasing every item they see on the wall. The painting will have been noted in a catalogue, subscriptions for which now cost hundreds of pounds, then it will have been viewed, in most cases involving a journey of over a hundred miles, then bid for at the sale, brought home, by a carrier if large, taken to the restorer for a clean and attention to the frame (or having to find an appropriate replacement), returned to the gallery and hung in the most suitable place. When sold, the VAT has to be accounted for and quite often the buyer will want a change of frame before arranging delivery via a specialised carrier. And, of course, there are the many items bid for unsuccessfully as well as those that have been purchased but remain unsold.

It is a tough old game, made tougher in recent years by the increasingly aggressive activities of the major auction houses. One of the most intense frustrations that can assail an art dealer is when, as happens with increasing frequency, he watches the work of an artist fetch more in the frenzied heat of an auction than an often better example by the same artist in his gallery is available at two-thirds of the price. This raises the question: why buy from a dealer ? The answers are (a) there is the legal guarantee that anything found to be incorrectly described within six years of purchase can be refunded, (b) an honest gallery specialising in an artist's work is better able to advise on relative quality, a fact well understood by those seeking to build a significant collection, and (c) the establishment of a good rapport with a gallery . The principal manipulators of market prices, especially for the lesser expensive works, are the auctioneers who provide 'estimates' which, although given little heed by the trade, strongly influence private buyers.

Kind people sometimes say how they admire what they see, recalling the comment of that great dealer of a past age, the late Bernard Berenson who, when someone admired what they were viewing in his gallery said 'But these, sir, are my failures', meaning, of course, that the successes had already all been sold.

Experiencing the machinations of the art world is a fascinating exercise involving the need to tread warily between cynicism and enthusiasm. One learns very quickly that there is little relationship between quality and financial worth. Market forces are dominated by wealth, often involving neither taste nor aesthetic appreciation. Furthermore, what hangs on the gallery wall is not necessarily a reflection of the owners' personal choice since the demand of a gallery's clientele is unlikely to coincide with the owner's taste and the clientele may be quite localised, especially in a rural environment. A recent example emphasised the point. For more than a year we had on our wall a good example of an important artist's work at a very reasonable price. Having failed to find a buyer after a considerable time, we placed it in an Edinburgh auction where it fetched a little more than we had been asking, purchased by an urban Scottish gallery who doubled the price and sold it within a month. Similarly, I have no doubt that because of the differences in local demand, some of that gallery's old stock would do well with us.

The most gratifying activities are selling good works to knowledgeable buyers and encouraging contemporary artists. The highlight of the first occurred in 1984. On one of her visits to Sotheby's, Dorothy became excited by the portrait of a young boy which she proceeded to buy for £66,000. She was confident it was a genuine work by the great English portraitist Thomas Gainsborough, but this was an opinion shared by neither Sotheby's nor, when on a visit to Balmoral, the Keeper of the Queen's Pictures, nor other leading art critics of the time, including one who publicly expressed his scepticism in London's *Evening Standard*. After the sale several dealers came up to tell her she had 'bought a wrong painting'. However, further research revealed that this was indeed one half of probably the first formal portrait painted by Gainsborough when he was no more than eighteen years old. On this basis we sold it for a very modest profit to the Gainsborough House Museum in the artist's birthplace at Sudbury in Suffolk.

A few years later the portrait of a young girl appeared at Sotheby's, attributed to the minor artist George Beare, having been consigned for sale from the trustees of an Edinburgh estate. The London art dealer Philip Mold, a specialist in early portraits, recognised it as the missing half of the Gainsborough we had sold. He purchased it for £4,400, selling it almost immediately to the museum where she is now re-united with her young brother. X-rays and texture analysis confirmed that the two portraits were indeed originally part of the same single work.

In his book *Sleepers*,[2] Mold features the portrait with a coloured plate within the text, replicated on the dust jacket, but, doubtless to preserve the reputation of the London art trade, our gallery was not given a mention. The text stated incorrectly that the boy had been 'bought at Christies' by the Gainsborough Museum. Our part of the story was subsequently covered more accurately in a *Sunday Times* colour supplement.

For eleven years, valuably assisted by Vivien Macmillan, I had been working on a comprehensive dictionary of Scottish artists. When the first edition was exhausted the publisher (The Antique Collectors Club) wanted to re-issue it without change. As there were revisions we needed to make, mainly to include

[2] Philip Mold, *Sleepers. In Search of Lost Old Masters*, Fourth Estate, London 1995

some contemporary artists missing from the first edition, but also to include a bibliography inadvertently missing from the first, we bought back the rights so that, with Vivien's renewed help, a second edition was produced, including over 11,000 entries, printed in Hong Kong and published by Rhod's burgeoning publishing house, The Glengarden Press. I like to believe that this will remain the definitive reference work for many years to come. An archive is being built up to include references to artists who have come to prominence, or have died, since publication.

One day in 1975, when the gallery was still very young, we had a visit from a wildlife artist whose work we considered remarkable. James Renny was born in Sri Lanka but moved to Zimbabwe in 1951. After graduating in Fine Art studies from the University of Witwatersrand he returned to Zimbabwe, living rough in the African bundu (bush), studying wildlife under the tutelage of an elderly African tracker. His attention to detail combined with fine draughtsmanship is breathtaking. We persuaded him to work toward an exhibition depicting the wildlife of the Scottish Highlands and in 1980 the Duke of Edinburgh paid us the honour of opening the one-man exhibition in our gallery. Within the first few days every picture was sold, purchasers including several members of the royal family. We were all so encouraged by this success that it was agreed to take James' second exhibition to London. The artist's second show was mounted in 1986, and was a great success with everything sold on the opening day, Sir Peter Scott among the buyers.

By 1974, with the gallery flourishing elsewhere in our home, the journal, which was now appearing every second week, and the conference series, both continued, two full-time secretaries helping me to cope. All this made our home an extremely busy place, with little inclination or time for any other activities. With a dozen ornamental waterfowl in the pond, two German Shepherd dogs and a Russian Blue cat, plus a social bridge group and a golf society to help organise, life was as full as it had ever been. Indeed, it always seemed odd that whereas at Ardachie, when Dorothy and I were in our early thirties, an hour was always reserved after lunch for reading, in our seventies such pleasure seemed an unthinkable luxury.

At the tea break one afternoon I mentioned Ardachie to Val. "Good heavens'" she said, "my uncle was the gamekeeper at Ardachie with Colonel Campbell." It gave us a memory in common for she knew Fort Augustus and some of our old retainers there, including Tom Campbell who had taught Dorothy to drive all those years ago.

A sentimental visit, albeit a brief one, brightened the summer of 2000. Nobby Clarke, of Ardachie days, had emigrated to Canada, joined the army, married and raised two attractive daughters. Before Nobby died he had mentioned to his family that the most beautiful place he knew was the bridge over the Tarff at Ardachie, beside the old keeper's cottage above Fort Augustus. His wife and daughters came on a pilgrimage to scatter Nobby's ashes beneath the bridge, a sentimental operation kindly assisted by Brian and Ann Steptoe, who were then living in the recently modernised keeper's cottage.

Together they erected a stone memorial plaque above the bank. This was a moving event for all of us, uniting in memory our two families across the years but separated for so long by the passage of time and the broad Atlantic. A feeling of great warmth was engendered by the knowledge that Nobby was a man who shared my love for Ardachie, a love so respected by his family whom we were delighted to have had the pleasure of meeting.

A source of considerable pleasure in the 1980s was that on one day every winter weekend, regardless of the weather, an old friend and retired teacher, Scott Sheret joined me and the dogs to explore the many hills and glens around our home. Every walk we followed a different route, never repeated, in conditions that were always varied. Our partnership was a good one because, apart from sharing the pleasure of hill walking, Scott was safe on icey slopers but had no sense of direction while I was a competent path finder but have no head for heights. Another feature of these mini-expeditions illustrated how different people are naturally attracted to different aspects of the environment. Scott was always fascinated by the different rocks and stones along the way, while another walking companion, an artist, was most attracted to the ever-changing cloud formations, another friend kept a wary eye for bird and animal droppings, another to whatever historical incidents and stories may have occurred from battles, cairns and caves to the routes and campsites of the old cattle drovers.

Occasionally, frivolity reared its cheery head, especially at Christmastime. Over a number of years the two boys and I joined four friends to play Diplomacy, a good war game invented at Harvard, when all the players wear the costume appropriate to the country they play. One year a party visiting the gallery through the snow were taken aback when, gazing through the window, they saw a figure like Napoleon in a tri-cornered hat, while another man appeared to be wearing a Turkish costume, brandishing a scimitar. The game lasts an entire day and was always greatly enjoyed except for the facts that it gave Dorothy a lot of work preparing the food, and the same person (Rhod) always won. Sadly, all good things have an ending and the sequence was broken when one of our number (Napoleon in the year just mentioned) died and two others no longer came north for Christmas.

One memorable autumn evening we were invited to dine with Algy Cluff and his current *amoretto* in his capacious Scottish country house near Huntly. During the meal I felt an occasional mild disturbance beneath the table, but thought nothing more about it until we retired to the library for a cigar and glass of port. Seated before the comfort of a roaring log fire my attention was drawn to the left leg of my suit. There was not only slobber all down the leg but a large hole had appeared around my left shin. It seemed that while we had been changing the world the dog had spent the meal chewing my lounge suit. Algy was suitably apologetic offering to pay for a replacement. I muttered that it was nothing really, I knew a very good local tailor who would be able to undertake the necessary repair. "Yes," Algy replied in his slightly haughty way, "I hear he is very good with the garments of game-keepers." I was suitably humbled. As the years have passed Algy and I have become good friends although, now that he has sold his Scottish base, opportunities for our meeting have declined. Since that dinner Algy has acquired a lovely, highly intelligent West Indian wife and produced three super children. He is unique among my friends and acquaintances in that his competence on the golf course equals my own.

Shortly after our arrival at Glengarden a few of our friends came together for occasional rounds of golf on both the matchless beauty of the Braemar course and the slightly more conventional holes at Aboyne. This led to an annual match between four of our party from Aboyne, genial martinet Major Ian Preston, John Berger, an anglicised American photographer with a lush red beard in the manner of George Bernard Shaw, convivial Mike O'Connor who had taken early retirement from his family business in order to enjoy life more fully, and diminutive Major Tough who was now a self-employed picture framer. The four from Ballater were Malcolm, Rhod, Brian Macpherson, our affable village postie, and myself. When travel, both temporary and permanent, led to replacements having to be found, the group gradually expanded until, in 1992, at the group's annual Christmas gathering, it was decided to formalise ourselves into the West Aberdeenshire Golfing Society, with a carefully constructed Constitution, a Magister and Secundus, annually elected, and a Scrivener and Bursarius elected *sine die.*

There were nineteen founder members and now, in 2008, there are forty-two. The transition from a small group of friends to a larger assembly, intended to make events easier to manage, has had the opposite effect. Whereas in its early days, the intimacy of friendship ensured participation, the cooler sentiment of acquaintanceship has diluted enthusiasm so that it has become more difficult to raise a team from forty than it was from eight.

The general level of performance, with a few significant exceptions, may be illustrated by one of our number, who when playing the old 14th hole at Aboyne, had his opening drive hit a large boulder directly in front of the tee, ricocheting back over his head, ending up out of bounds in a gorse bush.

There was also a more subtle influence at work. In the beginning, in 1986, the first competition was an internecine struggle between the men of Wester Aboyne and their neighbours from

Glengairn. This entered the world as the Hacker Cup, donated by the pseudonymous Sir John and Lady Hacker in memory, it is said, of their son Algernon, last seen disappearing down a rabbit warren adjacent to the 18th green at Braemar, searching for a driven golf ball. To the citation was added, as a prolegomenon, paraphrasing the late H.N.Wethered, 'the true-minded Hacker reaps his reward, he is the gentlest of all in the matter of prowess and, equally it is hoped, in his language and demeanour. He has few opportunities for inflicting pain on his fellow creatures because, owing to his technical defects, he has the least likelihood of being a conqueror. To those who dislike being beaten – and their name is legion – the hacker will be a genial benefactor, supporting their good opinion of themselves and encouraging their sense of wellbeing by placing them in harmony with their surroundings and indirectly, as in duty bound, assisting towards their spiritual refreshment. The hacker is, or ought to be, the happiest man on the links'.

The two days of the Hacker Cup are followed by a dinner. This throws up a difference between the two components of the Society, the members from Aboyne and those from Ballater. Whereas the former usually produce more of their members for dinner than for golf, the latter prefer golf to dining. Why, we often ask ourselves, should this be so – is it chance or is there a more subtle reason ?

Aboyne and Ballater are contiguous communities, but with clearly recognisable differences. Aboyne boasts a castle, wherein dwells the Marquis of Huntly, a cottage hospital, a community centre, a secondary school, supports a highly skilled dramatic society, a well supported music society, a rugby club, and a golf club. Their annual highland games are followed by a Ball, supported by a local landowner who is also the local councillor. Many of the houses are comparatively large, having been built by old money, with many of the current owners members of the angling/shooting set.

Ballater carries many more shops, no fewer than seventeen of them displaying a royal warrant (Windsor comes next with eleven), better hostelries, a golf club supported mainly by artisans, a good primary school, an absentee laird, Alwyn Farquharson, (though the Duke of Rothesay and Billy Connolly occasionally do a little shopping), it is a popular base for bus parties, and the houses are generally more modest than those in Aboyne, with a plethora of relatively small new properties, catering for the retired elderly.

These differences are inevitably reflected in the activities and attitudes of their respective inhabitants. The roles which humans enact are determined by the primary social institution into which they were born, our perceptions, our motives, our self-image. The experience of self is crucial, being basically reflected from our local peers to whose approbation and criticism we pay close attention. Thus Aboyne is a comparatively socially cohesive community, given to house parties and dinners, its citizens assuming a confident, slightly superior image of themselves and their environment. Ballater, on the other hand, produces a generality of less confident, slightly sardonic self-images, the village striving for improvement and popularity rather than quietly relishing its good fortune. Retired majors prefer Aboyne, retired segeant-majors choose Ballater.

Hence, in our golfing society, encompassing both communities, those of our number from Aboyne indulge in the camaraderie around the dinner table as much as on the golf course, while most of those in the Ballater team feel less comfortable dining together, preferring the less personal interaction involved in playing the game.

Allow me, dear reader, the indulgence of mentioning two achievements, both at Braemar which, although I say it myself, would be hard to equal, both having been suitably recorded in the annals of a golf magazine. Some years ago when snow lay in the glens and the greens were hard as rocks , I putted out of bounds. As the little mite sped across the frosted turf and disappeared beneath the frozen river that lay silently in wait beyond, a decision was born that as quickly became resolve. I would forsake the game for ever (or at least until the spring) and turn instead to my books.

This raised the question: why do we browse, collect, read and generally delight in bibliomania, and why particularly in the literature of the sport called golf ? Maybe it is for instruction – 'if all else fails read the instructions' – or we may seek entertainment, to enjoy the thought without being disappointed by the deed; perhaps it is for amusement, to savour the riches enshrined in the funny things of life; or we may find vicarious pleasure, rejoicing a touch when reading of the minister smilingly bestriding the final fairway 4 down, or castigating the deftness of a loser as he fluffs the final chip.

Conceivably, it is knowledge we pursue, by absorbing the history and traditions of the game enjoyment is heightened and wisdom born – vision, after all, depends on the ability to interpret what is seen; again, we may just love the feel and smell and touch of well- bound paper, the craft and art that goes into the making of a good book, the consummate thrill of identifying first editions, locating hidden bargains and unearthing unsuspected titles; a few of us, if we are honest, collect because that is our obsession, to find, record, possess and ever wallow in unending search. Another thought assails me. Some of us may nourish a secret interest in finance, reasoning to ourselves (and maybe to our spouses and bank managers as well) that every pound spent on literature is actually an investment, a hedge against inflation or the need for a latterday pension. For, when all is said and done, as the saloon keeper in northwest United States said during a prolonged blizzard, 'cheer up boys, whatever happens to the cattle, the books won't freeze' – unlike that green of mine all those years ago!

At the turn of the year, after the bells have chimed and the family is suitably fortified, and another log put on the fire, we play Winston Churchill's favourite parlour game. The usual form of the game is to invite the assembled company to produce correct definitions for unusual words and, when unknown, to invent a plausible definition. When the responses are read back, a point is scored for giving the correct answer and a point is also awarded the author of the definition most frequently chosen as being correct. We add to the flavour and richness of the fun by using only words with an amusing or unlikely meaning and by inviting definitions that, as well as being feasible, perhaps incorporating spurious derivations, carry a *double entendre* or are otherwise (we hope) hilarious. Examples might include 'pyknic' (a person with a thick neck, large abdomen and short legs), 'oda' (a room in a harem, so that an harem could be described as a place of many odas), 'pledget' (a small piece of fluff such as collects in the navel), 'sedeful' (virtuous), 'pilgarlic' (bald), 'cacoethes' (an itch to do something foolish). When one reflects that a well-educated person in Britain has a vocabulary of less than 14% of the English lexicon, one can appreciate the array of opportunity.[3]

* * * * * * * * *

Eventually, in 1996, with the conferences relinquished[4] and the journal secure in other hands, my last full time secretary, Val Farrelly and I both retired, her age and better judgement coinciding with my own decision. The self-effacing Val was one of the many full time secretarial treasures with whom I had been so luckily endowed, the last in a long line.

With all the children in place, life now became more measured. Feona, the high flier among us, is a workaholic, Director of Communications with WPP, the second largest marketing agency in the world; Malcolm was the long-suffering Director of Social Work in East Lothian until being uprooted by some unpleasant political machinations in 2007; Rhod has a number of irons in the fire, as well as being a partner in the gallery, having established himself as one of the leading golf book dealers worldwide and currently in the process of diversification.

The onset of the ageing process, once it becomes seriously tangible, does have some advantages. As one mellows, the

---

[3] It has been estimated that by April 2009 the English language will total one million words; at present the average Britisher uses less than 14,000 words, while a linguistically sophisticated person uses about 70,000. So the room for improvement is huge!

[4] One more conference was held in Turkey before the major foundations then withdrew their support and this, combined with the comparative disinterest of any of my successors, brought the series to a close. This seemed to me very disappointing, it is now twelve years since the last meeting and I still receive enquiries from people who profited from the series and want to know if and/or when it might be resuming.

pinpricks of life, the minor disappointments, become more easily tolerated while life's pleasures are no longer taken for granted. The shooting man stops shooting and supports the World Wildlife Fund, the doctor who spent years developing pathogens becomes a heart surgeon,[5] the poacher becomes a gamekeeper, the artful dodger becomes a charity worker. When we are young our life and the lives of other creatures around us are almost taken for granted, an unending and unthinking experience of 'being', but when the shadow of the old reaper begins to descend the preciousness of life, and the lives of others, is thrown into a sharper and more realistic relief. For as long as one has reasonable health there should always be a challenge ahead. I have noticed among friends that those most likely to survive are the ones with interests beyond their working preoccupations.

---

[5] A classic example is Dr Wouter Basson, an expert in the development of deadly germs, once described in the South African papers as 'Doctor Death', who later became a cardiologist saving lives in the Western Cape.

CHAPTER 8

An Excursus

The lost rootless masses of modern society: the restless, unhappy deification of earthly things that besets and distracts the modern world: the hysterical nationalisms; the idolising of leaders; the fanatic ideologies; the piddling love of gadgetry; the cults of violence . . . all the work of a philosophy of history which denies the existence of eternal truths.

[Jacques Maritain]

We are living in a demented world.

[Johan Huizinga]

Very few people realise how mad the world is today; it is only those standing a distance away from the confusing pattern of daily events who can see to what an extraordinary extent the present generation suffers from unreason.

[Abel J Jones]

In the mountains of truth walking is never in vain.

[Nietsche]

Higher criticism is the record of one's own soul, the only civilised form of autobiography, as it deals not with the events, but with the thoughts of one's life; not with life's physical accidents of deed or circumstance but with the spiritual moods and imaginative passions of the mind.

[Gilbert. The Critic as Artist]

Ideas have always held a strong fascination, none more than those associated with religion in general and the condition of man in particular, and in the crucial relationship between knowledge and action, an abiding theme that has not perhaps been too apparent in previous pages.

In a necessarily brief resumé of where, after seven decades, this has led me, thoughts can first be illuminated by the beacon lit by John Stuart Mill. In his autobiography[1] he wrote 'the practical reformer has continually to demand that changes be made in things which are supported by powerful and widely spread feelings, or to question the apparent necessity and indefeasibleness of established facts; and it is often an indispensable part of his argument to show how these powerful feelings had their origin, and how those facts came to seem necessary and indefeasible. There is therefore a natural hostility between him and the philosophy which discourages the explanation of feelings and moral facts by circumstances and association, and prefers to treat them as ultimate elements of human nature; a philosophy which is addicted to holding up favourite doctrines as intuitive truths, and deems intuition to be the voice of nature and of God, speaking with an authority higher than that of reason.'

If we set aside for a moment philosophical debate and our baggage of ideological preconceptions and ponder the world, we find on the one hand unmitigated evil among mankind, pain and injustice endemic throughout the natural world, and a solar system containing untold numbers of barren planets and other celestial bodies. On the other hand, there are the imponderables of beauty, truth and goodness, the mysteries of creation – most especially the mystery of mind. Analysing our perception of these phenomena, whether considered good, bad or neutral, there is the fact that human beings live on only three dimensions, those of space and time, irrespective of how these may be co-ordinated in modern physics. Now it is quite possible that there may be other dimensions 'out there' about which our perceptual apparatus can know nothing. For a seeker after truth this makes

---

[1]   p192.

any absolute belief such as atheism untenable. Mortals, who deny the validity of authority such as offered by some religions, can only reach a judgement upon what is experienced either directly or indirectly.

The creed of rationalism is flawed because it finds no room for intuition and the coruscating human spirit. We must beware of the arrogance of certainty, the abomination of fanaticism, the intellectual aridity of unthinking conformity.

The evils and apparent barrenness of much of the universe renders belief in a God Almighty most improbable, but this has to be balanced against the reality of goodness and spirituality. The Christian Church, for example, while we may reject its dogma, nevertheless plays an important role in tending the spirituality of man. But the notion of a God answers fewer questions than it asks. If we are persuaded to believe in some transcendent unknowable power then, it seems to me, we have also to recognise the influence of a force equally powerful but malevolent. The idea of a dualism between the powers of darkness and light has been around for centuries. It first reached prominence in the third century when taught by the Persian philosopher Manes, although the Manicheismic explanation that evil resides in matter with a divine central light that could be released by religion, for modern minds carries matters a step too far. We may not find the idea of a dualism attractive but this does not impair its validity.

In a recent book, former Bishop Holloway discusses in detail the evil of man and, although no longer a bishop of the church, considers religious belief a form of art, important in the understanding of life with all its pleasures and disasters, its goodness and its evil.[2] This approach, by ignoring the evils which are outwith the power of man, of which natural disasters are the prime example, allows the author to introduce free will and the eye of sympathy as the salvation of the good. The belief that religion of one sort or another can be a main armament in the conquest of evil fails to take into account the terrible history of the

---

[2]   Richard Holloway: *Between the Monster and the Saint*, Canongate, Edinburgh 2008.

world's religions as promoters of war, terror, torture, divisiveness, and intolerance of every kind. To regard religion as essentially a man made art form whose purpose is not to reach toward truth but to help cultivate understanding of what can be pragmatically understood, seems to me a purely academic exercise, unlikely to capture popular imagination or sympathy.

There is also the probability we should recognise that human nature is fundamentally flawed so that no amount of 'good' religion, wise philosophy or enlightened government can ever do more than paper over the cracks. Because of this worm at the heart of the human apple, greed and power can never be wholly conquered, only their affects ameliorated. The Czech writer Milan Kundera, speaking of goodness, struck a vital nail upon the head. 'True human goodness,' he wrote, 'can manifest itself, in all its purity and liberty, only in regard to those who have no power. The true moral test of humanity (the most radical, situated on a level so profound that it escapes our notice) lies in its relation to those who are at its mercy: the animals. And it is here that exists the fundamental failing of man, so fundamental that all others follow from it'.[3]

The question of design has been prominent in theological debate. But if we are to believe in a single intelligent force behind the Universe there is absolutely no good reason for regarding it as a force for good. We may not go as far as Russell who thought the evidence suggested the designer would have to be a fiend, but either we return to a dualist explanation, a divinely good force and a satanically evil one, or, if we insist on a single source, then the implication, far from confirming Christian belief in a good God, would be extremely chilling. Some argue that it is possible to experience directly the 'holy', an experience of sacredness that is *sui generis* a direct recognition like that of beauty which transcends the notion of dualism or doubt. Dr Otto in *The Idea of the Holy* maintains that direct experience of the holy in events, persons, things and thoughts are not only the origin of religious

---

[3] Quoted by Mark Rowlands in his entrancing, provocative book, *The Philosopher and the Wolf*, Granta Publications, London 2008, p.101.

feelings and beliefs among primitive peoples, but are the kernel of all that is of value in modern Christianity. To substitute a rational morality is to rob religious experience of its central core. But this feeling, and the supernatural power allegedly behind it, is not necessarily good. It may lead to action that those lacking such enlightenment would regard as evil. Thus, if it signifies anything, direct religious experience is but a vehicle that may be driven by the forces of darkness as well as those of light, irrespective of the fact that the experience will always be seen as righteous or sacrosanct by the subject him/her self. As C.J. Squire wrote, regarding the practice and power of prayer:

> To God the embattled nations sing and shout:
> 'Gott Strafe England' and 'God Save the King',
> 'God this, God that and God the other thing'.
> 'Good God', said God, 'I've got my work cut out.'

Many contend that leaving the search for truth on one side, civilisation is the better for Christian teaching and that when this is denied or neglected all kinds of evil and unpleasant consequences follow. Society becomes alienated without the lynchpin of Christian morality. Disregarding the inhuman and cruel notion of hell which is such a feature of Christian teaching,[4] a dispassionate view of Christ's character and moral injunctions reveal significant inconsistencies and a notion of justice that far from transcending his age, incorporated many of its features. There was a vindictive attitude to those who dissented from his teaching, not unusual among preachers, 'Ye serpents, ye generation of vipers, how can you escape the damnation of hell?'

The hell-fire punishment for sin is both cruel and irrational. Why were devils put into the Gadarene swine so that they ran into the sea? An omnipotent and good God would not have tolerated such behaviour. Similarly, how does one explain the fruitless fig tree 'He was hungry; and seeing a fig tree afar off having leaves, He came asking if haply He might find anything thereon; and

---

[4] 'Then shall he say also unto them on the left hand, Depart from me, ye cursed, into everlasting fire, prepared for the Devil and his angels. And these shall go away into everlasting punishment; but the righteous into life eternal'.

when He came to it He found nothing but leaves, for the time of figs was not yet. And Jesus answered and said unto it: "No man eat fruit of thee hereafter forever" '. Is this response not irrational and short-tempered ? Again, to take no thought for the morrow (Matthew ch.6, v.34) is hardly a percipient injunction.

In any case, the main tenets of Christian teaching have never been generally observed either by individuals or cultures. The edict 'Judge not lest ye be judged' is universally ignored. Another edict to 'resist not evil, but whosoever shall smite ye on the right cheek, turn to him the other also' is seldom observed so contrary is it to human nature. While this sentiment pre-dates Jesus by five or six hundred years it still fails to be observed. We are adjured to 'sell what thou hast and give to the poor', a fine maxim but one seldom followed.

A further reason to controvert much religious teaching has always seemed to me its conservative nature. Bertrand Russell put this succinctly; 'You find as you look around the world that every single bit of progress in humane feeling, every improvement in the criminal law, every step toward the diminution of war, every step toward better treatment of the coloured races, every moral progress that there has been in the world, has been consistently opposed by the organised churches of the world'.[5]

There is of course no denying that belief provides a great salve in times of misery and distress, as well as being a source of profound inspiration in artistic endeavour, but these facts are irrelevant to its truth. Sadly, human nature and social forces exert an influence that transcends religious belief. The cruelties of the Inquisition and the horrors of the holocaust were equally vile, one dominated by religious dogma, the other by irreligious fanaticism. As CP Snow reminded us, 'there have been many crimes committed in the name of duty and obedience – many more than in the name of dissent'.

Man needs a basis for the moral imperatives which influence if they do not always control or determine his actions. Moral rules

---

[5] Bertrand Russell, *Why I am not a Christian*, George Allen & Unwin Ltd, London, 1957, p15.

may be based on a religious creed or based upon what some have called social utility. Those based on authority may be conscious, embarking on a *jihad* or crusade, or maybe merely habitual as when, declining to practise birth control, marriage is preferred to cohabitation. But moral rules do not necessarily require authority or social utility, they can be based on self-evident premises not involving faith.

In my lifetime there has been a dissatisfaction among moral philosophers that because the traditional heuristic moral problem had been attempts to resolve the basis of obligation, the reason why I should do the actions which hitherto I had thought I ought to do, an insoluble anomaly had arisen. For the answer was always either that when I apprehend the facts I realise that by pursuing certain lines of conduct I was prompting my own advantage, which leaves one unenlightened as to why I ought to do anything which I did not want to do, or alternatively, that something that is perceived to be good would be realised in or by the action, equally unsatisfactory for what makes the act intrinsically good, is not its having a particular origin but its motive which cannot be included in our duty. Ought, said Kant, implies can, and a moral act can come only from conscious motives; if the motive is not there we cannot produce the act. Alternatively, if the sense of obligation is resolved into the sense of what is conducive to a good which is not itself an action, if it purports to explain the obligation and not merely explain it away, it must invest the idea of the good with autonomous authority, namely that what is good ought to be. But this has an implication which must be unsound since 'ought' can only refer to actions. In other words, the anomaly is that we either deduce what is right or we postulate an intuitive judgement 'this is right'. If we accept intuitionism the difficulty is overcome but if intuition is rejected we have still to face it.

In the western world there is an underlying presupposition that permeates much of moral philosophy. The world is attributed a meaning which allowed ethics to conceive the aims of mankind and of individual men and women as having a meaning within it. Its view of life is a conclusion derived from its view of the world. If we accept the world as it is in which the aims and objects of mankind and of individual men have a meaning also, this approach has dangers. As Albert Schweitzer reminded us, we can discover nothing of any purposive evolution in which our activities can acquire a meaning. The only advance in knowledge that is open to us is to describe ever more perfectly the events which make up the world. To apprehend the meaning of the whole is impossible. The last fact which knowledge can discover is that the world is a manifestation, in every way puzzling, of the universal will to live. Our view of the world must be a product of our view of life, not the other way round.

My preliminary attitude of mind which prompts the consequent chain of reasoning is that life requires discipline and rules, but that the thoughts which underlie and determine the discipline and the rules must in the last resort be extracted from life.

What is the most obvious fact in our world upon which we might base a theory of right and wrong in conduct ? This seems to me to be the universal will-to-live. The will-to-live always seems desirable and valuable, making its promotion and pursuit a reasonable moral end, an end which is neither pleasure nor help but self-development. Self-development implies an advance to a state of increased coherence, definitiveness and heterogeneity by the dual process of differentiation and specialisation of the parts and their integration into a whole by the formation of definite relations to one another. This is surely analogous to moral conduct which is also distinguished by its unitary composition and its striving after a determinate end.

I am not affirming the necessary desirability of life in all cases, but since the will to live is the most obvious cause of action it must become the most essential constituent of any ethical theory which does not admit the pre-eminence and infallibility of intuitive subsumption.

Here it is necessary to say a word about intuitionism, the notion that morals begin and end with an immediate discernment of the nature of right and wrong by understanding. Whereas agnosticism contends that we cannot know what lies behind implicit phenomena, intuition gives us hope that by 'sympathetic intelligence' we may have direct perception of reality as it is, Spinoza's *scientia intuitiva*. If the proof or justification of what 'ought to be' is my intuitive knowledge that it ought to be, clearly it becomes redundant to consider what ought to be, leaving us with the rather secondary question of why it ought to be. If, then, moral will and insight are fundamentally intuitive, free-will must be impossible. If, on the other hand, free-will and insight are fundamental qualities of our reasoning faculty, they declare themselves unable to judge between right and wrong actions without taking into account the consequences of the action and must, therefore, in certain cases cease to be intuitive as, for example, when consequences cannot be known until the act occurs. Similarly, it is impossible to separate an action from its motives, where motive connotes the act of will coupled with the judgement of anticipated consequences. There are, after all, such issues as extenuating circumstances, a bad act performed unconsciously is accepted as less blameworthy than the same act performed consciously. Furthermore, the insignificance of some moral judgements seems incompatible with them being intuitive. For example, there exists a tribe which has no word for chastity, does not know and cannot understand the concept; there is also a tribe which knows what it means but regards chastity as evil. Criteria of judgement are always changing and it seems to me an impertinent presumption to thrust blame on to what appears to us faulty or volatile intuition.

A theory of the world that excludes the supernatural (without necessarily denying it) has the inestimable advantage of accepting given fact in the natural world as its starting point.

The universal will-to-live does not imply the necessary desirability of life in all circumstances but it does affirm that the will-to-live is the most obvious cause of behaviour in the universe and thus, I would argue, the most essential ingredient of any ethical theory which denies the pre-eminence and infallibility of intuitive subsumption. The prime moral imperative is respect, regard and submission to this will-to-live. There is a profound sensitivity to the values that life has to offer. Love and appreciation of values take us deeper into the secrets of life and provide a more integrated view of its content than can other moral rules or moral reasoning not based on authority. This is not to argue that an ethical code is unnecessary. Love, as such, is transcendent but cannot by itself prescribe rules of action but the love of living creatures, of personalities and of animals finds its closest moral counterpart as respect for the universal will-to-live. This respect may be paid either positively by expansion or addition, or negatively by the removal and suppression of what may be a hindrance or a threat. We cannot know what ought to be but we can know what we ought to do. Conscience, for example, like humour, is a basic faculty unique to humans, able to be explained only in terms of itself.

It is true that a code of conduct which has as its end the positive expansion whenever possible of the will-to-live will on occasion be faced with serious quandaries. For example, an orchestral conductor may have to decide whether to sack a sub-standard violinist upon whose playing depends the fate of a family, or should the violinist be retained, allowing several lives to continue in their current existence but at the cost of lowering the quality and possible advancement of the remainder? Should one kill a mouse? The answers depend on other criteria. When there is no other question of value, such as shooting animals for amusement, the answer is simple, but in most cases the question is complex. First, respect for self-development *sui generis*; second, respect for other values in whatever order of priority an individual may decide.

Albert Schweitzer, the great Swiss doctor, philosopher and theologian, wrote of the painful enigma 'that I must live with reverence for life in a world dominated by a creative will which is also a destructive will, and destructive which is also creative. I can do nothing but hold to the fact that the will-to-live in me manifests itself as will-to-live which desires to become one with other wills-to-live. That is for me the light that shines in the darkness. I am thrown by reverence for life into an unrest such as the world does not know, but I obtain from it a blessedness which the world cannot give'.

For Schweitzer, the dilemma, although unanswerable, came to him by revelation. For others such as myself, denied revelation, we are forced to recognise an element of intransigent evil in the universe which has to be combated, not ignored or explained away. The mystery of the life-force must be revered, but equally the presence of its negation has to be recognised.

* * * * * * * * *

The second strain of thought that has long bemused me is the condition of man. Starting from the premiss that we are living in a dark age, Huizinga's 'demented world', and that this has no clearer reflection than in the state of contemporary art, my thinking has been influenced by Erik Fromm and Lewis Mumford, two prophets currently rather out of fashion. It is natural to believe that modern is best and that change is synonymous with progress, two preconceptions that demand challenge. In his provocative book *The Case for Modern Man* Charles Frankel[6] pointed out that we have lost our historical bearings. He refers to the peculiarly modern conviction 'that man can remake his life more effectively by the material reconstruction of his environment than by changing the philosophy he verbally professes . . . there is a new orientation for the enquiring mind – where once it started with limited doubts and ended with probable beliefs, it now moves between the poles of ultimate scepticism and absolute dogma. Emerson's dictum that things are in the saddle riding mankind to the devil has never been more true. Similarly, Montaigne's comment that 'the soul discharged her passions upon false objects, where the true are wanting'.

Toynbee refers to the ineluctable rise of technology. 'Technology', he reminds us 'is the fundamental dynamic element in modern western society. It affect everything from the size, shape, look and smell of our cities and suburbs to the mobility of populations, the character of social classes, the stability of the family, the standards of workmanship that prevail, and the direction and level of moral and aesthetic sensibilities. Technological innovations are regularly introduced for the sake of technological convenience, without establishing mechanisms for

---

6   Charles Frankel, *The Case for Modern Man*, Harper & Brothers, New York, 1956.

appraising or controlling or even cushioning their consequences.' Martyn Skinner stated the universality of such influence in verse.

> *Gone are the days when madness was confined*
> *By seas or hills from spreading through Mankind:*
> *When, though a Nero fooled upon a string,*
> *Wisdom still reigned unruffled in Peking.*

The question arises: can a society legitimately be described as sane or sick ? Sociological relativism tells us that pathology can only be ascribed to individuals when they fail to adjust to whatever society requires. But it has always seemed to me that a society which nourishes the needs of mentally healthy individuals can justifiably be considered a sane society, while a society which exhibits mass drug abuse, high levels of violence, suicide and crime, wild inequalities of income and a remarkable dilution of what are nowadays described as old-fashioned values must be considered sick. The attractiveness of Fromm's analysis is the extent to which it corresponds or explains social phenomena we can all recognise. The notion that freedom is the central characteristic of human nature complements the need for self-development which, I have argued, is the central core of the ethic of reverence for life. Complete personal freedom implies individuality, a challenging condition to fully enjoy. Pressures arise from all sides propelling against freedom. Freedom is most commonly weakened or avoided altogether by conformity, losing one's true identity among the herd. Fromm relates what he calls the escape from freedom to different forms of the family. He refers to symbiotic families wherein either the parents smother the child or the child smothers the parents, and withdrawing families. The latter may be either very demanding or submissively protective. The demanding family will exert all kinds of physical and mental pressure to achieve success for their children. In contemporary western society the submissive form is the most common. George Boeree describes such families, which are all too familiar; 'a father should be a boy's best buddy; a mother should be a daughter's soul mate . . . they are in fact no longer parents, just cohabitants with their children. The children, now without any real adult guidance, turn to their peers and to the media for their values. This is the modern, shallow television family.'

The circle of social alienation is intensified by the proliferation of single parents, children without a family at all, another skein in the unhealthy modern social weave.

In a sick society values become misplaced. For example, we speak of a million pound painting or a thousand pound costume, thus described from the consumptive point of view. The accent is on commercial value as a commodity which can be exchanged rather than its intrinsic worth or beauty. In a consumer society, as Ruskin reminded us in the 19th century, there are two main objects in life: whatever we have, to get more; and wherever we are, to go somewhere else. Not only do values change but they are seen as always relative and subjective. Their salience is therefore weakened. The subversion of morality largely through the influence of the social sciences is too large and momentous a topic to be developed here. But if ever I should come to write another volume that is one aspect of the modern world that I believe demands examination.

Without entering the minefield of defining what is denoted by the term 'art', one can consider the relationship between art, however defined, and society. It is a symbiotic relationship, the nature of society influences the kind of art produced by its aesthetically creative members, and they in turn exert influence on attitudes and behaviour. The disintegration of the middle ages was reflected in the work of Brueghel just as the disintegration of the modern world has been reflected by the greatest artist of the twentieth century, Pablo Picasso. In the words of Mumford, 'in every phase, Picasso's paintings have given a truer image of the world we live in than the so-called documentary realists, who show only what the most superficial eye sees'. When considering modern art it is extraordinary how many critics and public gallery custodians offer such panegyrics in their discussions and descriptions. Even as these words are being written, a gift of modern art reputedly worth £125 million on the open market, has been donated to the nation. Without wishing to denigrate this remarkable philanthropy, the paeans of praise from all quarters exalts the soulless, philistine, fragmented, ugly, and intentionally shocking nature of many of the works of art involved.

The accolades afforded so-called modernism are re-enforced by the operation of the marketplace. Wealth dominates fashion, because the immediate vision appeals to the *ingénues* with new money, exemplified by the popularity of contemporary Scottish artist Jack Vettriano, and because the purveyors of art naturally pander to what is fashionable, curators, mindful of the need to have their coffers replenished by rich benefactors, strengthen fashion even further. The biggest status symbols are valued at an international level,[7] sometimes as an alternative to paper money, sometimes as pure investment, sometimes as mere status symbols.

I am not thinking here of what constitutes great art, whether Ruskin's moralistic approach with his distinction between *aesthesis*, the enjoyment of merely sensuous pleasure and *theoria*, our response to beauty – or at the other end of the spectrum, John Berger's 'Realism', or any of the many other theories of art – but on the way artistic creation (however defined) reflects the nature of the society in which the artist lives. Again, how this may be reflected is subject to a multitude of interpretations, a psychoanalytic or Marxist analysis among many others. All the evidence seems to represent banality, shock for its own sake, the conscious denial of beauty or grace, spiritually arid materialism, often violence as an end in itself, always with the detachment of the object. My concerns hold good, not only for the graphic arts, but even more strikingly, with few honourable exceptions, in the realms of literature and music. Stridency, cacophony and vulgarity reign with critics offering judgements against only contemporary standards rather than against the pantheon of literary and musical tradition, while the few exceptions like Patrick O'Brian and Robin Jenkins in literature and Valentin Silvestov in music receive either

---

[7] For a detailed account of the factors involved in changes in artistic fashion, and their plotting, see Gerald Reitlinger, *The Economics of Taste*, especially volume II, Barrie and Rockcliffe, London, 1963, reprinted by Hacker Art Books, New York 1982.

a lukewarm reception or are completely ignored. Contemporary artists are much better at portraying the horrors of war than the rewards of peace. This is not, of course, to deny that occasional glimpses of saner times appear, as for example in the work of Peter Doig or the sculptures of Brancusi. But generally the nature of what passes as art attracts accolades from most critics mirroring the dark age in which we live.

There is another aspect to this. The separation of the artist from the consumer of art is a modern phenomenon. We no longer respond to the world with our senses in a meaningful, skilled, productive, active, shared way.

Ruskin came to the same conclusion a century and a half ago. 'We have studied and much perfected, of late, the great civilised invention of the division of labour; only we give it a false name. It is not, truly speaking, the labour that is provided, but the men. Divided into mere segments of men – broken into small fragments and crumbs of life; so that all the little pieces of intelligence that is left in a man is not enough to make a pin, or a nail, but exhausts itself in making the point of the pin and the head of a nail ..polished by the sand of human soul.'

This raises two equally vexatious questions. The first is whether great art can flourish, or even be created, in times of spiritual upheaval. The history of art suggests that this may be possible but only when renewal is in sight.[8]

In a bodacious and provocative slender volume,[9] the English philosopher Roger Scruton writes about encouraging cultural renewal. 'Young people are surrounded from the earliest age by music of an undemanding kind, designed as much to be overheard as to be listened to . . . To introduce young people to the musical culture of western civilisation – arguably one of the most lasting achievements of that civilisation and one in which the greatest treasure of sentiment has been instilled – it is necessary to

[8] For a detailed analysis interested readers are recommended Peter Watson, *From Manet to Manhattan:The Rise of the Modern Art Market*, Hutchinson, London, 1992.
[9] Roger Scruton, *Culture Counts*, Encounter Books, New York, 2007, pp 62 & 65/6.

proceed by careful steps. In particular, they have to learn to hear the movement that lies in music itself, and which is not reducible to a regular beat in the background . . . a signal launched from the tribe . . . In teaching young people the visual arts and to create artworks of their own, you are introducing them to a form of life in which the Master is the guide and the authority. You are unfolding before them another and quite different form of social membership from the one that they knew from their peers. You are teaching them to see the world with eyes that know what the world has meant and can still mean to the human heart.'

The second question is how best to cope with the darker sides of life within a mad, mad world. A positive response is demanded. We must recognise the truth of the human condition before doing what little any individual can hope to achieve toward the restoration of sanity, whether by teaching or writing or engaging in political exchange. Confronted by the choice between robotism or a more humanistic approach we must place our faith in the latter, in balance, toleration, harmony, and a society which nourishes the needs of free men and women, encouraging individuality rather than conformity, limiting the powers of the false idols of technology, returning closer to nature, exchanging political correctness (i.e. social conformity) and religious dogmas for a rational tolerance and reverence for life and the development of all living things. The destiny of mankind lies, not in any supernatural agency, but within the mind and soul of man himself.

CHAPTER 9

End Game

There's nothing can bring back the hour
Of splendour in the grass, of glory in the flower;
We will grieve not, rather find
Strength in what remains behind.

[William Wordsworth
'Ode: Intimations of Immortality' (1807), st. 10].

In a long voyage across the wide oceans of life, through tempests and in sunshine, the heuristic imprints of experience have been manifold. The vessel was made as seaworthy as any vessel can be by having two such caring, honest and loving parents, while the crew with which I have been blessed is a wonderful family with seldom a harsh word ever between us, sharing similar implicit values, all supporting each when one is overtaken by misfortune, and – not least important – sharing a similar sense of humour. Although travelling at different speeds and in diverse directions, the family has always marched to the same drummer.

Age increases sensitivity to the antipathies but decreases the level of hostility towards them. Similarly, delights, while more deeply appreciated, seldom arouse the ecstasies of youth. Among the antipathies, I continue to abhor climbers on the social ladder but no longer hope they will necessarily fall off, disdain pomposity without hoping for its implosion. More seriously, cruelty is an evil, inflicting it upon others perhaps the greatest sin of all, something to be condemned however and wherever it occurs, whether it be the torture of political prisoners[1] or the

---

[1] Amnesty International, 1 Easton Street, London, WC1V ODW.

factory farming of pigs.[2] It is too easy to give lip service to our disgust without seeking to do what little one individual can do to reduce the horrors. Donations to charity are, of course, very personal matters but examination of how they operate and what they achieve yield some surprising results.

For humans, cancer charities[3] have always been the best endowed for obvious reasons, but the case for supporting Amnesty International, for example, is less frequently considered. For animals, the number of wealthy pet owners, especially single elderly ladies, makes the RSPCA and the Cats Protection League both extremely popular – the annual budget of the latter is fifteen million pounds, but the World Society for the Protection of Animals,[4] for example, is less known. Another worthy recipient for animal lovers is the small Alternative Animal Sanctuary which has never yet had to turned away a homeless animal whether horse, goat, cat, dog or duck, all regular residents at their headquarters in the south of England. Similarly, the thought that almost three million sensitive animals – monkeys, mice, pigs and others – are killed every year in the UK alone is hurriedly cast out of mind. We do not wish to think about it or if we do we rationalise by saying to ourselves that this is just another example of inhumanity about which we can do nothing.

A crusade of the multitudes to promote euthanasia is long overdue. We do not allow our pets to suffer unnecessarily once they lose their dignity in terminal pain or excruciating disability, they are peacefully released, but in Britain humans are consigned to suffer for as long as society and its agents, the medical profession, can sustain life. When all dignity is lost and hope has fled, still the doctors fight. The reasons why euthanasia under strict control has never been permitted in Britain, except by the most humane doctors acting in secret, is partly due to the influence of the Christian Church,

---

[2]   Viva!, 8 York Court, Wilder Street, Bristol, BS2 8QH.
[3]   Charity incomes in Britain during 2006, the last date for which they are available shows Cancer Research at the top of the list with £423 million, followed by the British Heart Foundation £159 million, Marie Curie Cancer Care £103 million, Alzheimer's Society £37 million, Multiple Sclerosis Society £29 million, Parkinson's Disease Society £14 million, and Alzheimer's Research £3 million.
[4]   WSPA, 89 Victoria Embankment, London, SE1 7TP.

which preaches the sanctity of human life under all circumstances, regardless of pain or other forms of suffering, an edict reinforced by the medical profession which, as an organisation, has never been able to reconcile the Hippocratic Oath with the thought that extinguishing life can be more compassionate than prolonging it. As long ago as 1862 the poet Arthur Hugh Clough moderately beseeched the profession 'Thou shalt not kill; but needs't not strive officiously to keep alive'.

I have long been angered by the gross inequalities of wealth so long rampant in Britain. As Shelley reminded us 'titles are tinsel, power a corrupter, glory a bubble, and excessive wealth a libel on its possessor'. It is not just the width of the gulf that now separates the rich from the poor, although that is bad enough, but the absence of any criteria of value beyond market forces, to determine income.

Where is the logic that can defend an annual median income of £1.5 million for the top one hundred FSE directors or a premiership footballer for whom the average annual wage is £676,000, while a life-saving, caring nurse receives an average wage less than that of a garage mechanic. Academics such as Dickens and Swaffield and journalists such as Polly Toynbee have analysed the causes and details of the injustices but no sustained thought seems to have been given to methods of amelioration other than punitive taxation at the top and raising the minimum wage at the bottom. Furthermore, a direct link across all countries has been identified between wealth inequalities generally and health, though whether this is causal or merely correlational remains unclear.[5]

I am not advocating the kind of profound political change such as is demanded by left-wing Socialists, but the introduction of some mechanism whereby, in the name of justice, excesses are controlled. For example, it should not be beyond the capacity of a council of the great and the good to decree socially appropriate levels at both extreme ends of the financial spectrum. Their recommendations for capping at the very top of the scale and providing more realistic levels at the lower end could then be passed to the Treasury for appropriate action. Statutory control

---

[5] Since writing this I hear that Polly Toynbee is about to publish *Unworthy Earnings*.

would be needed. Many factors would have to be taken into account, considered by occupational categories, whilst avoiding attention to individual cases which would be impracticable.

A body such as I have envisaged would only be concerned with the extreme ends of the financial spectrum. Punitive taxation does not answer the problem because it ignores the lower end and fails to take into any account the question of social justice. It would also be psychologically more acceptable to determine the top echelons at source rather than extracting taxation after the receipt of income.

Resistance would be likely from many quarters but in the name of social justice this would have to be overcome. If, as a result, a few of our most financially successful entrepreneurs left the country, this would be a small price that would have to be paid, although the impulse behind most billionaire entrepreneurs is more often power than wealth. Investment income could not be included owing to the ease of evasion and the impossibility of monitoring.[6]

Living in a region diffused by the aura of royalty one is often asked for one's views on monarchy.

Monarchy is the seed bed of snobbery, the ground upon which class structure is built.

Dysfunctional within its own domestic orbit yet unifying for the reaches of the world beyond, thus reflecting the distinction between royals as people and royals as representatives. To touch the hem of royalty gives sustenance to many, a warm, harmless glow of pride to those who navigate a path to the holy garment. Before it grown men grovel and good men kneel. For the armed services and established religion a monarch is the shining font from which flows a sense of duty, obedience and reverence, the embodiment of national tradition. Soldiers fight and die not for England but for the Queen, the fountain head of honour and authority.

Nations require a talismanic image to exalt, an image of stability in a sea of change, an idealised icon to enflame and unify patriotism. For the United States it is the flag, for Great Britain it is the monarch.

<hr>

[6] S J Barbones, *Income Inequality and Population Health*, Social Science and Medicine, vol. 66, no 7, (2008) pp1614-1626.

On balance monarchy, although expensive, seems to me of national benefit – so long as we recognise that for as long as it exists a class structure will prevail. But we should not weaken at the knees in its presence nor be led to ignore greater intrinsic human worth in other social places.

J B Priestley once wrote a charming little book entitled *Delights*, each short chapter covering a special idiosyncratic pleasure. His account of one man's journey through life gives at least a passing mention to what have been the sources of greatest pleasure. On an early page his self-description resonated in my mind. 'I would not describe myself as a rebel', he wrote, 'for I have no fanaticism, but there is in me a streak of the jeering anarchist, who parts company even with his friends when they have succeeded to power'.

For an incurable romantic, pride of place among delights is of course, the family, working in all their different places, applying a wide variety of skills, sharing the ups and empathising over the downs, coming together whenever it matters and, sometimes, working together.

May 2006 produced two occurrences of important, lasting consequences. On May 21st, on my way to collect the Sunday papers, alighting from the car I tripped over an upturned curbstone and broke my right arm, a fractured humerus that has never mended, though happily without lasting pain. Exactly a week later, on May 28th, Feona celebrated her birthday in the best possible way: she married John. The ceremony and reception, which sadly I was still too traumatised to attend, were held in Licklyhead Castle, an ideal romantic location in the heart of rural Aberdeenshire. The castle, built in 1629 by John Forbes of Leslie, was large enough to hold seventy, an ideal number given that most of their friends lived in the south. John Petersen, the Welsh son of Britain's last gentleman champion pugilist, augments the family valuably with his unruffled wisdom born of forty years as a senior business executive.

Four perennial delights have been one's true friends, a lifelong attachment to dogs, especially graceful Scottish Deerhounds, jolly Bearded Collies and faithful, intelligent German Shepherds; the magical qualities of music when the soul reaches up to the stars, and the grandeur and majesty of the Scottish Highlands, given a choice, the western seaboard in the summer, the mountainous east in winter time.

Following closely behind, if one is forced to gradate, are the comfort and stimulation of good literature, consider the incomparable Walter Scott and Leo Tolstoy, the exciting allure of the theatre, limited in our own ancient days to the friendly elegance of the Pitlochry Festival Theatre with its annual repertoire of six carefully selected plays, and the quiet, independent, undemanding serenity of cats, Burmese and Russian Blues for preference. On a slightly lower level is friendly competition whether on the cricket ground, the golf course, the curling rink, the bridge or chess table, or around the Mah Jongg tableau:

> To strive for the impossible dream or to achieve some success at the last possible second is always a glorious moment: As the Chinese say *Hai-ti-low-yueh* (to catch the moon from the bottom of the sea).

* * * * * * * * *

For someone who has always, perhaps perversely, valued the living environment more than the nature of work, occasionally in life there comes the very special excitement of finding a new home, falling in love with a house and garden. We were fortunate enough to savour this unique joy four times: the inspirational Ardachie estate, elegant Deans Mill, remote but very comfortable Feardar with its glorious, uninterrupted kaleidoscopic views across the fields to majestic Lochnagar, and our final resting place, quiet Glengarden, wherein we have been happily going about our business for thirty-three years.

Forgive me, gentle reader, if at times I have seemed too didactic and at other times, when not completely diddly-squat, too inoculated with humour. If this impression sticks, please apply humour to the hortatories and empathy to the humour. Then we can all rest in peace with ourselves and, as far as humanly possible, with the world.

Another year draws almost to a close. May Tennyson's evocation regale our hearts:

> *Ring out the old, ring in the new,*
> *Ring, happy bells, across the snow:*
> *The year is going, let him go*
> ***Ring out the false, ring in the true.***

PHANTASY WITH A MORAL
(Dedicated to my friend)

Dimmed by the shadows of fortune,
Lost in the storms of a mood,
Crazed by its eerie reflection,
The hideous mind that lays nude.

Encouraged by help that was helpless,
Beguiled by the shape of its head,
The once thinking mind now lay thoughtless,
Live cells in a brain that was dead.

The tissues of theory redundant,
With throbs of a once horrid life;
The hairless, white skull without raiment,
Cruel glimmers of cold surgeon's knife.

Strange creaks of a hinge that is rusty,
Really the probes of the doctor,
The breaths of the dead that are musty,
Emotions of cold, queer disorder.

Foul stenches of displaced decay,
Alarmed by the seekers of health,
Crass searches which never repay,
Death comes – regardless of wealth.

Tired by smells of life that is dead,
Doctor trembles are taking the plunge,
The phantom rises – without any head,
And madly stabs the surgeon's lungs.

Dimmed by the shadows of fortune,
Lost in the storms of a mood,
Crazed by its eerie reflection,
The hideous mind that lays nude.

Encouraged by help that was helpless,
Beguiled by the shape of its head,
The once thinking mind now lay thoughtless,
Stiff statue on cold, icy bed.

–ooOoo–

THOUGHTS IN A YORKSHIRE WOODLAND

The chanted song of a springtime bird,
As darkly, in a forest heard,
The faint rustle of a tree-born breeze,
Yellow gorse by the moorland screes.
Morning's dew on a velvet lawn,
Grey day's return with virile dawn.
The soothing sound of a buzzing bee –
Yet Time still flows to eternity.

–ooOoo–

They met in a misty forest glade,
Antagonists of fortune,
That change might with a grace upbraid
The frailty of caution.

Five steps apart each dueller took,
The seconds roared "Hurray!"
And with a sad ephemeral look,
Commenced the bold affray.

For two long hours the battle raged,
With awful clashing sound;
Till suddenly, all eyes were raised
To spy the bloody ground.

Weakly to earth the fighter fell,
A tragedy of fate,
As carried near by steeple bell
Was news that came too late.

For as the victor cheer'd himself
At having slain another,
Misery came, like tax from wealth –
The dead man was his brother.

True sadness that, like shadows dark
Are always by our side;
Forever leave a stained mark
Upon our moral pride.

Then wiping eye with redden'd hand,
That quivered as a leaf,
The living knelt upon the land,
And kissed the face beneath.

–ooOoo–

I walk among hills made by heather;
In valley and glen do I stroll.
With the beasts of hide and of feather,
We few in the world with a goal.

Cold snows that in winter envelop
Bare summits in whiteness sublime,
The babies of spring that develop
With purpose that must be divine.

By tent I've pitched high in the hills,
With birds as they whistle around,
Soft silence entwining earth's ills,
Transcending the notes of a sound.

With flood and mist in the evening;
Grey dawn and the cool earth beneath.
To the ill and diseased of the city
These scenes I would gladly bequeath.
There is no finer way to cure man's ills,
Than sweet serenity, found only in hills.

–ooOoo–

Great minds and free,
Why should they think it so funny
If men decree
To deny their genius money?

Alas for the poor,
That those who govern their purses,
Makers of law
Are those who need spiritual nurses.

Why rule the rich?
For reasons that really are plain,
We've reached a pitch
Where money speaks louder than brain.

What can we do?
As change seems out of the question.
Try anything new?
But that is a bold suggestion.

One thing alone
Can save each invaluable soul;
So let us roam
Through wilds that so wistfully call.

–ooOoo–

Philosophers think as they dream of the Earth,
While other men read them for all they are worth;
But how can poor humans know which is the best,
When each eyes the other as some horrid pest?

–ooOoo–

MORE FROM THE LAIRG GHRU

I write in a dark, lonely glen,
With glimpses of Nature unfolding,
Noble thoughts engulfing the pen,
To write what my eyes are beholding.

But never was more desperate toil,
For true Beauty lies further than words,
And ink gets no higher than soil,
When great Art is described to the herds.

–ooOoo–

HOW MANY?

How many hearts have been broken?
How many hopes have been smashed?
How many fools have spoken?
How many innocents thrashed?
Too many.

How many makers of money?
How many killers of men?
How many dark lives once sunny?
How many? I do not ken.
Too many.

–ooOoo–

SOME QUERIES RAISED BY
THE PROSPECT OF ETERNITY

Earth's divinity and all that lies within;
Time's rocky waves cascading fortune's shore;
A sparrow's tweet above the din ---
Has all this happened once before?

–ooOoo–

A BIRD'S FAITHFULNESS AT ABERNETH

The mountain loch in a mist lay hidden,
Its grey eyes fasten'd up to heaven;
But as the darkness stole away,
In flew two gulls with the light of day.

Then to each nest each bird did fly,
One to mate, the other to die;
And as the waters calmly rippled,
A young bird by a stone lay crippled.

Yet disregarding how it stood,
It flew to fetch its brother food;
But ere it returned to Aberneth,
Its mate lay crippled too – with Death

–ooOoo–

SOME HIGHLAND THOUGHTS
WHILE CROSSING THE LAIRG GHRU

As through the mountain glen I wandered,
And echoing footsteps trod,
Thoughts of heaven came to me,
And the wherewithal of God.

This wilderness of sand and rock,
Witness to a Nation's plight?
If not, why burns of silver liquid
Engulf the soul with such delight?

That noble antler, that towering peak,
Do all these herald nought?
Or is this realm of deepest Nature
Not worth one jot of thought?

The magic of a starlit heaven,
Twinkling as it shines above,
Is this another wondrous notion,
Divorced from any human love?

The melting snows of joyous summer,
Quivering in the warmth of noon,
Is this the dread forerunner
Of a last, disastrous doom?

And yet with all these shadows passing,
Our minds must reign supreme;
The world is ours, and everlasting
Eternal witness to a reasoned Being.

–ooOoo–

SWEET SIMPLICITY

Fairies in the dying light,
Chasing cares away.
Mysteries of unending night,
Waiting for the day.
Rainbows burning bright the sky,
Firing every peak.
Music of a lover's sigh,
Kindly, yet so meek.
Mist that lies on mountain-top,
Whiteness of sublimity.
Crickets, as they gaily hop,
Lesson in humility.
Heaven comes on earth for me when all these reach tranquillity,
And manifest themselves with glee in Nature's sweet simplicity.

–ooOoo–

The length and breadth of feeling; happiness,
Discontent and joy. Each new night and day;
Each flower and tree --- all featureless,
Is this a re-enacted play?

The dark-veiled notion of a fate recast,
Wild storms, still calm, dry heat and rain,
A future running into past,
Why bring back all these things again?

But which of we poor striving fools can tell,
If this be circle false or flatten'd brim?
And who would want to know that Hell
Was the dread doom awaiting him?

–ooOoo–

JEALOUSY – THOU FOUL DEVOURING RAVEN

Jealousy, thou foul, devouring raven,
Creator of mischief, lies and lesser ills,
Which, sulking like a witch de-craven,
Emerges forth and swiftly kills.

When lacking goods that others have,
With a wish that you had them yourself,
Why, it is thee, black jealousy,
That fetches them – by stealth.

Too fearful and ashamed to dare to speak,
Thou sinuous monster, parasite and worm,
Thou reptile, bully, and base sneak,
From Hell you came – to soon return.

When lacking goods that others have,
Then, thro' cunning, taking them away,
Thou foul, self-devouring raven,
Remember – there always comes the Day!

–ooOoo–

PILGRIMS

To a distant land they have gone,
To a land of Hope and Art,
Where the earthly sun that shone,
Is but an age apart.
Where children play and men may roam,
Across vast tracts of space,
With hope to build a better home,
To start a finer race.
But – like all reforming souls,
The urge defeats the goal;
And, stricken by the boundless toils,
They go – to meet the soil.

–ooOoo–

Memories fleeting,
Failures sleeping –
Such is our mentality!

Excuses bleating,
Angers leaping –
Such is our mentality!

Crying, sighing,
Laughing, dying –
Such is our mentality!

–ooOoo–

Each new rose of summer-time;
Each new tender thought sublime;
Each and every autumn tree -
These are all delight for me.

–ooOoo–

Unto this land, sun-quenched and red,
There came a figure in grey;
He carried a crown upon his head
And his feet were made of clay.

Among the people, pink-skinned and black,
The figure moved and spoke;
He carried a weight upon his back
And upon his arms a cloak.

To all that was said, both stupid and wise,
The figure listened in awe;
He wore a shield before his eyes
And upon his chest a sore.

As they were working and at their play,
The figure talking among them;
He carried his burden all the way
And still he stayed among them.

'So little they have, so much do they lack',
The figure thought of those folk;
He carried a weight upon his back,
And upon his arm a cloak.

'This is our land – we're happy', they'd said.
He stood and mused 'Who are they?';
He carried a crown upon his head
And his feet were made of clay.

When the dawn uncovered this troubled man,
No figure was in the gleam;
'Who was he?', they asked, 'to leave so soon?',
'Perhaps 'twas only a dream'.

But the thoughts of some kept turning
To explain the figure away;

He wrent their hearts with a burning,
This grey figure, mould of clay.

Then one man, a black one, remembered,
The thoughts that had been enticed;
The figure of grey was engendered:
The Conscience of Man – before Christ.

15 April, 1960

–ooOoo–

I am uncomfortable, I am undone,
My hands feel heavy and my feet are numb.
The ears are deaf, the eyes are heavy,
The wind is high from a distend belly.
The question arises, but no answer found
How in a crisis can a square turn round?

–ooOoo–

O divinity! How reignest thou upon this brilliant scene?
Yon shimmering brook flowing bead-like to the sea.
This splendour is too great for mortals – and for me.
Here is no bitterness, no putrid lust or shame,
All worldly vice hath fled and evils can't remain,
O nature! of this thou art indeed the queen.

September, 1945

–ooOoo–

Swaying in the breeze,
To the rhythm of the trees,
Swinging in the branches,
To the tunes of little birds,
Springing on its haunches,
Is a monkey that has heard.
Footsteps in the forest,
As a white man marches.
This is what the animals have heard.
Every antelope and zebra,
Every elephant and crane,
All are very worried,
Lest with bullets they are slain.
For man has lost his glory,
As instead of playing games,
He happy is, not sorry;
He's come to shoot the cranes.
September, 1945

–ooOoo–

Calm and quiet lies the evening
In Nature's sweet repose.
And oft in the darkness of night,
I feel like one who knows
The secrets of an earthly bliss,
The meaning of a rose.

About soft grass with merry dew,
The silent night reclines.
The daylight splendour seen anew,
Amidst the dusky pines.
And in this scene I plainly see,
The meaning of a tree.
September 1945

–ooOoo–

TO MY FIRST DOG

Very many years have fled
Since last I saw my dark eyed queen
And very many moons will wane
Ere I can bring her home again.

Others came, but swiftly wed
Since last I saw by dark eyed queen
For lovers always come to these
Who loveless still breed many woes.

Thou sleek shadow, dark and slim
That hauntest me in every whim;
I happily content would be
To have thee back again with me.

September 1945

–ooOoo–

Somewhere alone;
Where the pine-trees chatter,
And the birches moan.

Some place apart;
Where musing doesn't matter,
And the rivers start.

Here's where I long to be!

Some hidden glade;
Where brooding linnets screech
On eggs they have laid.

Some autumn tree;
Where hues of brown reach
Gently to the sea.

Here's where I long to be!

September 1945

–ooOoo–

Our loves which steal the hours as they depart,
With anguish and sweet benefacted heart.
No true joys, but pure contented raptures
Which, though lasting but a day seem greater
Used when fortune may herself recapture
The bliss bestowed thro' our prime creator.
Some joys, like as weeds that e'er they flower,
Have withered and have left instead decay,
Worse than the health which begot the bower
And uglier made the place than th' day
When they began to grow; these too decline,
As their vigorous noon-day is approach'd,
And fading fast, feverishly pine
For the thrills they had so briefly poach'd

September 1945

–ooOoo–

The cruel condition of this hour's manhood,
Each jostling with his fellow to annexe
His neighbour's fortune; and by thrills of sex
Striving to reach a truer, nobler good.
Yet still with base design and wagging tongue
As every beast has since this world began.
Without a sacrilegious thought or word,
Swarms the street of life with the common herd.
No contemplation or sound, sane belief,
Just mad, troubled haste with no relief.
Alas! that this persistent parasite,
In which Satan seeks to shroud the right,
Should provide us with so gross a climax
As war – our manhood's bloody hangman's axe.

September 1945

–ooOoo–

A man owning no allegiance to a nation,
Just a gentle soul of my imagination.
A man so free from sin as God maketh him,
No vicious, wretched libelling; no dark entreaty;
Yet with truth and wisdom – and of sane sobriety,
Who does not nurse a hatred when he throws a kiss,
And contented, leads his life as near to bliss
As his poor earthly goods allow.
A man, sharp of wit, with subtle conversation,
Just a little imp of my imagination!

26 September 1945

–ooOoo–

How miserable to contemplate,
The inexorable mould of fate,
The sweetness of a baby ere
Its travails in this wearsome world begin.
Despair of a man when faced with fear,
As that vacuum death caresses him.
Great mountains, those very stern yet
Wondrous immortalities. They
Beget no offspring e'en though the velvets
Which enshrine their peaks give place to
New, from spring to spring. Here beauty
Lies in everlasting glory.
But for man? No future brooks
The damned gap twixt the grave
And ecstasy. His sons may grow
And prosper well, but happiness
Surely cannot penetrate the
Other side. For if this be false,
Then our life's ending would be a
Mockery, phantastic, monstrous.

No, tis far worse to be a man
Than a great, snow-capped mountain.

September 1945

–ooOoo–

E'en as dull gloom settles down
To enfold the countryside,
Within its cloven bosom,
The magic witch of life,
Creeps on and wreaks her havoc.
A young babe – all innocence
And faithful trust, when first its
Thrust, upon life's rotten stage;
Becomes acidified with age.
And whilst before its face show'd
Trust, with time its soul lay 'neath
A sadden'd fetter that is dust.
The brilliance of a flame – its
Use and warmth, do fade before
Time's sad, sickening approach.
So does frail innocence fade to
Evil. Where before was beauty, truth
Now rests mere ego, lust and shame,
This old decrepit play again!

September 1945

–ooOoo–

Oft as I have sat and gazed
Upon the playfulness of youth
And many hours have been amazed
How earthly sins have stood aloof
'Why?' sighed the soul which in me stirr'd
'Are young things truer things than old?'
And to my thoughts I was referr'd
To find writ there this truth in gold.
This world of ours – this world of shame
In which the prime rule is to gain
No matter whether ten men die
Or how wicked is the lie
Life's sport upon which all depends
Deals not with truth but dividends.
If one man cheats while fifty spurn
The fifty too must evil turn.
For tis far, far, easier to stray
Than to keep the noble, honest way.
As should <u>one</u> human lie or thieve
All others must to gain reprieve
Or bowing 'fore the wicked cry
Just quietly fade away and die.
And so this simple truth remains
Youth is clean but old age stains.

September 1945

–ooOoo–

ON BEING TRUE TO ONESELF

Is it wrong to wish to be in other places,
When the need and the open chance are near?
Is't wise to be quiet to other faces,
When the work and the beckoning day are here?

'Yes', says the mind – and men, 'tis wrong indeed',
'To destroy by neglect the present need';
Only the rich can afford to be wise,
And only the poor can afford to despise.

'But', feels the heart, 'do I wish to succeed',
'If this means planting an alien seed?'
Only the wise know where happiness lies,
And only the happy what wisdom decries.

1966

–ooOoo–

How green are the fields of my valley!
How pure run the waters beneath!
Is there a soul who would not tarry
To wander over my native heath?

There is no bliss, nor very greatest fame,
That ever could to this be matched.
To these all human goods remain the same,
As rustic cottage, poorly thatched.

Where is the man to himself so dumb,
Who never has to Nature gone?
That by her wisdom he might grow,
A humbler man for all to know.
How clearer still does this become,
When taking a glance at an Englishman!

–ooOoo–

Forgive me not if I am young and gay,
For the shadows of night are fast falling;
And the noon always brightens the day.
But if blown by the tempest of interest,
Thou findest me cold and untrue,
Forget me – for I'm not for you.

–ooOoo–

There is a mystery in places
Of a delicate, whispering hue,
Where a lonely memory traces
The pattern of fragrance one knew.

It may be a single reflection,
Or disarray, obtuse and dull,
But feelings that make the selection
Deny hope for thought to annul.

–ooOoo–

The deer stood high in the corrie,
Swept by the wind and the rain.
The eagle winged after its quarry,
Spanning the hill and the plain.

Down, 'neath the mist and the cloudbank,
Sharp by the heather and scree,
The cry of a lamb in a sheep fank
As plaintiff a note as could be.

We search'd all day on the hillside,
By every stone look'd we,
To find how the ewe mother had died
Or wherever she might be.

The deer stood high in the corrie,
Swept by the wind and the rain.
The eagle winged home with its quarry -
The ewe, so recently slain.

Down, 'neath the mist and the cloudbank
Sharp by the heather and scree,
The lamb still cried in the sheep fank,
As plaintiff a note as could be.

–ooOoo–

Was there ever a gleam more glorious
Or a silence more sublime
Than a mountain in the moonlight
In the snow of winter-time?

Was there ever a joy more deep and true
Or a beauty more inspired
Than nature on a frosty night
When you're old and growing tired?

Men tell so many truths and lies,
He fights and kills and maims,
But nature only softly sighs
And quietly still remains.

There may be time before we die
Before man's span expires –
To seek beyond our puny sky,
The message of the stars.

–ooOoo–

Index